VENTANA

THE Perl 5

Programmer's Reference

Windows 95/NT, Macintosh, OS/2 & UNIX

R. Allen Wyke & Luke Duncan

The Perl 5 Programmer's Reference
Copyright © 1997 by R. Allen Wyke and Luke Duncan

Library of Congress Cataloging-in-Publication Data
Wyke, Allen (R. Allen)
    The Perl 5 programmer's reference / R. Allen Wyke and Luke Duncan. — 1st ed.
        p. cm.
    ISBN 1-56604-750-1
    1. Perl (Computer program language) I. Duncan, Luke.
    QA76.73.P22W95 1997
    005.13'3—dc21   97-30090
                                    CIP

First Edition 9 8 7 6 5 4 3 2

Printed in the United States of America

Ventana Communications Group
P.O. Box 13964
Research Triangle Park, NC 27709-3964
919.544.9404
FAX 919.544.9472
http://www.vmedia.com

Ventana Communications Group is a division of International Thomson Publishing.

Limits of Liability & Disclaimer of Warranty
The authors and publisher of this book have used their best efforts in preparing the book and the programs contained in it. These efforts include the development, research, and testing of the theories and programs to determine their effectiveness. The authors and publisher make no warranty of any kind, expressed or implied, with regard to these programs or the documentation contained in this book.

The authors and publisher shall not be liable in the event of incidental or consequential damages in connection with, or arising out of, the furnishing, performance or use of the programs, associated instructions and/or claims of productivity gains.

Trademarks
Trademarked names appear throughout this book and on the accompanying compact disk, if applicable. Rather than list the names and entities that own the trademarks or insert a trademark symbol with each mention of the trademarked name, the publisher states that it is using the names only for editorial purposes and to the benefit of the trademark owner with no intention of infringing upon that trademark.

President
Michael E. Moran

**Vice President of
Content Development**
Karen A. Bluestein

**Director of Acquisitions and
Development**
Robert Kern

**Editorial Operations
Manager**
Kerry L. B. Foster

Production Manager
Jaimie Livingston

Art Director
Marcia Webb

Brand Manager
Jamie Jaeger Fiocco

Creative Services Manager
Diane Lennox

Acquisitions Editor
Neweleen A. Trebnik

Project Editor
Jennifer Huntley Mario

Development Editor
Michelle Corbin Nichols

Copy Editor
Judy Flynn

CD-ROM Specialist
Ginny Phelps

Technical Reviewer
Aaron Huslage

Desktop Publisher
Scott Hosa

Proofreader
Alicia Farris

Interior Designer
Jaimie Livingston

Cover Illustrator
Leigh Salmon

About the Authors

R. Allen Wyke wrote his first computer program at the age of 8, and has since programmed in many languages including Perl, Java, Visual Basic, Pascal, C, C++, and Lingo. He has developed Intranet web pages for a leading telecommunications company, and recently founded Beginners.com (http://www.beginners.com), a site dedicated to new Internet users.

Currently, Allen and his boa, Marcel, live in Durham, NC where he heads up CD-ROM production for Ventana Communications Group.

Luke Duncan is the Key Technology Developer at Ventana Communications Group in Research Triangle Park, NC. He has worked extensively with Perl on projects as simple as CGI scripts to large text processing scripts. He attended the University of North Carolina at Chapel Hill where he worked on the SunSITE project.

Acknowledgments

I would like to thank Neweleen Trebnik, Jennifer Huntley Mario, Michelle Nichols, Kerry Foster, Karen Bluestein, Ginny Phelps, Adam Newton, Simone Shannon, Marcell Marias, and everyone else at Ventana (Production, Sales, Marketing) whose combined efforts made this writing experience very enjoyable!

    I would also like to thank Luke Duncan for his excellent work, help, and professionalism in the creation of this book's contents.

    Finally, I would like to thank Chad Walsh, David Wheeling, and Travis Watson for being the best friends a guy could have. It is their support, pressure, and continual conversations that drive me to be who I am today.

—A.W.

I would like to thank everyone who had to put up with me while writing this book.

—L.D.

Dedication

To my father, the best hero a kid could have. To my mother, whose understanding and love have no end. Finally, to "my girl," Anne (not Ann). Her support, patience, inspiration, and undying love make my life complete. I love you all!

—A.W.

I would like to dedicate this book to a certain person, and you know who you are.

—L.D.

Contents

Jump Tables

Jump Table A—Listing by Function

Function	Category	Version	Page
&	Operator	Perl 4, Perl 5	1
&&	Operator	Perl 4, Perl 5	1
<	Operator	Perl 4, Perl 5	2
<<	Operator	Perl 4, Perl 5	3
<=	Operator	Perl 4, Perl 5	4
<=>	Operator	Perl 4, Perl 5	4
>	Operator	Perl 4, Perl 5	5
>>	Operator	Perl 4, Perl 5	6
>=	Operator	Perl 4, Perl 5	7
*	Operator	Perl 4, Perl 5	8
**	Operator	Perl 4, Perl 5	8
/	Operator	Perl 4, Perl 5	9
!	Operator	Perl 4, Perl 5	10
!=	Operator	Perl 4, Perl 5	10
^	Operator	Perl 4, Perl 5	11
.	Operator	Perl 4, Perl 5	12
=	Operator	Perl 4, Perl 5	12
==	Operator	Perl 4, Perl 5	13
-	Operator	Perl 4, Perl 5	14
->	Operator	Perl 5	15
—	Operator	Perl 4, Perl 5	15
%	Operator	Perl 4, Perl 5	16
|	Operator	Perl 4, Perl 5	17
||	Operator	Perl 4, Perl 5	17
+	Operator	Perl 4, Perl 5	18
++	Operator	Perl 4, Perl 5	19
?:	Operator	Perl 4, Perl 5	19
~	Operator	Perl 4, Perl 5	20
abs	Function	Perl 5	21
accept	System Call	Perl 4, Perl 5	21
alarm	System Call	Perl 4, Perl 5	22

Function	Category	Version	Page
and	Operator	Perl 5	22
atan2	Function	Perl 4, Perl 5	24
AUTOLOAD	Subroutine	Perl 5	24
BEGIN	Subroutine	Perl 5	26
bind	System Call	Perl 4, Perl 5	26
binmode	Function	Perl 4, Perl 5	27
bless	Function	Perl 5	27
caller	Function	Perl 4, Perl 5	29
chdir	Function	Perl 4, Perl 5	29
chmod	Function	Perl 4, Perl 5	30
chomp	Function	Perl 5	31
chop	Function	Perl 4, Perl 5	32
chown	Function	Perl 4, Perl 5	33
chr	Function	Perl 5	33
chroot	System Call	Perl 4, Perl 5	34
close	Function	Perl 4, Perl 5	34
closedir	Function	Perl 4, Perl 5	35
cmp	Operator	Perl 4, Perl 5	36
connect	System Call	Perl 4, Perl 5	37
continue	Loop Control	Perl 4, Perl 5	37
cos	Function	Perl 4, Perl 5	39
crypt	Function	Perl 4, Perl 5	39
DATA	Handle	Perl 4, Perl 5	41
dbmclose	Function	Perl 4, Perl 5	41
dbmopen	Function	Perl 4, Perl 5	42
defined	Function	Perl 4, Perl 5	43
delete	Function	Perl 4, Perl 5	44
die	Function	Perl 4, Perl 5	44
do	Loop Control	Perl 4, Perl 5	46
dump	Function	Perl 4, Perl 5	48
each	Function	Perl 4, Perl 5	49
else	Loop Control	Perl 4, Perl 5	50
elsif	Loop Control	Perl 4, Perl 5	51
END	Subroutine	Perl 5	52
eof	Function	Perl 4, Perl 5	53
eq	Operator	Perl 4, Perl 5	54
eval	Function	Perl 4, Perl 5	56
exec	Function	Perl 4, Perl 5	57
exists	Function	Perl 5	58
exit	Function	Perl 4, Perl 5	58
exp	Function	Perl 4, Perl 5	59
fcntl	System Call	Perl 4, Perl 5	60
fileno	Function	Perl 4, Perl 5	61

Function	Category	Version	Page
flock	System Call	Perl 4, Perl 5	62
for	Loop Control	Perl 4, Perl 5	63
foreach	Loop Control	Perl 4, Perl 5	64
fork	System Call	Perl 4, Perl 5	65
format	Function	Perl 4, Perl 5	66
formline	Function	Perl 5	67
ge	Operator	Perl 4, Perl 5	69
getc	Function	Perl 4, Perl 5	70
getgrent	System Call	Perl 4, Perl 5	71
getgrgid	System Call	Perl 4, Perl 5	71
getgrnam	System Call	Perl 4, Perl 5	72
gethostbyaddr	System Call	Perl 4, Perl 5	73
gethostbyname	System Call	Perl 4, Perl 5	73
gethostent	System Call	Perl 4, Perl 5	74
getlogin	Function	Perl 4, Perl 5	75
getnetbyaddr	System Call	Perl 4, Perl 5	75
getnetbyname	System Call	Perl 4, Perl 5	76
getnetent	System Call	Perl 4, Perl 5	76
getpeername	Function	Perl 4, Perl 5	77
getpgrp	System Call	Perl 4, Perl 5	78
getppid	Function	Perl 4, Perl 5	78
getpriority	System Call	Perl 4, Perl 5	79
getprotobyname	System Call	Perl 4, Perl 5	79
getprotobynumber	System Call	Perl 4, Perl 5	80
getprotoent	System Call	Perl 4, Perl 5	80
getpwent	System Call	Perl 4, Perl 5	81
getpwnam	System Call	Perl 4, Perl 5	81
getpwuid	System Call	Perl 4, Perl 5	82
getservbyname	System Call	Perl 4, Perl 5	83
getservbyport	System Call	Perl 4, Perl 5	83
getservent	System Call	Perl 4, Perl 5	84
getsockname	Function	Perl 4, Perl 5	85
getsockopt	System Call	Perl 4, Perl 5	85
glob	Function	Perl 5	86
gmtime	Function	Perl 4, Perl 5	86
goto	Function Loop Control	Perl 4, Perl 5	87
grep	Function	Perl 4, Perl 5	88
gt	Operator	Perl 4, Perl 5	89
hex	Operator	Perl 4, Perl 5	91
if	Loop Control	Perl 4, Perl 5	92
import	Method	Perl 5	93
index	Function	Perl 4, Perl 5	94
int	Function	Perl 4, Perl 5	95

Function	Category	Version	Page
ioctl	System Call	Perl 4, Perl 5	96
join	Function	Perl 4, Perl 5	97
keys	Function	Perl 4, Perl 5	98
kill	Function	Perl 4, Perl 5	98
last	Loop Control	Perl 5	100
lc	Function	Perl 5	101
lcfirst	Function	Perl 5	101
le	Operator	Perl 4, Perl 5	102
length	Function	Perl 4, Perl 5	103
link	Function	Perl 4, Perl 5	104
listen	System Call	Perl 4, Perl 5	104
local	Function	Perl 4, Perl 5	105
localtime	Function	Perl 4, Perl 5	107
log	Function	Perl 4, Perl 5	108
lstat	Function	Perl 4, Perl 5	108
lt	Operator	Perl 4, Perl 5	109
m	Operator	Perl 4, Perl 5	111
map	Function	Perl 5	112
mkdir	System Call	Perl 4, Perl 5	113
msgctl	System Call	Perl 4, Perl 5	114
msgget	System Call	Perl 4, Perl 5	114
msgrcv	System Call	Perl 4, Perl 5	115
msgsnd	System Call	Perl 4, Perl 5	115
my	Operator	Perl 5	116
ne	Operator	Perl 4, Perl 5	118
new	Subroutine	Perl 5	119
next	Loop Control	Perl 4, Perl 5	119
no	Declaration	Perl 5	120
not	Operator	Perl 5	121
oct	Operator	Perl 4, Perl 5	123
open	Function	Perl 4, Perl 5	123
opendir	Function	Perl 4, Perl 5	125
or	Operator	Perl 5	126
ord	Function	Perl 4, Perl 5	127
pack	Function	Perl 4, Perl 5	128
package	Declaration	Perl 5	130
pipe	System Call	Perl 4, Perl 5	131
pop	Function	Perl 4, Perl 5	132
pos	Function	Perl 5	133
print	Function	Perl 4, Perl 5	134
printf	Function	Perl 4, Perl 5	136
push	Function	Perl 4, Perl 5	137
quotemeta	Function	Perl 5	139

Function	Category	Version	Page
qw	Function	Perl 5	140
rand	Function	Perl 4, Perl 5	141
read	Function	Perl 4, Perl 5	142
readdir	Function	Perl 4, Perl 5	143
readlink	Function	Perl 4, Perl 5	144
recv	Function	Perl 4, Perl 5	145
redo	Function	Perl 4, Perl 5	146
ref	Function	Perl 5	146
rename	Function	Perl 4, Perl 5	147
require	Function	Perl 4, Perl 5	148
reset	Function	Perl 4, Perl 5	150
return	Function	Perl 4, Perl 5	151
reverse	Function	Perl 4, Perl 5	152
rewinddir	Function	Perl 4, Perl 5	153
rindex	Function	Perl 5	154
rmdir	Function	Perl 5	156
s	Operator	Perl 4, Perl 5	157
scalar	Declaration	Perl 4, Perl 5	158
seek	Function	Perl 4, Perl 5	159
seekdir	Function	Perl 4, Perl 5	160
select	Operator	Perl 4, Perl 5	161
semctl	System Call	Perl 4, Perl 5	162
semget	System Call	Perl 4, Perl 5	162
semop	System Call	Perl 4, Perl 5	163
send	Function	Perl 4, Perl 5	164
setpgrp	Function	Perl 4, Perl 5	165
setpriority	System Call	Perl 4, Perl 5	165
setsockopt	Function	Perl 4, Perl 5	166
shift	Function	Perl 4, Perl 5	167
shmctl	System Call	Perl 4, Perl 5	168
shmget	System Call	Perl 4, Perl 5	168
shmread	Function	Perl 4, Perl 5	169
shmwrite	Function	Perl 4, Perl 5	170
shutdown	Function	Perl 4, Perl 5	170
sin	Operator	Perl 4, Perl 5	171
sleep	Function	Perl 4, Perl 5	172
socket	Function	Perl 4, Perl 5	172
socketpair	Function	Perl 4, Perl 5	173
sort	Function	Perl 4, Perl 5	174
splice	Function	Perl 4, Perl 5	176
split	Function	Perl 4, Perl 5	177
sprintf	Function	Perl 4, Perl 5	178
sqrt	Function	Perl 4, Perl 5	179

Function	Category	Version	Page
srand	Function	Perl 4, Perl 5	179
stat	Function	Perl 4, Perl 5	180
study	Function	Perl 4, Perl 5	182
sub	Declaration, Operator	Perl 4, Perl 5	183
substr	Function	Perl 4, Perl 5	185
symlink	Function	Perl 4, Perl 5	185
syscall	System Call	Perl 4, Perl 5	186
sysopen	Function, System Call	Perl 5	186
sysread	Function, System Call	Perl 4, Perl 5	187
system	Function	Perl 4, Perl 5	188
syswrite	Function, System Call	Perl 4, Perl 5	188
tell	Function	Perl 4, Perl 5	190
telldir	Function	Perl 4, Perl 5	191
tie	Function	Perl 5	192
tied	Function	Perl 5	192
time	Function	Perl 4, Perl 5	193
times	Function	Perl 4, Perl 5	194
tr	Operator	Perl 4, Perl 5	195
truncate	Function	Perl 4, Perl 5	197
uc	Function	Perl 5	198
ucfirst	Function	Perl 5	198
umask	Function	Perl 4, Perl 5	199
undef	Operator	Perl 4, Perl 5	200
unless	Loop Control	Perl 4, Perl 5	201
unlink	Function	Perl 4, Perl 5	202
unpack	Function	Perl 4, Perl 5	203
unshift	Function	Perl 4, Perl 5	205
untie	Function	Perl 5	206
until	Loop Control	Perl 4, Perl 5	206
use	Declaration	Perl 5	207
utime	Function	Perl 4, Perl 5	208
values	Function	Perl 4, Perl 5	209
vec	Function	Perl 4, Perl 5	209
wait	Function	Perl 4, Perl 5	211
waitpid	System Call	Perl 4, Perl 5	212
wantarray	Function	Perl 4, Perl 5	213
warn	Function	Perl 4, Perl 5	213
while	Loop Control	Perl 4, Perl 5	214
write	Function	Perl 4, Perl 5	215
x	Operator	Perl 4, Perl 5	217
xor	Operator	Perl 5	217
y	Operator	Perl 4, Perl 5	219

Jump Table B—Listing by Category

Category	Function	Version	Page
Declaration	no	Perl 5	120
	package	Perl 5	130
	scalar	Perl 4, Perl 5	158
	use	Perl 5	207
Declaration, Operator	sub	Perl 4, Perl 5	183
Function	abs	Perl 5	21
	atan2	Perl 4, Perl 5	24
	binmode	Perl 4, Perl 5	27
	bless	Perl 5	27
	caller	Perl 4, Perl 5	29
	chdir	Perl 4, Perl 5	29
	chmod	Perl 4, Perl 5	30
	chomp	Perl 5	31
	chop	Perl 4, Perl 5	32
	chown	Perl 4, Perl 5	33
	chr	Perl 5	33
	close	Perl 4, Perl 5	34
	closedir	Perl 4, Perl 5	35
	cos	Perl 4, Perl 5	39
	crypt	Perl 4, Perl 5	39
	dbmclose	Perl 4, Perl 5	41
	dbmopen	Perl 4, Perl 5	42
	defined	Perl 4, Perl 5	43
	delete	Perl 4, Perl 5	44
	die	Perl 4, Perl 5	44
	dump	Perl 4, Perl 5	48
	each	Perl 4, Perl 5	49
	eof	Perl 4, Perl 5	53
	eval	Perl 4, Perl 5	56
	exec	Perl 4, Perl 5	57
	exists	Perl 5	58
	exit	Perl 4, Perl 5	58
	exp	Perl 4, Perl 5	59
	fileno	Perl 4, Perl 5	61
	format	Perl 4, Perl 5	66
	formline	Perl 5	67
	getc	Perl 4, Perl 5	70
	getlogin	Perl 4, Perl 5	75
	getpeername	Perl 4, Perl 5	77
	getppid	Perl 4, Perl 5	78
	getsockname	Perl 4, Perl 5	85
	glob	Perl 5	86

Category	Function	Version	Page
Function	gmtime	Perl 4, Perl 5	86
	grep	Perl 4, Perl 5	88
	index	Perl 4, Perl 5	94
	int	Perl 4, Perl 5	95
	join	Perl 4, Perl 5	97
	keys	Perl 4, Perl 5	98
	kill	Perl 4, Perl 5	98
	lc	Perl 5	101
	lcfirst	Perl 5	101
	length	Perl 4, Perl 5	103
	link	Perl 4, Perl 5	104
	local	Perl 4, Perl 5	105
	localtime	Perl 4, Perl 5	107
	log	Perl 4, Perl 5	108
	lstat	Perl 4, Perl 5	108
	map	Perl 5	112
	open	Perl 4, Perl 5	123
	opendir	Perl 4, Perl 5	125
	ord	Perl 4, Perl 5	127
	pack	Perl 4, Perl 5	128
	pop	Perl 4, Perl 5	132
	pos	Perl 5	133
	print	Perl 4, Perl 5	134
	printf	Perl 4, Perl 5	136
	push	Perl 4, Perl 5	137
	quotemeta	Perl 5	139
	qw	Perl 5	140
	rand	Perl 4, Perl 5	141
	read	Perl 4, Perl 5	142
	readdir	Perl 4, Perl 5	143
	readlink	Perl 4, Perl 5	144
	recv	Perl 4, Perl 5	145
	redo	Perl 4, Perl 5	146
	ref	Perl 5	146
	rename	Perl 4, Perl 5	147
	require	Perl 4, Perl 5	148
	reset	Perl 4, Perl 5	150
	return	Perl 4, Perl 5	151
	reverse	Perl 4, Perl 5	152
	rewinddir	Perl 4, Perl 5	153
	rindex	Perl 5	154
	rmdir	Perl 5	156
	seek	Perl 4, Perl 5	159
	seekdir	Perl 4, Perl 5	160

Category	Function	Version	Page
Function	send	Perl 4, Perl 5	164
	setpgrp	Perl 4, Perl 5	165
	setsockopt	Perl 4, Perl 5	166
	shift	Perl 4, Perl 5	167
	shmread	Perl 4, Perl 5	169
	shmwrite	Perl 4, Perl 5	170
	shutdown	Perl 4, Perl 5	170
	sleep	Perl 4, Perl 5	172
	socket	Perl 4, Perl 5	172
	socketpair	Perl 4, Perl 5	173
	sort	Perl 4, Perl 5	174
	splice	Perl 4, Perl 5	176
	split	Perl 4, Perl 5	177
	sprintf	Perl 4, Perl 5	178
	sqrt	Perl 4, Perl 5	179
	srand	Perl 4, Perl 5	179
	stat	Perl 4, Perl 5	180
	study	Perl 4, Perl 5	182
	substr	Perl 4, Perl 5	185
	symlink	Perl 4, Perl 5	185
	system	Perl 4, Perl 5	188
	tell	Perl 4, Perl 5	190
	telldir	Perl 4, Perl 5	191
	tie	Perl 5	192
	tied	Perl 5	192
	time	Perl 4, Perl 5	193
	times	Perl 4, Perl 5	194
	truncate	Perl 4, Perl 5	197
	uc	Perl 5	198
	ucfirst	Perl 5	198
	umask	Perl 4, Perl 5	199
	unlink	Perl 4, Perl 5	202
	unpack	Perl 4, Perl 5	203
	unshift	Perl 4, Perl 5	205
	untie	Perl 5	206
	utime	Perl 4, Perl 5	208
	values	Perl 4, Perl 5	209
	vec	Perl 4, Perl 5	209
	wait	Perl 4, Perl 5	211
	wantarray	Perl 4, Perl 5	213
	warn	Perl 4, Perl 5	213
	write	Perl 4, Perl 5	215
Function Loop Control	goto	Perl 4, Perl 5	87
Function, System Call	sysopen	Perl 5	186

Category	Function	Version	Page
Function, System Call	sysread	Perl 4, Perl 5	187
	syswrite	Perl 4, Perl 5	188
Handle	DATA	Perl 4, Perl 5	41
Loop Control	continue	Perl 4, Perl 5	37
	do	Perl 4, Perl 5	46
	else	Perl 4, Perl 5	50
	elsif	Perl 4, Perl 5	51
	for	Perl 4, Perl 5	63
	foreach	Perl 4, Perl 5	64
	if	Perl 4, Perl 5	92
	last	Perl 5	100
	next	Perl 4, Perl 5	119
	unless	Perl 4, Perl 5	201
	until	Perl 4, Perl 5	206
	while	Perl 4, Perl 5	214
Method	import	Perl 5	93
Operator	!	Perl 4, Perl 5	10
	!=	Perl 4, Perl 5	10
	%	Perl 4, Perl 5	16
	&	Perl 4, Perl 5	1
	&&	Perl 4, Perl 5	1
	*	Perl 4, Perl 5	8
	**	Perl 4, Perl 5	8
	+	Perl 4, Perl 5	18
	++	Perl 4, Perl 5	19
	-	Perl 4, Perl 5	14
	->	Perl 5	15
	.	Perl 4, Perl 5	12
	/	Perl 4, Perl 5	9
	<	Perl 4, Perl 5	2
	<<	Perl 4, Perl 5	3
	<=	Perl 4, Perl 5	4
	<=>	Perl 4, Perl 5	4
	=	Perl 4, Perl 5	12
	==	Perl 4, Perl 5	13
	>	Perl 4, Perl 5	5
	>=	Perl 4, Perl 5	7
	>>	Perl 4, Perl 5	6
	?:	Perl 4, Perl 5	19
	and	Perl 5	22
	cmp	Perl 4, Perl 5	36
	eq	Perl 4, Perl 5	54

Category	Function	Version	Page
Operator	ge	Perl 4, Perl 5	69
	gt	Perl 4, Perl 5	89
	hex	Perl 4, Perl 5	91
	le	Perl 4, Perl 5	102
	lt	Perl 4, Perl 5	109
	m	Perl 4, Perl 5	111
	my	Perl 5	116
	ne	Perl 4, Perl 5	118
	not	Perl 5	121
	oct	Perl 4, Perl 5	123
	or	Perl 5	126
	s	Perl 4, Perl 5	157
	select	Perl 4, Perl 5	161
	sin	Perl 4, Perl 5	171
	tr	Perl 4, Perl 5	195
	undef	Perl 4, Perl 5	200
	x	Perl 4, Perl 5	217
	xor	Perl 5	217
	y	Perl 4, Perl 5	219
	^	Perl 4, Perl 5	11
	|	Perl 4, Perl 5	17
	||	Perl 4, Perl 5	17
	~	Perl 4, Perl 5	20
	—	Perl 4, Perl 5	15
Subroutine	AUTOLOAD	Perl 5	24
	BEGIN	Perl 5	26
	END	Perl 5	52
	new	Perl 5	119
System Call	accept	Perl 4, Perl 5	21
	alarm	Perl 4, Perl 5	22
	bind	Perl 4, Perl 5	26
	chroot	Perl 4, Perl 5	34
	connect	Perl 4, Perl 5	37
	fcntl	Perl 4, Perl 5	60
	flock	Perl 4, Perl 5	62
	fork	Perl 4, Perl 5	65
	getgrent	Perl 4, Perl 5	71
	getgrgid	Perl 4, Perl 5	71
	getgrnam	Perl 4, Perl 5	72
	gethostbyaddr	Perl 4, Perl 5	73
	gethostbyname	Perl 4, Perl 5	73
	gethostent	Perl 4, Perl 5	74

Introduction

The Practical Extraction and Reporting Language (Perl) is by far one of the most widely used languages for parsing and World Wide Web (WWW) purposes. Its roots lie in awk, C, sh, and sed languages yet its implementation is far easier than any other object oriented language.

Created by Larry Wall, Perl is by nature a practical interpreted language. Its principal functionality was originally for parsing text-based data and generating summaries or results of this data. With the explosion of the Internet, we have seen Perl's hands in Common Gateway Interface (CGI) programming and the processing of form data. Even with newer compiled and scripting languages evolving, such as Java, JavaScript, and VBScript, Perl's worth has not fallen. It proves to thousands of programmers everyday that its functionality, ease of use, and ease of implementation are ever needed.

What's New in Perl 5?

So what are the newest features in our favorite programming language? Although programming techniques is not the topic of this book, we feel it necessary to list the relevant new features of Perl 5:

- **AUTOLOAD, BEGIN, and END.** These are routines that execute according to their conditions rather than by being explicitly called. See their entries in the *Perl Commands* section for more information on their implementation.

- **Integration into C and C++ Applications.** Your scripts can be embedded into your C and C++ applications and can call or be called by your interface routines.
- **Library Modules.** The library is now in the form of Perl modules which allows multiple and more defined access.
- **Multiple Database Module Accesses.** This feature allows you to access various database modules at the same time in the same script.
- **Object Oriented.** Packages now function as classes, as well as other added functions, to form the syntax to a more OOP tradition.
- **POSIX Support.** Included in a module that provides access to POSIX routines and definitions.
- **Subroutine Calls.** Can now be done without the preceding & if the routine has already been defined. If it hasn't been defined, then you can declare references, such as '**sub myRoutine,**' that give you access to the routine without the preceding &.
- And more. . . .

With the addition of these features, which make Perl 5 a considerable rewrite of the language, there are new functions and commands. The following is a list of the latest additions to Perl commands:

->	lcfirst	ref
abs	map	rindex
bless	my	rmdir
chomp	new	sysopen
chr	no	tie
exists	not	tied
formline	or	uc
glob	package	ucfirst
import	pos	untie
last	quotemeta	use
lc	qw	xor

Supported Platforms

Perl was originally designed for the UNIX operating system and is generally distributed as the source code rather than as binary executables. This allows you the ability to tailor your installation to your needs and requirements and helps you maintain a certain degree of portability for the language.

There are, however, a few third-party binary distributions out there. The most common are Perl for Win32, for 32-bit Windows systems, and MacPerl, for the MacOS. Along with these binaries, actual source code is available for multiple ports, including OS/2, VMS, Macintosh, Windows 16- and 32-bit, Windows NT, and others. Keep in mind that the language relies heavily on the system in which it is running. In these non-native ports you may find that some of the functions and other commands work differently or may not work at all. Be sure to check the Perl documentation for any deployment issues on these systems, and keep an eye out for any new developments that could help you in your quest.

To keep a current tab on the most recent ports, visit the Perl home page at http://www.perl.com/perl.

What's Inside

The Perl 5 Programmer's Reference was written by programmers for programmers to simplify and organize the language's syntax. As with many programming languages, Perl has a multitude of built-in functions, commands, and modules, each with its own meaning and syntax. This book is not written for a programmer wanting to learn the semantics of the language, but rather as a true reference for the functions and commands it contains.

As we Perl programmers know, most all the documentation on this wonderful interpreted language is "how to" meshed with pure documentation. There is a lack of true, dedicated reference books on the shelves today, yet their relevance is unmatched. This is where Ventana's Programmer's Reference series comes to the rescue. Ventana has developed a series whose sole purpose is to be the dictionary to the languages that a given programmer loves most. In the case of our book, Perl gets all the attention.

We have developed this book with the assumption that when Perl programmers need help on a particular problem, they want it now. They do not want to filter through hard-to-understand documentation with examples that are too complex. You will notice that even though this book is for intermediate and advanced users, its definitions and examples are quite easy to follow and understand. The reasoning behind this simplistic approach is that our examples and definitions give you a true feel for a command. The entries do not serve just as a reference, but are written in a manner to allow you to understand how the command works as well as how to implement it. We do not attempt to tell you how to program. Programming is much like one's handwriting; it is unique to each programmer. An understanding of how a function works is much more important than the result. If you know how it works, you will understand the result; however, the reverse is not always true. This methodology will also aid those programmers who are learning the language or have only used it to a small degree.

In the following pages you will have access to an alphabetized list of these reserved words, each accompanied with syntax, description, examples, list of parameters, return values, and a list of any related commands where appropriate.

Note: The term *reserved words* is used to represent any predefined functions, commands, and special variables. Likewise, the terms *command* and *functions* will be used interchangeably to represent any Perl word that performs a function.

The approach we have taken, as you can see, is quite unique. Our intentions were to create the ultimate reference for Perl, but to do so in a comprehensible way. Before we get started, we would like to take a bit more of your time to discuss some of the organization and conventions used in this book.

Entry Organization

Each entry in this reference book has several internal fields. We have tried to include as much relevant information in these fields as possible without further confusing the programmer. Do note that there are some occasions where the fields are not relevant. In these instances, they were simply left out. The following is a list of the fields accompanied with a brief description of what they contain:

- **Icons.** These icons are located to the right of the entry's name and denote the version of Perl that supports the entry.

- **Syntax.** Each Perl reserved word has its own unique syntax. This syntax defines what type of arguments, if any, are to be passed to the commands. In defining the syntax, we have tried to maintain names that correspond to their type and usage. Please see the next section of this Introduction for any conventions used in this section.

- **Usage.** You can't use the command if you do not know what it does. This section contains the definitions to the commands as well as any special notes or tips.

- **Examples.** You may find this section the most helpful. It contains examples of the defined commands and is included to help you understand their functionality. Often times, simple *print* statements are used to demonstrate this functionality.

- **Parameters.** This field contains the type of arguments that you may be passing to the functions. Again, please see the section on *Conventions* for any conventions used in this section.

- **Value.** This field contains the return type of the function. Once again, please see the section on *Conventions* for any conventions used in this section.

- **See Also.** The final field in each entry contain a list of any related functions.

Conventions Used

As any programmer knows, everyone has their own interpretation of a language. Perl programmers are no different. Being amongst the Perl programming population exposes the Perl programmer to various terms, lingo, and conventions. Since a reference book should address any programmer of Perl, we feel it is necessary to document the conventions we used in this book to clarify any cloudy terminology. The following is a list of terms we use as well as a description of each:

- **Alphanumeric.** Signifies that this instance can contain all numeric characters (0-9) as well as alphabetic (A-Z and a-z).
- **Array.** A list of elements that are referenced via their indexed location. The first location in an array is known as index position 0.
- **Associative array (Hash).** This type of array creates an alias, or key, for each entry in the array. This allows you to access the entry in a method other than by explicitly calling it by its indexed location.
- **Boolean.** The value can be used as conditions for boolean operations.
- **CODE.** Designates the area occupied by *CODE* to contain any relevant code as the programmer sees fit.
- **Condition.** Used in loop initialization to determine if the loop is to be entered or not. This entry is based on the assessment of the *condition*.
- **EXPRESSION.** Place holder in those functions that can evaluate arguments of any value type.
- **FILE_VARIABLE.** Used to represent a handle for a file.
- **Filename.** A string that contains the exact filename to be used (i.e., "test.txt").
- **Handle.** Serves as an alias to a file, set of data, or socket connection. This is used so that manipulation can be done via a handle rather than by the explicitly declared name.
- **List.** A list of data, usually separated using the comma operator.
- **Numeric.** Signifies a numeric value.
- **Properties.** Used on occasions that a function will return various properties of various types, rather than a single type of data.
- **Scalar.** Signifies a scalar value.
- **SOC_VARIABLE.** Used to represent a handle for a socket connection.
- **String.** Signifies a string value.
- **System Call.** Used to signify that the command uses the system's version of the program of the same name. If you are running Perl on a ported platform, be sure that your system supports these calls.

In addition to the terms we just defined, we also tried to maintain a form of consistency across the entries. This includes the following:

- *italics.* This type of formatting is used when we reference other functions, commands, and special variables. This is done to help the reader interrelate the various functions.
- **Bold.** Used to signify text that should be entered at the command line.
- **Tips and Notes.** These are sub-entries throughout the text that are used to describe various types of implementations for the entry in which they are contained.

Moving On

Now that you understand the layout of the book and its entries and you have had a crash course in its conventions and terminology, you are ready to go forward. The following pages will take you in and out of the syntax of Perl as well as help pave the road to a better understanding of its semantics. We truly hope that this book will lighten up any dark areas you have, and that it will expose any hidden beasts in Perl. Enjoy!

— R. Allen Wyke
— Luke Duncan

Perl Commands

1

&

Syntax   *num1* & *num2*

Usage   The & bitwise logical operator performs and returns a bitwise AND on the arguments passed. A 0 is returned if the arguments passed are not equal.

Examples   This example assigns a number to *$one* and *$two*. The two variables are then compared and the *print* statement prints a result to the user's screen:

```
# define 2 numeric variables
$one = 8;
$two = 8;

# print the result, 8, of the & operator
print($one & $two);
```

Parameters   numeric

Value   numeric

See Also   or, Appendix C (Operators)

&&

Syntax   *element1* && *element2*

Usage   The *&&* logical operator returns 1 if *element2* and *element1* exist. If only one or neither exist, then a *NULL* is returned. This is commonly used to verify the existence of variables in your script as well as to return the second argument based on this existence.

     For those of you who are unfamiliar with logical operations, a *truth table* can be constructed based on the possible arguments passed. By looking at a truth table of the possible results, you could determine the result of an *&&* operation. See the entry for *and* in the Perl Commands section of this book for a similar table.

Examples This example assigns a number to *$j* and then compares this variable to an undefined *$i*. Since *$i* is undefined, the nonexistent string will be printed:

```
# define a variable
$j = 1;

# but there is no '$i'!
if ($i && $j){
   print('$i exists!\n');
}else{
   print('$i does not exist!'."\n");
}
```

Parameters numeric

Value boolean
numeric

See Also and, Appendix C (Operators)

<

OPERATOR

PERL 4 PERL 5

Syntax *numeric1 < numeric2*

Usage The < numeric comparison operator tests the arguments passed to see if the first argument is less than the second argument. If the first argument is less than the second, the returned result is 1. If the second argument is less than the first or the two arguments are equal, then a *NULL* is returned.

Examples This example assigns a number to *$num1* and *$num2*. These two variables are then compared and a result based on the comparison is printed:

```
# define the variables
$num1 = 4;
$num2 = 3;

# determine if first argument is less than second
if ($num1 < $num2){
   print('$num1 is less than $num2'."\n");
}else{

   # this line will be printed to the user's screen
   print('$num2 is less than $num1'."\n");
}
```

<<

Parameters   numeric

Value   numeric

See Also   lt, Appendix C (Operators)

<<

OPERATOR

PERL 4   PERL 5

Syntax   *numeric << num*

Usage   The << bitwise shift operator shifts the bits of *numeric* to the left by *num* bits. The newly created undefined bit locations are buffered with 0's, with the result of this shift returned.

Examples   This example assigns a number to *$num1*, then prompts the user to enter the number of bits they wish to shift the variable. The result is calculated and printed to the user's screen:

```
# define variable
$numeric = 1;

# prompt user for bit shift value
print("How many bits to the left would you like to shift $ numeric?:
    ");
chop($shift = (<STDIN>));

# print results
print($numeric << $shift);
```

Parameters   numeric

Value   numeric

See Also   >>, Appendix C (Operators)

<=

Syntax   *numeric1* <= *numeric2*

Usage   The <= numeric comparison operator tests the arguments passed to see if the first argument is less than or equal to the second argument. If the first argument is less than the second or the two arguments are the same, the returned result is 1. If the second argument is less than the first, then a *NULL* is returned.

Examples   This example assigns a number to *$num1* and *$num2*. These two variables are then compared and a result based on the comparison is printed:

```
# define the variables
$num1 = 4;
$num2 = 3;

# determine if first argument is less or equal to second
if ($num1 <= $num2){
   print('$num1 is less than or equal to $num2'."\n");
}else{

   # this line will be printed to the user's screen
   print('$num2 is less than $num1'."\n");
   }
```

Parameters   numeric

Value   numeric

See Also   le, Appendix C (Operators)

<=>

Syntax   *numeric1* <=> *numeric2*

Usage   The <=> numeric comparison operator compares *numeric1* to *numeric2*. If the two strings are the same, the returned result is 0. If *numeric* is greater, 1 is returned, and if *numeric2* is greater, -1 is returned.

Examples   This example shows how the <=> operator can distinguish between numeri-cal arguments:

```
# define two numeric variables
$i = 1;
$j = 1;

# print the result of their comparison
print(($i <=> $j)."\n");
```

Parameters   numeric

Value   numeric

See Also   cmp, Appendix C (Operators)

>
                                                                   OPERATOR

PERL 4   PERL 5

Syntax   *numeric1 > numeric2*

Usage   The > numeric comparison operator tests to see if the first argument passed is greater than the second argument passed. If it is, then a 1 is returned; a *NULL* is returned if the second argument is greater than or equal to the first argument.

Examples   This example assigns a number to *$one* and *$two*. The numbers are then compared, and *print* function prints a result based on the comparison:

```
# define 2 numeric variables
$one = 1;
$two = 2;

if ($one > $two){
   print("$one is greater than $two\n");
}else{

   # this line will be printed
   print("$two is greater than $one\n");
}
```

Parameters   numeric

Value   numeric

See Also   gt, Appendix C (Operators)

>>

OPERATOR

PERL 4   PERL 5

Syntax   *numeric >> num*

Usage   The >> bitwise shift operator shifts the bits of *numeric* to the right by *num* bits. The result of this shift is returned.

Examples   This example assigns a number to *$num1*, then prompts the user to enter the number of bits they wish to shift the variable. The result is calculated and printed to the user's screen:

```
# define variable
$numeric = 3;

# prompt user for bit shift value
print("How many bits to the right would you like to shift $ numeric?:
    ");
chop($shift = (<STDIN>));

# print results
print($numeric >> $shift);
```

Parameters   numeric

Value   numeric

See Also   <<, Appendix C (Operators)

>=

Syntax   *numeric1 >= numeric2*

Usage   The >= numeric comparison operator tests to see if the first argument passed is greater than or equal to the second argument passed. If the first argument is greater than or equal to the second argument, then a 1 is returned. If the second argument is greater, a 0 is returned.

Examples   This example assigns a number to *$one* and *$two*. These two variables are then compared and the *print* function outputs a result based on the comparison:

```
# define two numeric variables
$one = 1;
$two = 2;

# test to see if the first variable is greater or equal
if ($one >= $two){
   print("$one is greater than or equal to $two\n");
}else{

   # this line will be printed
   print("$two is greater than $one\n");
}
```

Parameters   numeric

Value   numeric

See Also   ge, Appendix C (Operators)

*

Syntax   *numeric1 * numeric2*

Usage   The * multiplication operator multiplies *numeric1* by *numeric2* and returns the result of the multiplication.

Examples   This example defines two numeric variables, then prints the multiplication result to the screen:

```
# define two numeric variables
$num1 = 2;
$num2 = 3;

# print the multiplied result, '6', to the screen
print($num1*$num2);
```

Parameters   numeric

Value   numeric

See Also   Appendix C (Operators)

**

Syntax   *numeric ** num*

Usage   The ** exponential operator raises *numeric* to the power of *num*.

Examples   This example defines a numeric variable and prompts the user for a power to raise it. The result of the variable raised to the numeric power is then evaluated and printed to the user's screen:

```
# define variable
$numeric = 2;
```

```
# prompt user for power
print("To what power would you like to raise $numeric?: ");
chop($power = (<STDIN>));

# print result
print($numeric ** $power);
```

Parameters numeric

Value numeric

See Also Appendix C (Operators)

/

Syntax *numeric1 / numeric2*

Usage The / division operator divides *numeric1* by *numeric2* and returns the result of the division.

Examples This example defines two numeric variables, and then prints the division result to the screen:

```
# define two numeric variables
$num1 = 6;
$num2 = 3;

# print the divided result, '2', to the screen
print($num1\$num2);
```

Parameters numeric

Value numeric

See Also Appendix C (Operators)

!

Syntax   `!EXPRESSION`

Usage   The *!* unary negation operator negates the *EXPRESSION* passed. This is often used to control the conditions to enter loops.

Examples   This example sets a variable to 0, then prints its negation value to the screen:

```
# define numeric variable
$myNum = 0;

# print '1' to the screen
print(!$myNum);
```

Parameters   expression

Value   negated expression

See Also   Appendix C (Operators)

!=

Syntax   `numeric1 != numeric1`

Usage   The *!=* numeric comparison operator tests the arguments passed to see if they are *not* equal. If the two strings are the same, then *NULL* is returned. If they are not equal, a 1 is returned.

Examples   This example assigns numbers to two variables. The two variables are then compared, and the *print* function prints a result based on the comparison. The result of this example prints the "not equal" string to the user's screen:

```
# define 2 variables with numeric values
$num1 = 4;
$num2 = 3;
```

```
# test to see if they are equal
if ($num1 != $num2){

   # this line is printed
   print('$num1 and $num2 are not equal'."\n");

}else{
   print('$num1 and $num2 are equal'."\n");
}
```

Parameters   numeric

Value   numeric

See Also   ne, Appendix C (Operators)

^

OPERATOR

PERL 4   PERL 5

Syntax   *num1 ^ num2*

Usage   The ^ bitwise logical operator performs and returns a bitwise exclusive OR on the arguments passed.

Examples   This example assigns a number to *$one* and *$two*. The two variables are then compared and the *print* statement prints a result to the user's screen:

```
# define 2 numeric variables
$one = 1;
$two = 0;

# print the results, 1, of the ^ operator
print($one ^ $two);
```

Parameters   numeric

Value   numeric

See Also   Appendix C (Operators), xor

Syntax   *element1 . element2*

Usage   The . concatenation operator concatenates *element2* to the end of *element1* and returns it.

Examples   This example defines three variables as strings. The concatenation operator is called in the *print* function to "append" the strings together:

```
# define 3 variables
$one = "Hello ";
$two = "Perl ";
$three = "World!\n";

# print the variables concatenated together
# prints 'Hello Perl World!'
print($one . $two . $three);
```

Parameters   expression

Value   expression

See Also   Appendix C (Operators)

=

Syntax   *EXPRESSION = value*

Usage   The = assignment operator assigns *value* to *EXPRESSION*. This operator is used to assign scalar values, array contents, list values, etc. It can also be used in conjunction with other operators to perform a numeric function on itself and reassign the result to the same variable. See the Operators section of Appendix C for the type of functions you can use, and see the second example for a better understanding of this type of implementation.

Examples   This example assigns values to several types of variables:

```
# define variables
$numeric = 999;
$string = ("Hello Perl World!\n");
%assocArray = ("One", 1, "Two", 2, "Three", 3);
$list = ("Robert", "Bettie", "Sandra", "Valerie", "Evelyn", "Emily",
  "Alex");
```

This example shows how you can perform a numeric function and self assignment in one statement:

```
# define a numeric variable
$num = 5;

# add 6 to $num and reassign it
$num += 6;

# print '11' to screen
print("$num\n");
```

Parameters   expression
value

Value   value

See Also   Appendix C (Operators)

==   OPERATOR

PERL 4   PERL 5

Syntax   *numeric1 == numeric2*

Usage   The == numeric comparison operator tests *numeric1* and *numeric2* to see if they are equal. If the two strings are the same, the returned result is 1. If they are not equal, a 0 is returned.

Examples   This example assigned a number to *$num1* and *$num2*. These two variables are then compared and the *print* function prints a result based on the comparison. The result of this example prints the "are equal" string to the user's screen:

```
# define 2 variables
$num1 = 3;
$num2 = 3;
```

```
# compare the variables
if ($num1 == $num2){

   # this line will be printed
   print('$num1 and $num2 are equal'."\n");

}else{
   print("Not equal\n");
}
```

Parameters numeric

Value numeric

See Also eq, Appendix C (Operators)

—

OPERATOR

PERL 4 **PERL 5**

Syntax *numeric1 - numeric2*

Usage The - subtraction operator subtracts *numeric2* from *numeric1* and returns the result of the subtraction.

Examples This example defines two numeric variables, then prints the subtraction result to the screen:

```
# define two numeric variables
$num1 = 6;
$num2 = 3;

# print the subtracted result, '3', to the screen
print($num1 - $num2);
```

Parameters numeric

Value numeric

See Also Appendix C (Operators)

OPERATOR

PERL 5

Syntax   `$arr_ref->[index];`

`$hash_ref->{'key'};`

`$symbol_ref->method();`

`$symbol_ref->variable;`

Usage   The -> arrow operator is used as an infix dereferencing operator. It is used
so you can access what an array or symbolic reference points to. This allows
you to access keys or indices of the array or methods and variables of a
symbol without having to dereference it explicitly before accessing the data
you care about.

Examples   The following example creates an anonymous array reference and accesses
the indices of it.

```
$array_ref = ['a', 'b', 'c', 'd', 'e'];
print "1st index is ", $array_ref->[0], "\n";
```

Parameters   reference

See Also   Appendix C (Operators)

—— ——   OPERATOR

PERL 4   PERL 5

Syntax   *numeric--*

Usage   The -- numeric auto-decrement operator decreases the value of *numeric* by 1.
This is often used to control the number of loop iterations you wish to
perform on a given loop.

Examples   The following example initializes a variable and prints it to the screen. The
variable is then decremented and again printed to the screen:

```
# define numeric variable and print it to the screen
$myNum = 3;
print("$myNum\n");
```

%

```
# decrement your number and print the new value
$myNum--;
print("$myNum\n");
```

Parameters   numeric

Value   numeric

See Also   ++, Appendix C (Operators)

%

Syntax   *numeric1 % numeric2*

Usage   The % modulus division operator divides *numeric1* by *numeric2* and returns the remainder of the division.

Examples   This example defines two numeric variables, then prints their modulus division result to the screen:

```
# define two numeric variables
$num1 = 5;
$num2 = 3;

# print the modulus division result, '2', to the screen
print($num1 % $num2);
```

Parameters   numeric

Value   numeric

See Also   Appendix C (Operators)

|

Syntax   *num1 | num2*

Usage   The | bitwise logical operator performs and returns a bitwise OR on the arguments passed.

Examples   This example assigns a number to *$one* and *$two*. The two variables are then compared and the *print* statement prints a result to the user's screen:

```
# define 2 numeric variables
$one = 8;
$two = 0;

# print the result, 8, of the | operator
print($one | $two);
```

Parameters   numeric

Value   numeric

See Also   or, Appendix C (Operators)

||

Syntax   *element1 || element2*

Usage   The || logical operator returns 1 if either element exists, and a *NULL* if neither exist. It is commonly used to verify the existence of variables in your script as well as in returning the second argument based on this existence.
For those of you who are unfamiliar with logical operations, a "truth table" can be constructed based on the possible arguments passed. By looking at a truth table of the possible results, the result of an || operation can be determined. See the entry for *or* in the Perl Commands section of this book for a similar table.

Examples   This example prompts the user for a number between 1 and 5. The | | operator is used to see if the user entered 1 or 5 and prints a result based on the evaluation:

```
# prompt for a number
print("Enter a number between 1 and 5? (y/n): ");
chop($input = (<STDIN>));

# determine what the user entered
if(($input == 1) || ($input == 5)){
  print("You entered 1 or 5!\n");
}else{
  print("You entered 2, 3 or 4.\n");
}
```

Parameters   expression

Value   boolean
numeric

See Also   or, Appendix C (Operators)

+

OPERATOR

PERL 4   **PERL 5**

Syntax   *numeric1 + numeric2*

Usage   The + addition operator adds *numeric1* by *numeric2* and returns the result of the addition.

Examples   This example defines two numeric variables, then prints the addition result to the screen:

```
# define two numeric variables
$num1 = 6;
$num2 = 3;

# print the added result, '9', to the screen
print($num1 + $num2);
```

Parameters   numeric

Value   numeric

See Also   Appendix C (Operators)

++

Syntax   *numeric++*

Usage   The ++ numeric auto-increment operator increases the value of *numeric* by 1. This is often used to control the number of loop iterations you wish to perform on a given loop.

Examples   The following example initializes a variable and prints it to the user's screen. The variable is then incremented and again printed to the screen:

```
# define numeric variable and print it to the screen
$myNum = 0;
print("$myNum\n");

# increment your number and print the new value
$myNum++;
print("$myNum\n");
```

Parameters   numeric

Value   numeric

See Also   --, Appendix C (Operators)

?:

Syntax   *CONDITION ? TRUE : FALSE*

Usage   The *?:* conditional operator evaluates *CONDITION*. If it passes evaluation, *TRUE* will be returned. If it fails evaluation, *FALSE* will be returned.

Examples   The following example defines two return variables and asks the user if their name is Bryant. The conditional operator is used to evaluate their input:

```
# define the return variables
$true = "Hello Bryant!\n";
$false = "You're not Bryant!\n";
```

~

```
# prompt user to see if their name is bryant
print("Is your name Bryant? (y/n): ");
chop($input = (<STDIN>));

# determine what the user entered
$result = ($input eq "y") ? $true : $false;

# print result of evaluation
print("$result\n");
```

Parameters   condition
           expression

Value   expression

See Also   if, for, Appendix C (Operators)

~

OPERATOR

PERL 4   **PERL 5**

Syntax   *~numeric*

Usage   The ~ unary compliment operator performs a bitwise complement on the *numeric* passed.

Examples   This example defines a numeric variable then prints its bitwise complement to the screen:

```
# define numeric variable
$num1 = 2;

# print the complement (-3) to the screen
print(~$num1);
```

Parameters   numeric

Value   numeric

See Also   Appendix C (Operators)

abs

Syntax   abs(*num*)

Usage   The *abs* function is an arithmetic function that returns the absolute value of the element passed to it. The absolute value of the element can be thought of as its positive representation or its distance from zero. If the element is originally positive, then the value remains the same.

        This type of function is most commonly used for error checking input strings. Its application in CGI programming could ensure that the proper values are passed for processing.

Examples   The following example assigns 56 to *$absValue*:

```
$absValue = abs(-56);
```

Parameters   numeric

Value   numeric

See Also   atan2, cos, exp, log, sin, sqrt

accept

Syntax   accept(*SOC_VARIABLE2, SOC_VARIABLE1*)

Usage   The *accept* network function waits for the *SOC_VARIABLE2* process to connect with process *SOC_VARIABLE1*, at which time it will return the address of the process requesting the connection. The first connection must be made using the *socket* function and then bound to its address using *bind*.

        Like most Perl functions, *accept* returns a true or false based on a successful connection. This allows you to check the success of the connection via a *die* function call.

Examples   This example returns the address of the *newConnection* after a connection to *currConnection* has been made:

```
$connAddress = accept(newConnection, currConnection) || die("Error:
    unable to accept connection");
```

A

Parameters	handle
Value	boolean
See Also	bind, connect, getpeername, getsocketname, getsockopt, listen, recv, send, shutdown, socket, socketpair

alarm

SYSTEM CALL

PERL 4   PERL 5

Syntax	`alarm(num)`
Usage	The *alarm* system function sends a *SIGALARM* to the user's computer after the specified *num* of seconds. Do note, however, that the seconds are initiated based on the user's computer. If, when the alarm is initialized, a second has partially elapsed on the user's computer, then it is possible that the user may receive the alarm some fraction of a second fast.
Examples	The following example sends an alarm to the user's computer after 60 seconds:

```
alarm(60);
```

Parameters	numeric

and

OPERATOR

PERL 5

Syntax	`element1 and element2`
Usage	This logical operator returns *element2* if *element1* exists. If it does not exist, then a NULL is returned. Perl's *and* is not a bitwise operator but rather a supposed low-precedence version of the *&&* operator. It could be commonly used to verify the existence of variables in your script as well as to return the second argument based on this existence.

For those of you who are unfamiliar with logical operations, a *truth table* can be constructed based on the possible arguments passed. By looking at a truth table of the possible results, you could determine the result of an *and* operation.

A

I have created a truth table that takes two elements, *element1* and *element2*, as the arguments passed to it. Below each column, I have listed all possible cases that the two elements could encounter, while the right column contains the result of using the *and* operator on the two columns. As you can see, the *and* operator only returns a *TRUE* (non-zero in a Perl implementation) result when both of the arguments are *TRUE*. As stated earlier, however, the Perl *and* simply returns *element2* if *element1* exists. A NULL assignment would be used for any *FALSE* results.

Truth Table		
element1	*element2*	*element1* and *element2*
FALSE	FALSE	FALSE
FALSE	TRUE	FALSE
TRUE	FALSE	FALSE
TRUE	TRUE	TRUE

Examples   This example assigns a number to $j and then compares this variable to an undefined $i. Since $i is undefined, the nonexistent string will be printed:

```
$j = 1;

# but there is no '$i'!
if ($i and $j){
   print('$i exists!\n');
}else{
   print('$i does not exist!'."\n");
}
```

Parameters   alphanumeric

Value   boolean
numeric

See Also   cmp, eq, not, or, undef, xor, Appendix C (Operators)

atan2

A

Syntax   `atan2(num1, num2)`

Usage   The *atan2* arithmetic function returns the arc tangent of *num1*/*num2* in the range of -π to π. The arc tangent is the inverse function of the tangent of the angle created by the two passed numbers.

Examples This example prints the arctangent of 1 and 1 concatenated with a newline to the screen:

`print(atan2(1,1)."\n");    # approximately '0.785398'`

Parameters numeric

Value   numeric

See Also abs, cos, exp, log, sin, sqrt

AUTOLOAD

Syntax   `AUTOLOAD{`
          `    CODE`
          `    }`

Usage   AUTOLOAD is the default subroutine that loads if you make a call to a nonexistent routine. This can be a helpful debugging tool if you place a *die* function call in the *CODE* that will allow you to exit the program under favorable circumstances and with the knowledge of where the incorrect subroutine call was made.

          $AUTOLOAD, which holds the name of the incorrectly called routine, is passed to the *AUTORUN* subroutine. In addition to the name of the routine, the information passed to the routine, when applicable, is stored in array @_.

A

Examples   This example demonstrates how effective use of the *AUTOLOAD* subroutine can make it possible to safely exit your script with the name and information of the routine making the call:

```
AUTOLOAD{
   die("Error: invalid subroutine called: $AUTOLOAD\n@_");
}
```

Parameters   array
string

Value   code

See Also   BEGIN, END

B

BEGIN

Syntax
```
BEGIN{
    CODE
    }
```

Usage   The *BEGIN* subroutine allows you to specify *CODE* to be executed before your regular script begins.

Examples   This example uses the *print* function to tell the user that the execution of the current script has begun:

```
BEGIN{
    print("You have now begun\n");
    }
```

See Also   AUTOLOAD, END

bind

Syntax   bind(*SOC_VARIABLE*, *NAME_VARIABLE*)

Usage   The *bind* function attempts to assign *NAME_VARIABLE* to the previously opened socket, *SOC_VARIABLE*. If the assignment fails, *FALSE* is returned.

Examples   This example assigns the name *$socketOne* to the connection *SOC*. If the assignment fails, the program will quit displaying the *die* string to the user's computer:

```
bind(SOC, $socketOne) || die ("Assignment failed\n");
```

Parameters   handle

See Also   accept, connect, getpeername, getsocketname, getsockopt, listen, recv, send, shutdown, socket, socketpair

binmode

Syntax   binmode(*FILE_VARIABLE*)

Usage   The *binmode* function lets your script know that you wish to access the file specified by the handle passed in binary form. Since Perl has the ability to parse binary files in addition to the usual text, you may find it more appropriate to declare the file binary in your script. This process should occur immediately after the file is opened to ensure no improper manipulation can occur.

Examples   This example opens the file *data.binary* under the handle *INPUTFILE*. After this association takes place, *binmode* is called:

```
open(INPUTFILE, 'data.binary');
binmode(INPUTFILE);
```

Parameters   handle

See Also   open

bless

Syntax   bless(*OBJECT*, *CLASS*)

           bless *OBJECT*

Usage   The *bless* function makes an *OBJECT* an instance of *CLASS*. If no *CLASS* is specified, as in the second syntax definition, *OBJECT* is made an instance of the current class.

> **Tip**
>
> *It is best to explicitly declare the CLASS rather than assuming you will make the proper calls to the functions within it. This will ensure your method can be inherited and can save you many hours of debugging and incorrect implementation.*

Examples   The following example declares *$class* and *$var* and then calls the *bless* function to make the *$var* an instance of *$class*:

```
sub new{
    my $class = sample;
    my $var = {};
    bless $var, $class;
    return $var;
}
```

This example shows how you can use the *bless* function without explicitly declaring a *CLASS*:

```
sub new{
    my $var = {};
    bless $var;
    return $var;
}
```

Parameters   class
                object

See Also   my, new, sub

caller

Syntax
: ```
caller()
caller(num)
```

Usage
: The *caller* function returns the package name, filename, and line number of the subroutine that is being executed. This information is then used by the Perl debugger to help pinpoint bad calls to subroutines.
: If you want to show previous stack frames (frames other than the current one), you can pass a *num* to the function. This number signifies the number of previous frames you want to display.

Examples
: This example returns information about the routine in which it is executed to the corresponding variables, which makes it easy to access each individual piece of information:
: ```
caller = ($packageName, $fileName, $line);
```
: This example returns information about the routine in which it is executed:
: ```
$subDebug = caller();
```

Parameters
: numeric

Value
: string

See Also
: Appendix C (Debugger Commands)

# chdir

Syntax
: ```
chdir(string)
```

Usage
: The *chdir* function changes the current working directory to the directory defined in the *string* passed to it. This is particularly useful when performing recursive file manipulation that is not solely located in the working directory.
: Since, like most Perl functions, the *chdir* function returns a true or false based on a successful change of directories, it is possible to do error checking based on these changes in conjunction with the *die* function.

Examples   This example changes your current working directory:

```
chdir ('/usr/local/bin');
```

Parameters   string

Value   boolean

See Also   chroot, closedir, opendir

chmod

Syntax   chmod (*num, @list*)

chmod (*num, filename1, filename2*)

Usage   The *chmod* function is used to change the permissions on a file (or a list of files). The permission code is passed as the first argument followed by the list of files to be changed as the second argument.

> **Tip**
>
> *It is possible to assign the implementation of the function to a variable in order to verify the number of changes that occur. This is helpful in verifying that all the changes you sought to make were actually made.*

Examples   This example changes the permission of the test.pl file to an executable on a UNIX machine:

```
chmod(700, 'test.pl');
```

This example returns the number of changes that were made in the list *@list* to the variable *$numChanges*:

```
$numChanges = chmod (700, @list);
```

Parameters   list
numeric
string

See Also   chown, flock

chomp

FUNCTION

PERL 5

Syntax
: ```
  chomp(@list)
  ```
  ```
  chomp(string)
  ```
  ```
  chomp
  ```

Usage
: The *chomp* function, which is very similar to the *chop* function, removes any trailing newline ("\n") characters and then returns the number of characters removed. It does not, however, remove every last character, only the newlines.

  If a list was passed to the *chomp* function, then any trailing newline in each entry will be removed.

  This function helps to ensure that the information you will be processing will have no unwanted information, which could lead to improper data reporting.

Examples
: This example removes any trailing newline characters from *$input* and places the value of the removed end of lines in *$numNewline*:

  ```
  print("Enter your name: ");
  $input = <STDIN>;

  $numNewline = chomp($input);
  print($numNewline."\n");   # prints '1' to screen
  ```

  As mentioned earlier, it is also possible to remove all trailing newlines from an entire list of strings. This example takes *@list* and removes any trailing newlines:

  ```
  chomp(@list);
  ```

Parameters
: string
  list

Value
: numeric

See Also
: chop
  ```

chop

C

Syntax chop(*@list*)

chop(*string*)

chop

Usage The *chop* function removes and returns the last character of the argument passed to it. If a list is passed to *chop*, the last character of each entry is removed.

The *chop* function is most commonly used to remove the newline character from the input line. This helps to ensure that the information you will be processing will have no unwanted characters, which could lead to improper data reporting.

It is also possible to use the *chop* function without any arguments passed. This type of usage is usually contained in a loop that is processing the data of an opened file; for example, in the body of a *while* loop.

Examples This example assigns c, which is the last character in the string "abc," to the variable *$lastChar*:

```
$example = "abc";

$lastChar = chop($example);
print($lastChar."\n");  # print 'c' to screen
```

As mentioned earlier, it is also possible to remove the last character from an entire list of strings. This example takes a list and removes the last character of each entry:

```
chop(@list);
```

Parameters string
list

See Also chomp, split

chown

Syntax
```
chown(num, num, @list)
chown(num, num, filename1, filename2)
```

Usage Much like the *chmod* function, the *chown* function allows the script to change the user and group permissions for the specified files. The files can be listed individually or in an array of filenames. The two preceding *num*'s are the user's ID and the group's ID.

Examples This example changes the permissions for users and groups based on a *$userID* and a *$groupID* that must be previously assigned. The IDs are numerical and, on a UNIX system, are generally located in the passwd file:

```
@list = ('file1', 'file2');
chown($userID, $groupID, @list);
```

Parameters list
numeric
string

See Also chmod

chr

Syntax `chr(num)`

Usage The *chr* function returns the ASCII character of the *num* passed to it. It is helpful in converting non-keyboard characters to their ASCII representation via decimal numbers.

Examples This example allows your script to contain the → (arrow) character even though there is no key representation. You may, however, not be able to print this character to the screen. It will depend on the system on which you are running your script:

```
chr(26);
```

Parameters	numeric
Value	character
See Also	Appendix C (ASCII Character Set)

C

chroot

SYSTEM CALL

PERL 4   PERL 5

Syntax   chroot(*directory*)

Usage   The *chroot* function changes the root directory in which you are working. But be careful; once this function has been called and implemented, you can no longer return to the directory in which you were working previously. Also, be sure you have the correct permissions to make the change that you are seeking to make.

Examples   This example will change the root directory in which you are working to the /ftp directory:

```
chroot ('/ftp');
```

Parameters   string

See Also   chdir, closedir, opendir

close

FUNCTION

PERL 4   PERL 5

Syntax   close(*FILE_VARIABLE*)

Usage   The *close* function will close the previously opened *FILE_VARIABLE* file. If the file is currently undergoing manipulation, such as being piped to another process, *close* will wait until that process has completed its execution before closing the file.

Examples   This example shows a file opened with the *open* function and then immediately closed using the *close* function. The *die* function call ensures that the file was successfully opened:

```
open(NEWFILE, 'newfile.txt') || die ("Error opening!\n");
close(NEWFILE);
```

Parameters   handle

See Also   closedir, flock, open, opendir

closedir

FUNCTION

PERL 4   PERL 5

Syntax   `closedir(DIR_VARIABLE)`

Usage   The *closedir* function will close the previously opened *DIR_VARIABLE* directory. The *DIR_VARIABLE* directory is originally opened with the *opendir* command and should be closed with the closedir command to comply with proper programming techniques. Failure to do so may result in a slower script or misread information.

Examples   This example opens a directory with the *opendir* function, assigns it to a *DIR_VARIABLE*, and then closes it with the *closedir* function:

```
opendir(CURRDIR, '/cgi-bin');
closedir(CURRDIR);
```

Parameters   handle

See Also   close, open, opendir

cmp

Syntax   *alphanum1* cmp *alphanum2*

Usage   The *cmp* comparison operator compares *alphanum1* to *alphanum2*. As you would imagine, this operator is also case sensitive. Use it to distinguish between strings of varying capitalization.

   If the two strings are the same, the returned result is 0. If *alphanum1* is greater, 1 is returned, and if *alphanum2* is greater, -1 is returned.

Examples This example assigns a string to two variables. The two variables are then compared, and the *print* function prints the result of the comparison:

```
$i = "test3";
$j = "test2";
print(($i cmp $j)."\n");   # prints '1'
```

   This example shows how the *cmp* operator can distinguish between strings of various cases:

```
$i = "Test";
$j = "test";
print(($i cmp $j)."\n");   # prints '-1'
```

   This example shows how the *cmp* operator can distinguish between numerical arguments:

```
$i = 1;
$j = 1;
print(($i cmp $j)."\n");   # prints '0'
```

Parameters alphanumeric

Value   numeric

See Also   eq, gt, le, lt, ne, not, xor, Appendix C (Operators)

connect

PERL 4   PERL 5

C

Syntax   connect(*SOC_VARIABLE*, *NAME_VARIABLE*)

Usage   The *connect* function sets up a connection between *SOC_VARIABLE*, which
         has already been created, and *NAME_VARIABLE*, which is the address with
         which you wish to connect.
              Be sure the *NAME_VARIABLE* is bound to the socket by using the *bind*
         function and that the *SOC_VARIABLE* socket connection is in *listen* mode.
         The socket connection must then be ready to *accept*.

Examples The following example shows an attempt to connect socket *SOCKET* to
          $address. The *die* function call ensures that the connection was successfully
          created:

          connect(SOCKET, $address) || die ("Error Connecting!\n");

Parameters handle
            string

Value   boolean

See Also accept, bind, getpeername, getsocketname, getsockopt, listen, recv, send,
          shutdown, socket, socketpair

continue

PERL 4   PERL 5

Syntax   while (*CONDITION*){
             CODE
         }continue{
             CODE
         }
         ─────────────
         until (*CONDITION*){
             CODE
         }continue{
             CODE
             }

C

Usage The *continue* element of loop control is executed at the end of each loop, just before returning to the beginning. It is often used in *while* and *until* loops to mimic the last argument of a *for* loop, which usually is the auto-increment or -decrement.

Note also that the *continue* element of the loop control is *not* executed if the loop is exited using a *last* function call.

Examples This example shows a *continue* implementation on a *while* loop. The example initializes *$i* to 1 and then prints the loop number to the screen. After each iteration through the loop, the *continue* section increments the loop counter and prints the new value of *$i*:

```
$i = 1;

while ($i < 5){
    print ("Loop number $i\n");
}continue{
    $i++;
    print('$i is now '.$i."\n");
}
```

This example shows a *continue* implementation on an *until* loop. The example initializes *$i* to 1 and then prints the loop number to the screen. After each iteration through the loop, the *continue* section increments the loop counter and prints the new value of *$i*:

```
$i = 1;

until ($i > 5){
    print ("Loop number $i\n");
}continue{
    $i++;
    print('$i is now ', $i."\n");
}
```

Parameters code

See Also Appendix C (Loop Control), do, else, elsif, for, foreach, if, last, next, require, until, use, while

cos

Syntax   cos(*num*)

Usage   The *cos* arithmetic function takes the cosine, in radians, of a number. In a right triangle, the cosine is the ratio of the length of the hypotenuse to the length of the side adjacent to an acute angle.

Examples   The following example assigns the cosine of 3.14, which is approximately π, to $cosVar. The result will be approximately -1... of course this will not be exact due to my approximation in π, but you get the idea:

```
$cosVar = cos(3.14);
print("$cosVar\n");      # prints '-0.999998'
```

Parameters   numeric

Value   numeric

See Also   abs, atan2, exp, log, sin, sqrt

crypt

Syntax   crypt(*string*, *alphanumeric*)

Usage   The *crypt* function allows you to encrypt *string* according to the NBS Data Encryption Standard algorithm, or DES. To use this function, you pass the *string* to be encrypted using the syntax noted, while the function takes *alphanumeric* characters as an encryption key. The *alphanumeric* characters are two characters specified by the programmer that are imported into the algorithm to provide a "customizable" encryption.

Examples   This example will encrypt a user's inputted string and display it to the screen:

```
print("Enter String: ");
chop ($passWord = <STDIN>);
print("Enter Encryption: ");
chop ($salt = <STDIN>);
print(crypt($passWord, $salt),"\n" );
```

Parameters   string
alphanumeric

Value   string

C

DATA

PERL 4   PERL 5

Syntax   `<DATA>`

Usage   The *DATA* handle refers to any text that is located after the *__END__* token in your script or anything after the *__DATA__* token in a required file. It allows you to perform various functions, suc as placing any input data and your script in the same file even though it is not recommended. This restricts your script to using only the explicitly declared data accompanying it and does not allow you to implement the program on other data.

Examples   The text referred to as *DATA* is placed into the variable *$input* and then printed to the user's screen. This also allows it to be further accessed anywhere within the script via this variable:

```
# place 'DATA' in a variable
$input = <DATA>;

# print 'Here is my data' to screen
print($input);

# define DATA
__DATA__
Here is my data
```

Value   alphanumeric

See Also   Appendix B

dbmclose

PERL 4   PERL 5

Syntax   `dbmclose(%array)`

Usage   The *dbmclose* function closes the connection between the DBM (Data Base Management) file and *%array*.

> **Tip**
>
> *Note that this function has subsequently been replaced in Perl 5 with the* untie *function, but it was left in to ensure that Perl 4 scripts would still have the ability to run in version 5. I do not recommend using this function since it will most likely be removed in future releases of Perl.*

Examples   The following example shows the DBM file being opened using *dbmopen* and then immediately closed using *dbmclose*:

```
# open a database connection
dbmopen(%dbmArray, '/database/current', 5444);
```

```
# close the database connection
dbmclose(%dbmArray);
```

Parameters   array

See Also   dbmopen, tie, untie

dbmopen

FUNCTION

PERL 4   PERL 5

Syntax   dbmopen(*%array, string, num*)

Usage   The *dbmopen* function makes a connection between the DBM (Data Base Management) file and *%array*. The *num* portion passed to the function contains the permissions necessary to access the DBM file. If the file which you are trying to access does not exist and the permission you entered is valid, then a file will be created based on the name and permission for which you were searching.

> **Tip**
>
> *This function has subsequently been replaced in Perl 5 with the* tie *function, but it was left in to ensure that Perl 4 scripts would still have the ability to run in version 5. I do not recommend using this function since it will most likely be removed in future releases of Perl.*

Examples   The following example shows the DBM file being opened using *dbmopen* and then immediately closed using *dbmclose*:

```
# open a database connection
dbmopen(%dbmArray, '/database/current', 5444);
```

```
# close the database connection
dbmclose(%dbmArray);
```

Parameters	array
	numeric
	string

See Also	dbmclose, untie, tie

defined

Syntax	defined(*alphanumeric*)
	defined(*$array[num]*)

Usage The *defined* function will return a 0, false or a nonzero, true based on contents of the argument passed to it for evaluation. If the argument does not contain an alphanumeric value, then a 0 will be returned. If it does contain an alphanumeric value, then a nonzero, or true, value will be returned. This is helpful in determining if an array you have created has values in each indexed position.

Examples This example checks to see if the fourth entry in *$entry[]* has been defined. The results of running this script prints "Not Defined" since positions 0 through 3 are the only ones defined:

```
# define an array
@entry = (1, 2, 3, 4);

# check to see if there is an entry at position 4
if (defined($entry[4])){
   print("Defined\n");
}else{

   # this line will be printed
   print("Not Defined\n");
   }
```

Parameters	alphanumeric
	array
	numeric

Value	numeric

See Also	undef

delete

Syntax   `delete %array{alias}`

Usage   The *delete* function deletes an entry in an associative array. The alias, or
         "key," that you wish to delete is passed to the function and removed from
         the array. The deleted alias, which includes the name association and the
         element, is then returned which can, of course, be assigned to a variable and
         used for later manipulation.

Examples The following example shows the creation of *%asscArray* followed by an
         alias being deleted and stored in *$delStored*. The result is printed to the
         screen:

```
%asscArray = ("var1", 1, "var2", 2, "var3", 3);
$delStored = delete $asscArray{"var2"};

# prints '2' to screen
print("$delStored\n");
```

Parameters array
           alias

Value   string

See Also exists, unlink

die

Syntax   `die(string)`

         `die(@list)`

Usage   The *die* function sends the contents of *string* or *@list* to STDERR and ceases
         the execution of the program. *Die* is commonly used to verify that actions,
         such as opening a file or directory, are completed correctly. If the file is
         unable to be opened, for example, then the string or list will be printed to the
         user's screen.

If you include a newline character (\n) at the end of the *die* string, your error message will be printed verbatim to the user's screen. If you omit the newline character, the filename and line number of your script will be concatenated to your string. This appears in the form "*die_string* at *filename* line *num*" where *die_string* is the string you declared in your *die* function call, *filename* is the name of your script, and *num* is the line number where the error occurred.

> **Tip**
>
> *Having several instances of* die *in your script can be a helpful debugging tool. It presents information that pinpoints your execution problems.*

Examples   The following example prints the *die* string to the user's screen if the file /etc/passwd is not opened successfully:

```
open(PASS, '/etc/passwd') || die ("Error opening file\n");
```

The second example shows how you can declare a list of strings to display as the *die* string. This allows you to create a single list and call it in various *die* functions. Leaving off the newline character will display the line number and filename to the screen for easier debugging.

As in any list, you can have multiple entries separated by commas and set off by double or single quotations, depending on your intent. This example, however, has only one entry for simplicity's sake:

```
@dieList = ("Error ");
open (PASS, '/etc/passwd') || die (@dieList);
```

Parameters   string
list

Value   STDERR

See Also   exit, warn

do

Syntax
```
do{
    CODE
    }until(CONDITION)

do{
    CODE
    }while(CONDITION)

do SUB()

do SUB(EXPRESSION)

do string
```

Usage
In the first two syntax definitions, the loop control statement will execute the contents of *CODE* based on *CONDITION*. Since these conditions are located after the loop is encountered, you are assured that the code in the loop will be executed at least once.

The third and fourth syntax definitions describe how the *do* function can be used to call a subroutine. The first of the two definitions shows how to call a routine that requires no information to be passed. The second passes *EXPRESSION*, which represents any type of information that your subroutine needs to execute properly.

The final syntactical definition passes only a string to the *do* function. In this instance, the *do* function will include a library module defined by *string*. Including a Perl library module gives you access to all the functions in that library as if they were native to the language.

> **Tip**
>
> *The* do string *implementation has subsequently been replaced by* require *in Perl 4 and even more recently by* use *in Perl 5. Do note, however, that there are run-time differences between* do, use, *and* require.
>
> *Also note that you cannot use the* last, next, *and* redo *functions with the* do *function because of the nature of the* do *function.*

Examples
This *do...until* example executes the print statement until $i is greater than 5:

```
$i = 1;
do{
    print("This is loop number $i\n");
    $i++;
} until($i > 5);
```

This example is a *do...while* loop that compares an entry from the user with the predefined variable, *$verify*. The user will continually be prompted until the correct entry is made. Note the difference between the notation for this string comparison and the notation in the first example with a numeric comparison:

```
do{
   print("What is the magic word? ");
   $verify = <STDIN>;
} while($verify ne "please");
```

This example prompts the user to input two numbers which are then passed to a subroutine via the *do* function. The results are returned and printed to the user's screen. Notice that *&* is left off these subroutine calls and is in essence replaced with *do*:

```
# prompt user for a number
print("Enter the first number: ");
$a = (<STDIN>);
chop($a);

# prompt user for a second number
print("Enter the second number: ");
$b = (<STDIN>);
chop($b);

# pass numbers to subroutine 'greatest' via do
$result = do greatest($a,$b);

# print result of subroutine
print("$result is the greater of the two numbers you entered\n");

# subroutine
sub greatest{
   if ($a < $b){
      return $b;
   }else{
      return $a;
   }
}
```

This final example shows how the *do* function can be used to add access to a Perl library. As mentioned earlier, this implementation of the *do* function has been effectively replaced with *require* and *use*:

```
do 'find.pl';
```

Parameters   string
subroutine

See Also   continue, else, elsif, for, foreach, if, Appendix C (Loop Control) require, until, use, while, next

dump

D

Syntax   dump *SECTION*

Usage   The *dump* function causes the script to do an immediate core dump to the system. This dump is usually done after all of your initialization of required files and variables are complete. Using the *undump* program (which is available on some platforms), the dump can be transformed into a binary file containing your information. This will provide faster access to your code and quicker scripts since their contents have already been transformed into binary machine code.

   SECTION is the location in your code that signifies where the binary needs to start after executing the initialization that was used to create it. In short, you dump the slow section of your script, passing it a location that signifies where the dump ended. This in turn tells the executing binary where to start after it is complete to ensure nothing is repeated.

Examples   This example performs a core dump after all initialization, defining the location for the binary to start up when executed:

```perl
# define variables
require 'bigfloat.pl';
$passwd = "help";
@list = ("a", "b", "c");
%array = ("one", 1, "two", 2, "three", 3);

# create the core dump
dump INITIALIZED;

# dump everything prior to this point
INITIALIZED:
print("Start here after binary execution is complete.\n");
```

Parameters   section

See Also   BEGIN

each

E

Syntax   each(*%array*)

Usage   The *each* function returns an entry *%array* that comprises an alias and an element. In an associative array, each entry is a combination of an element, as with most arrays, and a name association or alias. The alias allows you to reference the element by the name association rather than by the index number of the entry.

Calling the *each* function returns a complete entry in the form of a list with both alias and element. Subsequent calls iterate through the array returning entries until the array is exhausted. The final call to the array returns an empty entry.

The iteration through the array is dependent on how the array is arranged, and it is not guaranteed to return the entries in any specific order. While this might be of no use in returning an ordered list, it still can serve the purpose of returning all entries when order is of no importance.

Examples   This example first defines *%iterateThru* and then prints each of the entries as the *each* function iterates through the array:

```
# define associative array
%iterateThru = ('one', 1, 'two', 2, 'three', 3);

# read the key and value into variables
while(($alias, $entry) = each(%iterateThru)){

   # print key and value to screen
   print("$alias = $entry\n");
}
```

Parameters   array

Value   list

See Also   foreach, keys, values

else

E

Syntax
```
if (CONDITION){
    CODE
}else{
    CODE
}
```

Usage   The *else* loop control element is implemented as a default for the *if* loop when *if* does not meet its conditions. The syntax shows an *if* loop control statement, which will execute the contents of *CODE* based on *CONDITION*. If this *CONDITION* is not met, then the following *else* block of *CODE* will execute.

Note that since these conditions are located before the internal portion of the loop is encountered, the code in the loop may not be executed.

Examples   The following example prompts the user for a password. If the user enters the correct password, then the "Success" message will be printed to the user's screen. If the user enters an incorrect password, then the "Failure" message will be printed to the screen.

Note that the *chop* function is called to remove the newline character at the end of the user's input:

```
# define the password
$password = "test";

# prompt the user for the password
print("Please enter a password: ");
$input = <STDIN>;
chop($input);

# see if the user inputted the correct password
if ($input eq $password){
    print("Success!\n");
}else{
    print("Failure!\n");
}
```

Parameters   code

See Also   continue, do, elsif, for, foreach, if, Appendix C (Loop Control), require, until, use, while, next

elsif

Syntax
```
if (CONDITION){
   CODE
}elsif(CONDITION){
   CODE
}else{
   CODE
}
```

Usage   The syntax shows the *if* loop control statement, which will execute the contents of *CODE* based on *CONDITION*. If this *CONDITION* is not met, then the following *elsif* control statement will have its *CONDITION* tested. If this control statement passes, then its *CODE* will be executed. If it fails, then the *else* block of *CODE* will execute as a default.

Note that since these conditions are located before the internal portion of the loop is encountered, the code in the loop may not be executed.

Examples   The following example sets up two passwords in the *$password* and *$password2* variables. The user is then prompted to enter a password. If the user enters one of the correct passwords, then a "Success" message, along with the password, will be printed to the screen. If the user enters a password not defined, then the "Failure" message will be printed to the screen.

Note that the *chop* function is called to remove the newline character at the end of the user's input:

```
# define 2 passwords
$password = "test";
$password2 = "test2";

# prompt the user for a password
print("Please enter a password: ");
$input = <STDIN>;
chop($input);

# determine which password was used if correct
if ($input eq $password){
   print("Success! You entered $password\n");
}elsif($input eq $password2){
   print("Success! You entered $password2\n");
}else{
   print("Failure!\n");
}
```

Parameters   code
              condition

See Also   continue, do, else, for, foreach, if, Appendix C (Loop Control), require, until,
              use, while, next

END

E

Syntax   END{
              CODE
              }

Usage   The *END* subroutine allows you to specify *CODE* that will be executed at the
          end of your script.

Examples This example uses the *print* function to tell the user that the execution of the
          current script has ended. The comments in the center of the script would be
          replaced with any code you want to execute:

```
print("The script is running!\n");

#---------------------------
# All of your other code goes here
#---------------------------

# executed last, before script terminates
END{
    print("The script is finished!\n");
}
```

See Also AUTOLOAD, BEGIN

eof

Syntax
```
eof(FILE_VARIABLE)
eof()
eof
```

Usage   The *eof* function returns a nonzero when the end of a file is reached. You can test the status of a specific file by passing *FILE_VARIABLE* to the function, or you can test the status of the file you are currently working with using *eof* with no parentheses. If you have passed multiple files, as in command-line arguments, you will need to use *eof()* to ensure access to the correct file.

   Without the parentheses, an end of file will be detected at the end of the first file passed. The parentheses, in effect, tells the script that there are more entries to look at before testing for an end of file. Then, after the last file is read in, the script will check for the end of file.

Examples   This example opens a file under the handle, FILEIN. A variable is initialized to counter the number of lines in the file before the end of file is reached. A *while* loop is used to iterate through the file. In the body of this loop, the counter is incremented and its value is printed to the user's screen. When the end of file is encountered, *print* sends a message to the screen alerting the user that an end of file has occurred:

```
# open a file for reading
open(FILEIN, "test.txt") || die("Error: unable to open file");

# initialize a line counter
$counter = 0;

# read the contents of the file one line at a time
while(<FILEIN>){

    # increment the counter
    $counter++;

    # print current line number on newline
    print("$counter\n");

    # when eof is reached, print this line
    if(eof(FILEIN)){
        print("This is the end of this file.");
    }
}
```

In the instances where a single file is to be passed to the script in the command line, we use the *eof* syntax to check for the end of file. This example iterates through the lines of the inputted file until an end of file is found, at which point the *print* sends a message to the screen alerting the user that an end of file has occurred:

```
while(<>){
    if(eof){
        print("This is the end of this file.");
    }
}
```

When multiple files are passed in the command line, you can assume that the user does not want the script to stop execution after the first file has been processed. Your script should evaluate each of the files before looking for the end of file. In this case, you should use the *eof()* call and include the parentheses. This example shows how you would implement this function call based on multiple files being passed in the command line:

```
while(<>){
    if(eof()){
        print("This is the end of the last file passed.");
    }
}
```

Parameters   handle

Value   boolean

eq

OPERATOR

PERL 4   PERL 5

Syntax   *alphanum1* eq *alphanum2*

string1 eq *string2*

Usage   The *eq* comparison operator tests *alphanum1* and *alphanum2* to see if they are equal. As you would imagine, this operator is also case sensitive, which allows you to be able to distinguish between equal strings with different capitalization.

If the two strings are the same, the returned result is 1. If they are not equal, a 0 is returned.

eq • **55**

Examples   This example assigns a number to *$num1* and *$num2*. These two variables are then compared and the *print* function prints a result based on the comparison. The result of this example prints the "are equal" string to the user's screen:

```
# define 2 variables
$num1 = "3";
$num2 = "3";

# compare the variables
if ($num1 eq $num2){

   # this line will be printed
   print('$num1 and $num2 are equal'."\n");

}else{
   print("Not equal\n");
}
```

This example shows how *eq* can distinguish between strings of various cases. The result of this example prints the "not equal" string to the user's screen:

```
# define 2 strings with different case
$string1 = "One";
$string2 = "one";

# compare the strings
if ($string1 eq $ string2){
   print('$string1 and $string2 are equal'."\n");
}else{

   # this line will be printed
   print("Not equal\n");
}
```

Parameters   alphanumeric
string

Value   numeric

See Also   cmp, gt, le, lt, ne, not, Appendix C (Operators), xor

eval

FUNCTION

PERL 4   PERL 5

Syntax   eval(*string*)

eval(*function*)

Usage   The *eval* function interprets the string or function passed to it as if it was a separate script altogether. The string is not restricted to a series of alphanumeric characters; instead it defines what the alphanumeric characters make up. This could be anything from a function call, as in the second definition, to a mathematical computation.

Eval literally executes the string in the same manner it would execute if in the script. This allows the result of the execution, in the form of a string, to be verified or stored in a variable for later usage and can be used in instances when you don't necessarily know what type of data you are going to receive.

Examples   This example puts the square root of 13 into *$result*. This can, of course, be done without the use of *eval*, but it demonstrates the functionality of returning a result to a variable. Other operations, such as implementing *print*, can be evaluated using *eval* with the result being placed in the variable:

```
$result = eval(sqrt(13));
```

Parameters   string
function

Value   alphanumeric

See Also   exec, system

exec

PERL 4   PERL 5

Syntax   exec(*string*)

exec(*@list*)

Usage   The *exec* function executes a program that is specified in the first entry of the list passed and executes it with the additional arguments following the first entry. Before the program is initiated, the current script, which calls *exec*, is terminated. By allowing you to pass arguments to the programs you wish to execute, *exec* can, for example, open files in programs or open specific instances of programs.

Examples   This example passes a single string to the function so the function can initiate and run the program:

```
# opens Netscape on a Windows machine when it is in
# your path
exec("netscape");
```

This example defines a list that has the program's name in the first entry followed by the options you wish to pass to it:

```
# define the list
@progArg = ("netscape","-mail");

# opens Netscape Mail on a Windows machine when Netscape
# is in your path
exec(@progArg);
```

Parameters   list

string

See Also   eval, flock, system

exists

Syntax   exists(*%array*{*alias*})

Usage   The *exists* function tells you if *alias* is in *%array*. This is, in effect, the associative array version of *defined*.

Examples   The following example checks to see if the alias, *four*, is in *%example*. Since it is not, the *else* portion of the if statement will be printed to the user's screen:

```
# define an associative array
%example = ('one', 1, 'two', 2);

# check to see if 'four' is in the list
if (exists $example{"four"}) {
   print ("Yes, this is in the array.\n");
}else{

   # this line will be printed
   print ("No, this is not in the array.\n");
}
```

Parameters   array
            string

Value   boolean

See Also   defined

exit

Syntax   exit(*num*)

Usage   The *exit* function exits the currently running script with error code *num*. This is a helpful debugging method to alert you to the type of error your script has encountered.

Examples   The following example exits this script's execution with an error code of 1 when the user inputs incorrect data:

```
# prompt the user to enter the name of a planet
print("Please enter the name of our planet: ");
$entry = (<STDIN>);
chop ($entry);

# see if the user entered 'earth'
if ($entry ne 'earth'){
   exit(1);
}else{
   print("You are correct sir!");
}
```

Parameters   numeric

Value   string

See Also   dir, warn

exp

FUNCTION

PERL 4   PERL 5

Syntax   exp(*num*)

Usage   The *exp* arithmetic function takes the natural logarithm of *num*.

Examples   This example takes the natural logarithm of 2 and puts it in *$result*, which it then prints to the screen:

```
# pass an number to the exp function
$result = exp(2);

# approximately '7.38905'
print("$result\n");
```

Parameters   numeric

Value   numeric

See Also   abs, atan2, cos, log, sin, sqrt

fcntl

Syntax   fcntl(*FILE_VARIABLE*, *COMMAND*, *string*)

Usage   The *fcntl* function calls the system *fcntl* function. It is used to provide control over an open file handle. The third argument is optional and depends on the *COMMAND* passed to the function. You need:

use Fcntl;

at the top of your script to load the correct *COMMAND* definitions. If *fcntl* isn't implemented on the machine running your script or it is implemented incorrectly, using this function will result in a fatal error or it may damage your file system.

The possible commands may be:

- **F_DUPFD.** The function returns a new file descriptor that is the same as the file handle. The descriptor will be numbered with the lowest available file descriptor greater than the argument passed as the third argument.

- **F_FREESP.** The function frees disk space from a section of the file referred to by the file handle. The section is specified by the third argument and must be a packed variable. Please see your system documentation on *fcntl* for more information on this argument.

- **F_GETFD.** The function returns the close-on-exec flag associated with the file handle.

- **F_GETFL.** The function returns the file handle status flags.

- **F_GETLK.** The function is locked as requested in the packed variable passed as the third argument. See your system documentation for more information on this variable.

- **F_SETFD.** The function sets the close-on-exec flag associated with the file handle to the third argument. It can be either 0 or 1.

- **F_SETFL.** The function sets the status flag associated with the file handle to the third argument.

- **F_SETLK.** The function sets or clears a file section lock described by the packed variable passed as the third argument.

- **F_SETLKW.** This is the same as F_SETLK except that if a read or write lock is blocked by other locks, it waits until the section is available to be locked.

Examples   This example returns the status flag of the file handle and sets it to the scalar *$ret*:

```
use Fcntl;
$ret = fcntl(FILE1, F_GETFL);
```

Parameters   handle
string

Value   numeric

See Also   fork, your system documentation on *fcntl*

fileno

FUNCTION

PERL 4   PERL 5

Syntax   `fileno(FILE_VARIABLE)`

Usage   The *fileno* function returns the assigned handle number of *FILE_VARIABLE*. Each time you open a file and assign it a handle, Perl assigns a number to that handle to keep track of the order in which the files where opened.

The first three handle numbers (0, 1, and 2) are reserved for *STDIN*, *STDOUT*, and *STDERR* respectively, but it is possible for these assignments to change if multiple files are opened and closed for them. By default, the first handle you assign will start with a handle number of 3.

If the handle passed to *fileno* has not opened or was closed before the function was called, then an undefined is returned. This undefined is the same as an *undef* implementation.

Examples   This example opens two files, *test.txt* and *test2.txt*, in the same directory as the script. After the files have been successfully opened, their handle number and a concatenated newline are printed to the screen by using *print* and *fileno*:

```
# open the files for reading
open(FILE1, 'test.txt') || die ("Error: File #1");
open(FILE2, 'test2.txt') || die ("Error: File #2");

# will print '3' to screen
print (fileno(FILE1)."\n");

# will print '4' to screen
print (fileno(FILE2)."\n");

# this handle is not defined and will print ' ' to screen
print (fileno(FILE3)."\n");
```

Parameters	handle
Value	numeric
See Also	undef

flock

F

Syntax	flock(*FILE_VARIABLE*, *SYS_OP*)

Usage   The *flock* function performs an advisory lock, defined by the system operation *SYS_OP*, on *FILE_VARIABLE*. *Flock* will return a numeric value based on the success of its implementation.

Be sure to check the manual pages, if you are on a UNIX system, to ensure that you passed the proper system operation to *flock* and to define the returned numeric value. Generally, the following table can be used to determine the type of lock you wish to implement:

Variable	Type
1	shared
2	exclusive
4	non-blocking
8	unlock

Examples   This example opens a file under the handle *FILE1* and then prints the result of passing an exclusive *SYS_OP* to *flock*:

```
# open a file for reading
open(FILE1, 'test.txt') || die ("Error: opening file");

print (flock(FILE1, 2)."\n");
```

| Parameters | handle
numeric |
|---|---|
| Value | numeric |
| See Also | chmod, close, exec, fcntl, open, your systems documentation on *flock* |

for

PERL 4   PERL 5

Syntax
```
for(EXPRESSION; CONDITION; CONTROL){
    CODE
}

for(EXPRESSION1,EXPRESSION2; CONDITION1,CONDITION2;
    CONTROL1,CONTROL2){
    CODE
}

for(;;){
    CODE
}
```

Usage   The *for* loop control, one of the most commonly used looping methods for recursive loops, is made of three sections. In the syntax definitions, *EXPRESSION* defines a loop variable to initialize the loop. This is usually a variable assignment that is incremented in *CONTROL* and compared in *CONDITION* to ensure the relevance of the loop.

It is also possible, as seen in the second syntactical definition, to iterate through multiple variables. This is achieved by separating each variable in each section of the *for* loop control by a comma. Note that if you pass more than one *CONDITION*, the loop exits completely when any of the conditions are satisfied. Also note that it is not necessary to have the same number of components for each section. For example, you can pass multiple *EXPRESSION*s and *CONTROL*s and still have only one *CONDITION* statement.

The third syntactical definition demonstrates the ability of Perl to create *for* loops with the absence of any section. This allows the user to create infinite loops or to have the ability to assign the sections within the body of the loop.

Examples   This *for* loop initializes $i to 0, increments it upon the completion of each iteration, and verifies that the condition, $i < 5, is still valid. In the body of the loop, there is a print statement, executed at each iteration, that prints out the value of $i concatenated with a newline character. This loop prints out the numbers 0 through 4 on a new line and then exits the script:

```
for($i = 0; $i < 5; $i++){
    print($i."\n");
}
```

This example shows how multiple variables can be passed in each section of the *for* loop. It initializes and increments the three variables while checking the condition of two of them. Since the $k condition will be met before the i condition, the loop will exit before the fifth loop. This example prints out the numbers 0 through 3 for each variable on a new line and then exits the script:

```
for($i = 0, $j = 0, $k = 0; $i < 5, .$k < 4; $i++, $j++, $k++){
    print($i."\t".$j."\t".$k."\n");
}
```

This example creates an infinite loop that will continue to run until it is exited from inside the loop itself. I have told the loop to quit, using *last*, when i is greater than 5. This example prints up to the number 6 and then exits the infinite loop. This is usually done for loops that must perform recursive tasks on the file or files given. Such recursion is commonly found when manipulating data structures:

```
# define a loop variable outside the for loop
$i = 0;

# define a section for the last function to return to
# and start the looping
LOOP: for(;;){
        $i++;
        print($i."\n");
        last LOOP if $i > 5;
}
```

Parameters   code
conditions
expressions

See Also   continue, do, else, elsif, foreach, if, Appendix C (Loop Control), require, until, use, while, next

foreach

Syntax
```
foreach $variable(@list){
    CODE
}
```

Usage   The *foreach* function iterates through *@list* for every *$variable*. In short, the loop iterates as many times as there are items in *@list*. So if the list has five items, then the loop executes five times. This is helpful when you wish to perform the same manipulation on each item of the list without explicitly declaring the number of items in the list.

Examples   This example defines *@list* and then prints a sentence followed by the current item of the list:

```
# define an array of names
@list = ("Allen", "Anne", "Dane", "Robert");

# print the contents of the array as long as there
# are entries
foreach $list(@list){
   print("The current name is $list\n");
}
```

Parameters   list

See Also   continue, do, else, elsif, for, if, Appendix C, "Reference Tables & Lists," require, until, use, while, next

fork

SYSTEM CALL

PERL 4   PERL 5

Syntax   `fork`

Usage   The *fork* function creates a new child process that inherits the attributes of the calling parent process. The new child process has its own identification, ID, which is returned by *fork*.

Examples   This line assigns the new child's process ID to *$childID*:

```
$childID = fork;
```

Value   numeric

See Also   fcntl, your system documentation on *fork*

format

Syntax
```
format NAME_VARIABLE =
    HEADER_FORMAT
    variables
    .
```

Usage
The *format* function allows a programmer to format output. Since
NAME_VARIABLE defines each instance of *format*, it is possible to define
several different types of formatting that can be called. This can be useful in
displaying the same data in various forms.

The *HEADER_FORMAT* contains the information that tells Perl how the
format is to look. It designates the number of characters, the justification, and
the type of character to be passed per line. These are, in effect, the columns
for your information.

The *variables* passed to the format function are the variables you wish to
print out. This is the actual data that falls under the columns you have
defined in the *HEADER_FORMAT*.

The final line of the *format* function is the period (.). This signifies that all
of your information has been entered and that any following lines are not
part of the *format* function definition.

Examples
This example opens an information file that contains a person's *name*, *age*,
and *social security number* on each line. An example line is listed here:

```
Allen 24 555555555
```

After opening this file, the program reads each line, splits the information,
and assigns it to the appropriate variable.

As you can see, there are two different format declarations,
NAME_FIRST and *AGE_FIRST*. Each declaration instructs the output to
be printed with a seven-character name, a three-character age, and an
eight-character social security number; however, the order in which this
information is printed to the user's screen is different. The $~ assignment is
used to select the format desired:

```
# open a file to read data from
open(FILE1, 'students.txt') || die ("Error: opening file\n");

# define a "name first" format
format NAME_FIRST =
@<<<<<< @<<   @<<<<<<<<
$name,    $age, $ssn
.     # be sure to include this period, "."!

# define an "age first" format
```

```
format AGE_FIRST =
@<<< @<<<<<< @<<<<<<<<<
$age, $name,    $ssn
.    # be sure to include this period, "."!

while(<FILE1>){
   ($name, $age, $ssn) = split;

   # use 'Age First' format
   $~ = "AGE_FIRST";

   write;
}
```

Parameters   handle
formatting information
variable(s)

See Also   formline, Appendix C (Formatting), write

formline

FUNCTION

PERL 5

Syntax   formline(*string*, *@list*)

Usage   The *formline* function allows you to call a defined format held in *string* and apply it to *@list*. Unlike *format*, this function allows you to call other defined formats that do not have explicitly declared values. The values to be used are declared in *@list*. This formatted list is then stored in $^A, the Accumulator.
In *format*, you pass the formatting characteristics followed by the values you wish to format. The *formline* function allows you to call the formatting characteristics and then pass the values you wish to format. Using this method allows you to reuse specific formats without explicitly assigning them to a set of values.
It is also possible to define the format to be used in the function rather than defining it in *string* as a variable.

Examples   This example opens an information file that contains a person's *name*, *age*, and *social security number* on each line. An example line is listed here:

```
Allen 24 555555555
```

After opening, it is then *split* into the appropriate groups and passed to *formline* to be formatted. The final print statement prints the contents of the Accumulator concatenated with a newline:

```
# open a file for reading the data
open(FILE1, 'test.txt') || die("Error: opening file\n");

# define format
$format = ("@<<<<<  @<<  @<<<<<<<<<<");

while(<FILE1>){
   ($name, $age, $ssn) = split;
   formline ($format, $name, $age, $ssn);
}

# print results via accumulator
print($^A."\n");
```

F

Parameters	list
	string

Value	true

See Also	format, Appendix C (Formatting), write

ge

Syntax   *alphanum1* ge *alphanum2*

string1 ge *string2*

Usage   The *ge* comparison operator tests to see if the first argument passed is greater than or equal to the second argument passed. If the first argument is greater than or equal to the second argument, then a 1 is returned. If the second argument is greater, a 0 is returned.

As you would imagine, this operator is also case sensitive, which allows you to distinguish between equal strings with different capitalization.

Examples   This example assigns a number to *$ one* and *$ two*. These two variables are then compared and the *print* function outputs a result based on the comparison:

```
# define two numeric variables
$one = 1;
$two = 2;

# test to see if the first variable is greater or equal
if ($one ge $two){
   print("$one is greater than or equal to $two\n");
}else{

   # this line will be printed
   print("$two is greater than $one\n");
}
```

This example shows how *ge* can distinguish between strings of various cases:

```
# define 2 string variables
$one = "one";
$two = "One";

# test to see which string is greater
if ($one ge $two){

   # this line will be printed
   print("$one is greater than or equal to $two\n");

}else{
   print("$two is greater than $one\n");
}
```

G

Parameters	alphanumeric
	string

Value	numeric

See Also	cmp, eq, gt, le, lt, ne, not, Appendix C (Operators), xor

getc

FUNCTION

PERL 4   PERL 5

Syntax   getc(*FILE_VARIABLE*)

getc

Usage   The *getc* function gets one character at a time from *FILE_VARIABLE*. If, as in the second syntactical definition, no handle is passed, then the character is taken from *STDIN*. This function begins with the first character and proceeds with successive characters.

Examples   This example opens *test.txt* under the handle *FILE*. After a successful *open*, the *getc* function gets the first character of the file and prints it, concatenated with a newline character, to the screen. The second *getc* accesses the next character in *FILE* and prints it to the screen in the same manner as the first call:

```
# open a file for reading
open(FILE, 'test.txt') || die("Error: opening file\n");

# prints first character in FILE
print(getc(FILE)."\n");

# prints second character in FILE
print(getc(FILE)."\n");
```

Parameters	handle

Value	alphanumeric

See Also	read, seek, sysread

getgrent

SYSTEM CALL

PERL 4   PERL 5

Syntax   `getgrent`

Usage   The *getgrent* function is called when you wish to read from the */etc/group* file or its equivalent. It returns, in this order, the name, password, group ID, and group members listed in the file.

Examples   This example shows the group file being read using *getgrent*. While it is being read, the name field, concatenated with a newline character, will be printed to the screen:

```
while (($name, $password, $groupID, $users) = getgrent){
   print ($name."\n");
}
```

Value   properties

See Also   getgrgid, your system documentation on *getgrent*

getgrgid

SYSTEM CALL

PERL 4   PERL 5

Syntax   `getgrgid(`*num*`)`

Usage   The *getgrgid* function returns the name, password, group identification, and list of members of the group ID passed.

Examples   This example returns the associated information, in the proper variables, for the group number that is supplied by the user:

G

```
# prompt user for group ID
print("Please enter group ID to get information on: ");
$input = <STDIN>;

# remove trailing newline
chop($input);
($name, $password, $groupID, $memberList) = getgrid($input);
```

Parameters   numeric

Value   properties

See Also   getgrent, getgrnam, your system documentation on *getgrgid*

getgrnam

Syntax   getgrnam(*string*)

Usage   The *getgrnam* function returns the name, password, group ID, and a list of the members of the group passed.

Examples   This example prompts the user to enter a group name on which to get information. After entering a group name, the associated information for that group is assigned to variables for script manipulation:

```
# prompt the user for a group name
print("Please enter group name to get information on: ");
$input = <STDIN>;

# remove trailing newline
chop($input);
($name, $password, $groupID, $memeberList) = getgrnam($input);
```

Parameters   string

Value   properties

See Also   getgrent, gergrid, your system documentation on *getgrnam*

gethostbyaddr

Syntax gethostbyaddr(*ADDRESS*, *num*)

Usage The *gethostbyaddr* networking function searches your */etc/hosts* or correspond-ing file and returns the name, any aliases, address type, length, and address of *ADDRESS*. Since the address is generally packed into four-byte segments, you will have to unpack the data before reading.

As for the *num* passed to this function, it designates the type of address you are searching for. To determine the types for which you can search, you should check your */usr/include/netdb.h* or corresponding file for the possible values to pass.

Examples See the Socket example in the Perl Modules section of this book for a detailed example that uses *gethostbyaddr*.

Parameters numeric

Value properties

See Also gethostbyname, getnetbyaddr, getnetbyname, pack, your system documenta-tion on *gethostbyaddr*

gethostbyname

Syntax gethostbyname(*string*)

Usage The *gethostbyname* networking function searches your */etc/hosts* or corre-sponding file and returns the name, any aliases, address type, length, and address of *string*. The *string* is the alphanumeric alias that is associated with your numeric IP address.

Examples   See the Socket example in the Perl Modules section of this book for a detailed example that uses *gethostbyname*.

Parameters   string

Value   , properties

See Also   gethostbyaddr, getnetbyaddr, getnetbyname, your system documentation on *gethostbyname*

G gethostent

SYSTEM CALL

PERL 4   PERL 5

Syntax   gethostent

Usage   The *gethostent* networking function searches your */etc/hosts* or corresponding file and returns all the names, any aliases, address types, lengths, and a list of addresses in this file.

Examples   This example shows the host file being read using *gethostent*. While it is being read, the name field, concatenated with a newline character, will be printed to the screen:

```
while (($name, $alias, $addressType, $size, @address) = gethostent){
    print ($name."\n");
}
```

Value   properties

See Also   gethostbyaddr, gethostbyname, getnetbyaddr, getnetbyname, your system documentation on *gethostent*

getlogin

PERL 4   PERL 5

Syntax   `getlogin`

Usage   The *getlogin* function gets the current login name, which is extracted from the */etc/utmp* file of the user executing the script.

Examples   This example prints the login name, concatenated with a newline character, to the user's screen:

```
print(getlogin."\n");
```

Value   string

See Also   getpwuid

getnetbyaddr

PERL 4   PERL 5

Syntax   `getnetbyaddr(ADDRESS, ADDRESSTYPE)`

Usage   The *getnetbyaddr* networking function searches your */etc/networks* or corresponding file and returns the name, any aliases, address type, length, and address of *ADDRESS*. Since the address is packed into four-byte segments, you will have to unpack the data before reading.

As for the *num* passed to this function, it designates the type of address for which you are searching. To determine the types you can search for, you should check your */usr/include/netdb.h* or ãrresponding file for the possible values to pass.

Examples   This example simply returns the network information from the loopback setting and prints it to *STDOUT*. The Socket library is imported to bring in some standard variables for use in the script. You see the *AF_INET* in the example. I could just as easily use 2 instead, but the program wouldn't be as readable:

```
use Socket;
($name, $aliases, $addrtype, $netaddress ) = getnetbyaddr('127',
    AF_INET);
print ("$name $aliases $addrtype $netaddress\n");
```

Parameters   numeric

Value   properties

See Also   gethostbyaddr, gethostbyname, getnetbyname, getnetent, your system
documentation on *getnetbyaddr*

getnetbyname

SYSTEM CALL

PERL 4   PERL 5

Syntax   getnetbyname(*string*)

Usage   The *getnetbyname* networking function searches your */etc/networks* or corresponding file and returns the name, any aliases, address type, and address of
string. The *string* is the alphanumeric alias that is associated with your
numeric IP address.

Examples   This example is similar to the one with *getnetbyaddr* except that the function
call and the Socket module aren't necessary since the address type isn't
needed with *getnetbyname*:

```
($name, $aliases, $addrtype, $netaddress ) = getnetbyname ('loopback');
print ("$name $aliases $addrtype $netaddress\n");
```

Parameters   string

Value   properties

See Also   gethostbyaddr, gethostbyname, getnetbyaddr, getnetent, your system
documentation on *getnetbyname*

getnetent

SYSTEM CALL

PERL 4   PERL 5

Syntax   getnetent

Usage   The *getnetent* function is called when you wish to read from the */etc/networks*
file or its equivalent. It returns the name, any aliases, the address type, and
the network listed in this file.

Examples This example shows the network file being read using *getnetent*. While it is being read, the name field, concatenated with a newline character, will be printed to the screen:

```
while (($name, $alias, $addressType, $network) = getnetent)
   print ($name."\n");
}
```

Value properties

See Also gethostbyaddr, gethostbyname, getnetbyaddr, getnetbyname, your system documentation on *getnetent*

getpeername

FUNCTION

PERL 4 PERL 5

Syntax getpeername(*SOC_VARIABLE*)

Usage The *getpeername* networking function allows you to return the peer connection address of the connection specified in *SOC_VARIABLE*. If the returned address is packed, you have to unpack the data before reading.

Examples This example prints the peer address, concatenated with a newline character, of the previously defined *SOCKET* to the user's screen:

```
print(getpeername(SOCKET)."\n");
```

Parameters handle

Value string

See Also accept, getsocketname, pack, unpack

getpgrp

Syntax   `getpgrp(num)`

Usage   The *getpgrp* function returns the process group ID of the process specified by *num*. Calling this function without passing the *num* argument will default the function implementation to act on process ID 0.
   Note that you will get a fatal error if the system you are running doesn't support *getpgrp*.

Examples   This example returns the process group ID of this script. I could have left off the 0 argument since *getpgrp* defaults to 0 when no argument is passed:

```
print(getpgrp(0)."\n");
```

Parameters   numeric

Value   numeric

See Also   getppid, your system documentation on *getpgrp*

getppid

Syntax   `getppid`

Usage   The *getppid* function returns the process ID of the parent process that is calling *getppid*. So, when executed in a script, a call to the *getppid* function will return the process ID of the running script.

Examples   This example prints the process ID, concatenated with a newline character, of the script containing the print statement:

```
print (getppid."\n");
```

Value   numeric

See Also   getpgrp

getpriority

Syntax   `getpriority(type, process)`

Usage   The *getpriority* function returns the current priority of process *process*. The *type* argument signifies the user, process, or process group for which you wish to retrieve the priority of *process*.

   Note that you will get a fatal error if the system you are running doesn't support *getpriority*.

Examples   This example shows how you would find out the priority of the current process:

`$priority = getpriority(0, $$);`

Parameters   numeric

Value   numeric

See Also   your system documentation on *getpriority*

getprotobyname

Syntax   `getprotobyname(string)`

Usage   The *getprotobyname* networking function returns the protocols name, any aliases, and the protocol number of the protocol *string* passed.

Examples   See the Socket example in the Perl Modules section for a detailed example that uses *getprotobyname*.

Parameters   string

Value   properties

See Also   getprotobynumber, your system documentation on *getprotobyname*

getprotobynumber

Syntax	getprotobyname(*num*)
Usage	The *getprotobynumber* networking function converts the protocol defined by *num* into its name, any aliases, and the protocol number.
Examples	See the Socket example in the Perl Modules section for a detailed example that uses *getprotobynumber*.
Parameters	numeric
Value	properties
See Also	getprotobyname, your system documentation on *getprotobynumber*

getprotoent

Syntax	getprotoent
Usage	The *getprotoent* function is called when you wish to read from the */etc/ protocols* file or its equivalent. It returns the name, any aliases, and the protocol number in this file.
Examples	This example shows the protocols file being set, read, and closed. While it is being read, the name field, concatenated with a newline character, will be printed to the screen:

```
while (($name, $alias, $protocolNum) = getprotoent){
   print ($name."\n");
}
```

Value	properties
See Also	Your system documentation on *getprotoent*

getpwent

Syntax   getpwent

Usage   The *getpwent* function is called when you wish to read from the */etc/passwd* file or its equivalent. It returns the name, password, user ID, group ID, disk quota, any comments, the user's full name, directory, and the shell listed in this file.

Examples   This example shows the password file being read using *getpwent*. While it is being read, the name field, concatenated with a newline character, will be printed to the screen:

```
while (($name, $password, $userID, $groupID, $diskQuota, $comments,
    $userFullname, $directory, $shell) = getpwent){
    print ($name."\n");
}
```

Value   properties

See Also   getpwnam, your system documentation on *getpwent*

getpwnam

Syntax   getpwnam(*string*)

Usage   The *getpwnam* networking function searches your */etc/passwd* or corresponding file and returns the name, password, user ID, group ID, disk quota, any comments, the user's full name, directory, and shell of *string*. This *string* is the login ID of the user for which you wish to retrieve information.

Examples   This example prompts the user for a username and then, after *chop*ping off the newline character, passes the name to *getpwnam*. The final line of the script prints the user's ID to the screen:

```
# prompt user for ID they wish to get information on
print("Retrieve ID for: ");
$entry = (<STDIN>);

# remove newline
chop($entry);
```

```
($name, $password, $userID, $groupID, $diskQuota, $comments,
   $userFullname, $directory, $shell) = getpwnam($entry);

# print user's ID
print ($userID."\n");
```

Parameters   string

Value   properties

See Also   getpwent, getpwuid, your system documentation on *getpwnam*

G

getpwuid

SYSTEM CALL

PERL 4   PERL 5

Syntax   getpwid(*num*)

Usage   The *getpwuid* networking function searches your */etc/passwd* or corresponding file for the user's identification and returns the name, password, user ID, group ID, disk quota, any comments, the user's full name, directory, and shell of *num*. The *num* is the ID of the user for which you wish to retrieve information.

Examples   This example prompts the user for a user ID and then after *chop*ping off the newline character, passes the ID to *getpwuid*. The final line of the script prints the user's name to the screen:

```
# prompt user for name to get information on
print("Retrieve user name for: ");
$entry = (<STDIN>);

# remove newline
chop($entry);
($name, $password, $userID, $groupID, $diskQuota, $comments,
   $userFullname, $directory, $shell) =  getpwuid($entry);

# print user's name
print ($name."\n");
```

Parameters   numeric

Value   string

See Also   getpwent, getpwnam, your system documentation on *getpwuid*

getservbyname

SYSTEM CALL

PERL 4 PERL 5

Syntax getservbyname(*string*, *stringProtocol*)

Usage The *getservbyname* networking function searches your */etc/services* or corresponding file for *string* and returns the name, any aliases, the port number, and the protocol name for *stringProtocol*. The *stringProtocol* specifies the protocol name for which you wish to retrieve information.

Examples This example prompts the user to input a server name and type and then prints the server port number based on the arguments passed:

```
# prompt user and remove newline character
print("Enter server name: ");
$servName = (<STDIN>);
chop($servName);

# prompt user and remove newline character
print("Enter server type: ");
$type = (<STDIN>);
chop($type);

($name, $alias, $portNum, $protoName) = getservbyname($servName,
    $type);
print("The port number is: $portNum\n");
```

Parameters string

Value properties

See Also getservbyport, getservent, your system documentation on *getservbyname*

getservbyport

SYSTEM CALL

PERL 4 PERL 5

Syntax getservbyport(*num*, *stringProtocol*)

Usage The *getservbyport* networking function searches your */etc/services* or corresponding file for port *num* and returns the name, any aliases, a port number, and the protocol name. The *stringProtocol* specifies the protocol name for which you wish to retrieve information.

Examples   This example prompts the user to input a server port and type and then prints the server name based on the arguments passed:

```
# prompt user for server port number
print("Enter server port: ");
$servPort = (<STDIN>);
chop($servPort);

print("Enter server type: ");
$type = (<STDIN>);
chop($type);

($name, $alias, $portNum, $protoName) = getservbyport($servPort,
    $type);
print("The port name is: $name\n");
```

Parameters   numeric
string

Value   properties

See Also   getservbyname, getservent, your system documentation on *getservbyport*

getservent

SYSTEM CALL

PERL 4   PERL 5

Syntax   getservent

Usage   The *getservent* networking function iterates through the */etc/service* file and returns the names, any aliases, the port numbers, and the protocol names.

Examples   This function prints the corresponding information for the system in which this script is run:

```
($name, $alias, $portNum, $protoName) = getservent;
print("$name\t$alias\t$portNum\t$protoName\n");
```

Value   properties

See Also   getservbyname, getservbyport, your system documentation on *getservent*

getsockname

FUNCTION

PERL 4 PERL 5

Syntax   getsockname(*SOC_VARIABLE*)

Usage   The *getsockname* networking function allows you to return the socket connection address of the connection specified in *SOC_VARIABLE*. Since the returned address may be packed, you may have to unpack the data before reading.

Examples   This example prints the socket address, concatenated with a newline character, of the previously defined *SOCKET*:

```
print(getsockname(SOCKET)."\n");
```

Parameters   handle

Value   string

See Also   accept, getpeername, unpack

getsockopt

SYSTEM CALL

PERL 4 PERL 5

Syntax   getsockopt SOCKET, LEVEL, OPTION

Usage   The *getsockopt* function queries the SOCKET for OPTION and returns its value. If an error occurs, an undefined value is returned. See *setsockopt* for more detailed information.

Examples   See *setsockopt* for an example of *getsockopt*.

Parameters   Socket handle, numeric, string

Value   scalar

See Also   setsockopt, your system documentation on *getsockopt*

glob

Syntax glob(*pattern*)

Usage The *glob* function expands the *pattern* passed to it the same way the shell would. If no pattern is passed, it uses *$_*.

Examples The following example is the same as typing **ls *.pl** in your shell without the formatting:

```
@perl = glob "*.pl";
print ("@perl\n");
```

Parameters string

Value string

gmtime

Syntax gmtime(*timeFormat*)

Usage The *gmtime* function returns the system time into seconds, minutes, hours, month day, month, year, week day, and year day and indicates whether it is daylight savings time. This returned time is in the form of the Greenwich time zone.

Examples This example returns *time* in all the appropriate variables, at which time the information they contain is printed to the user's screen. An *if* loop is used to determine if it is daylight savings time:

```
($seconds, $minutes, $hour, $monthDate, $month, $year, $weekDay,
    $yearDate, $dayLightSavings) = gmtime(time);

# print the output
print("The time is: $hour:$minutes:$seconds\n\n");
print("It is the $weekDay day of the week,\n");
print("the $monthDate day of month $month,\n");
print("the $yearDate day of the year,\n");
```

```
# determine if it is daylight savings time
if($dayLightSavings){
   print("and it is daylight savings time.\n");
}else{
   print("and it is not daylight savings time.\n");
}
```

Parameters time format

Value properties

See Also time

goto

FUNCTION LOOP CONTROL

PERL 4   PERL 5

Syntax goto *SECTION*

Usage The *goto* function goes to a defined *SECTION* in your script and is often used to "jump" from one segment of your script to another without implementing any of the code in between.

    Do note that the use of *goto* will probably disappear in a future release of Perl since it handles subroutines and packages better than implementing the *goto* function.

Examples This example asks the user if he or she would like to start at the front or back of the script. Depending on the user's entry, the script will "jump" to the preferred location and print a short statement to the screen:

```
# prompt user for decision
print("Would you like to start at the FRONT or BACK? ");
$entry = (<STDIN>);
chop($entry);

# determine "jump"
if($entry eq "FRONT"){
   goto FRONT;
}elsif($entry eq "BACK"){
   goto BACK;
}else{
   print("You made an incorrect entry, please restart\n");
   goto STOP;
}
```

```
# define 'FRONT'
FRONT:
   print("You went to the front\n");
   goto STOP;

# define 'END'
BACK:
   print("You went to the back\n");
   goto STOP;

# end execution here
STOP:
   print("The End!\n");
```

G

Parameters   section

See Also   Appendix C (Loop Control)

grep

Syntax   grep(*pattern*, *@list*)

Usage   The *grep* function searches *@list* for *pattern*. In a list context, if any matches
are found, the string is returned by *grep*; in a scalar context, *grep* will return
the number of entries that it found.

Examples   This example defines *@list* with some random numbers and strings and then
prompts the user to enter in a character for which the *grep* function will
search. The final line of the script prints the number of occurrences of the
character :

```
# define list
@list = (1, 2, "hello", 4, "Perl", 5, 3, 3, "four");

#prompt user for input
print("Please enter a character to search for: ");
$entry = (<STDIN>);
chop($entry);

# search for character
$numEntries = grep(/[$entry]/, @list);

# print results
print("There were $numEntries occurrences of your character\n");
```

This example shows how each occurrence found can be held in a list for later manipulation:

```
# define list
@list = (1, 2, "hello", 4, "Perl", 5, 3, 3, "four");

#prompt user for input
print("Please enter a character to search for: ");
$entry = (<STDIN>);
chop($entry);

# search for character and place occurrences in list
@found = grep(/[$entry]/, @list);

# print results
$result = join("\n", @found);
print("$result\n");
```

Parameters   list
pattern

Value   numeric
string

See Also   split

gt

OPERATOR

PERL 4   PERL 5

Syntax   *alphanum1* gt *alphanum2*

string1 gt *string2*

Usage   The *gt* comparison operator tests to see if the first argument passed is greater than the second argument passed. If it is, then a 1 is returned; a *NULL* is returned if the second argument is greater than or equal to the first argument.

As you would imagine, this operator is also case sensitive, which allows you to distinguish between strings that are equal, but are passed with capitalization and strings with various case.

Examples   This example assigns a number to *$one* and *$two*. The numbers are then compared, and *print* function prints a result based on the comparison:

```
# define 2 numeric variables
$one = 1;
$two = 2;

if ($one gt $two){
   print("$one is greater than $two\n");
}else{

   # this line will be printed
   print("$two is greater than $one\n");
}
```

This example shows how *gt* can distinguish between strings of various cases:

```
$one = "one";
$two = "One";

if ($one gt $two){

   # this line will be printed
   print("$one is greater than $two\n");

}else{
   print("$two is greater than $one\n");
}
```

Parameters   alphanumeric
string

Value   numeric

See Also   Appendix C (Operators), cmp, eq, ge, le, lt, ne, not, xor

hex

PERL 4   PERL 5

Syntax	hex(*string*)
Usage	The *hex* operator returns the hexadecimal value of *string*. If you pass a string that contains a white space, only the characters before the white space will be evaluated. Also note that hexadecimal representation can include any numeric value and any character from *A* to *F*.
Examples	This example prints the hexadecimal value of "A45F9," concatenated with a newline character, to the user's screen:

```
# print '673273' to screen
print(hex("A45F9")."\n");
```

Parameters	string
Value	numeric
See Also	oct

H

if

Syntax
```
if (CONDITION){
    CODE
}
```
```
if (CONDITION){
    CODE
}else{
    CODE
}
```
```
CODE if(CONDITION)
```

Usage   The *if* loop control statement executes the contents of *CODE* based on *CONDITION*. In the second syntactical definition, if this *CONDITION* is not met, then the following *else* block of *CODE* executes. The third definition shows a single line implementation of *if*, where *CODE* is executed if *CONDITION* is satisfied. As you might guess, other loop control statements can be used in conjunction with *if*.

Note that, since these conditions are located before the internal portion of the loop is encountered, the code in the loop may not be executed.

Examples   The following example prompts the user for a password. If the user enters the correct password, then the "Success" message will be printed to the user's screen. If the user enters an incorrect password, then the "Failure" message will be printed to the screen.

Note that the *chop* function is called to remove the newline character at the end of the user's input:

```
$password = "test";

print("Please enter a password: ");
$input = <STDIN>;

# remove newline
chop($input);

if ($input eq $password){
    print("Success!\n");
}else{
    print("Failure!\n");
}
```

This example shows the use of the single definition of *if*. In this short script, the user is prompted for input. If the user enters "y", then the *if* statement will prove to be true and a string will be printed to the screen:

```
print ("Would you like to print text to the screen? ");
$entry = (<STDIN>);

# remove newline
chop($entry);

# print if user enters 'y'
print("Here it is!\n") if ($entry eq "y");
```

Parameters   code

See Also   continue, do, else, elsif, for, foreach, Appendix C (Loop Control), require, unless, until, use, while, next

import

METHOD

PERL 5

Syntax   import *CLASS*

import *CLASS @list*

Usage   The *import* declaration is effectively the same as the *use* declaration. If you wish to "uninclude" a module that you have previously included using the *use* or *import* declaration, then you pass the module name to *no*.

You can also pass a list of symbols that you want to import from the module, as in the second syntactical definition, so as not to clutter your namespace unnecessarily.

Examples   This example shows a module being included and then unincluded:

```
# include the module
import MyModule;

# uninclude the module
no MyModule;
```

This example only imports one method from the module:

```
import MyModule qw("func1");
```

Parameters   class
              list

See Also   no, require, use

index

Syntax   index(*string*, *substring*, *num*)
          index(*string*, *substring*)

Usage   The *index* function searches *string* for *substring* and returns the numeric location of its first character. Passing *num* allows you the ability to assign the location to start the search, which will reduce the amount of searching that has to take place. Also note that if there are multiple occurrences of the string you are searching, then the location of the last occurrence will be returned.

Examples   This example defines *$string* and then implements the *index* function on the variable. The final statement prints the result to the screen:

```
$string = "My name is Allen";
$return = index($string, "Allen");

# prints '11' to screen
print($return."\n");
```

Parameters   numeric
              string

Value   numeric

See Also   rindex, substr

int

Syntax   `int EXPRESSION`

Usage   The *int* function is responsible for returning the integer value of *EXPRES-SION*. It is often used to ensure that the value you seek, after implementing an arithmetic operator, is an integer.

Examples   This example assigns a string and a couple of numerical values to variables, which are then evaluated using *int*. The first comparison does not implement *int* but is there to show the difference in output. After these new results are generated, they are printed to the user's screen:

```
# define the variables
$num = 685;
$float = 33.5;
$alphanumeric = "Is that you 007?";

# implement 'int' function and stored in another variable
$result = $num*$float;
$resultInt = int($num*$float);
$resultAlphanumeric = int($alphanumeric);

# print results to screen which will be as follows:
# '22947.5 22947   0'
print("$result\t$resultInt\t$resultAlphanumeric\n");
```

Parameters   numeric

Value   numeric

ioctl

Syntax   ioctl(*FILE_VARIABLE*, FUNCTION, VARIABLE);

Usage   The *ioctl* function allows you to run a system-specific function on a file handle. This function is only useful on UNIX machines. To load the appropriate function definitions, you can import the *ioctl*-bundled module like:

use ioctl;

The VARIABLE you pass to this function will depend on the function you call. It can either be used as an argument to FUNCTION or where the return value of the FUNCTION is stored. See your system documentation on *ioctl*, *streamio*, and *termio* for more information on the functions you can call and what type of arguments they take. You generally use pack and unpack to set and retrieve values to pass as the argument.

The *ioctl* function returns an undefined value when an error occurs processing the *ioctl* call. It returns 0 if the system call returned 0. It returns any number returned by the system call if any.

Parameters   handle

Value   numeric

See Also   fcntl, Modules: ioctl, your system documentation on *ioctl*

join

Syntax   join(*expression*, *@list*)

Usage   The *join* function creates a string of the items in *@list* that are separated by *expression*. This is, in effect, the complete opposite of the *split* function.

Examples   This example creates a string that has each entry of *@names* separated by a newline character and the string "Name: ". The output of this code is shown in the comment section after the *print* statement:

```
# define an array of names
@names = ("Allen", "Anne", "Dane", "Robert");

# create list has 'Name' in between each entry
$list = join("\nName: ", @names);

print ("Name: ".$list."\n");
# the following is printed to the user's screen
# Name: Allen
# Name: Anne
# Name: Dane
# Name: Robert
```

This example shows how you list the first 10 characters of the alphabet separated by commas:

```
# define array of first 10 characters in alphabet
@alpha = ("a", "b", "c", "d", "e", "f", "g", "h", "i", "j");

# create list using join, where the entries are separated
# by commas
$list = join(",", @alpha);

# print the list to the screen
print ("$list\n");
```

Parameters   expression
list

Value   string

See Also   split

keys

FUNCTION

PERL 4   PERL 5

Syntax   `keys(%array)`

Usage   The *keys* function returns all the aliases of *%array*. Although they are in no specific order, each alias is listed.

Examples   This example defines *%array* and then prints out all the aliases on a newline. Notice that the *join* function is used to insert newline characters between each alias. Without it, a continuous string is printed to the screen:

```
# define an associative array
%array = ('one', "1", 'two', "2", 'three', "3");

# print the 'keys' to the array on new lines
print (join("\n", keys(%array))."\n");

# the output will be as follows:
# three
# two
# one
```

Parameters   array

Value   array

See Also   each, values

K

kill

FUNCTION

PERL 4   PERL 5

Syntax   `kill(num, @list)`

`kill(string, @list)`

`kill(@list)`

Usage   The *kill* function sends the signal *num* or the signal name, *string*, to the list of processes in *@list*. To pass a single process to be killed, you would simply pass a list with a single entry. After sending, the function then returns the number of processes that received the *kill* signal.

If you implement this function by passing the signal name, be sure to surround the name in single quotes and leave off the preceding signal *num*. It is also possible, as in the third syntactical definition, to include the signal as the first entry of *@list*.

Examples   This example takes a predefined list of processes and sends a signal to each of them. The number of processes that received the signal is held in the variable *$numKilled*:

```
$numKilled = kill(1, @processes);
```

This example shows how a single process can be killed using the name of the signal. Again, the number of processes that received the signal is held in the variable *$numKilled*:

```
$numKilled = kill('STOP', $process);
```

This example initializes a list whose first element is the signal that needs to be sent to the resulting processes. This type of action is commonly used when scripts have to perform a *kill* on multiple processes that run together. Once again, the number of processes that received the signal is held in the variable *$numKilled*:

```
@killProcess = ("1", $process1, $process2, $process3);
$numKilled = kill(@killProcess);
```

Parameters   list
numeric
string

Value   numeric

See Also   exit, warn

K

last

Syntax   `last` *SECTION*

`last`

Usage   The *last* loop control function, when implemented, breaks out of the loop defined by *SECTION*. This allows the programmer to exit the desired loop when needed rather than exiting based on predefined conditions. If *SECTION* is not defined, as in the second syntactical definition, then the *last* loop control statement exits the current innermost loop. Passing *SECTION* allows you the ability to not only exit this loop, but also to exit any number of nested loops.

Do note that if you have a *continue* implementation after the body of the loop, it will *not* be entered if the loop is exited via a *last* function call.

Examples   This example initializes a variable, *$i*, to 0 then enters a *while* loop. After incrementing the loop variable, the *last* loop control checks to see whether the variable is equal to 2 via a single line *if* statement. If the *last* loop control is not implemented, the script prints the loop number to the screen and continues looping. When the loop variable is 2, the *print* statement is skipped and the loop is exited:

```
# initialize a variable
$i = 0;

LOOP:while ($i < 5){
        $i++;

        # prints only one iteration due to the
        # 'last' implementation
        last LOOP if ($i eq "2");
        print ("Loop number $i\n");
        }
```

Parameters   section

See Also   Appendix C (LoopControl), do, else, elsif, for, foreach, if, next, require, use, while

lc

FUNCTION

PERL 5

Syntax   lc(*string*)

Usage   The *lc* function converts and returns the lowercase version of the *string* passed.

Examples This example defines a string of mixed case in *$string*. The string is then passed to *lc* and its output is printed to the user's screen. A concatenated newline character is added to return the user's prompt to a newline:

```
$string = "This IS A strING of MIXed CaSe";

# print 'this is a string of mixed case'
print(lc($string)."\n");
```

Parameters string

Value   string

See Also   m, lcfirst, s, tr, y

lcfirst

FUNCTION

PERL 5

Syntax   lcfirst(*string*)

Usage   In much the same manner as the *lc* function, *lcfirst* creates a lowercase conversion on the string passed. This function, however, converts only the first character of *string* to lowercase.

Examples This example defines a string of mixed case in *$string*. Since *lcfirst* only changes the first character to lowercase, the rest of the string is left intact. A concatenated newline character is added to the output to return the user's prompt to a new line:

```
$string = ("THIS IS A strING of MIXed CaSe");

# print 'tHIS IS A strING of MIXed CaSe'
print(lcfirst($string)."\n");
```

Parameters	string
Value	string
See Also	m, lc, s, tr, y

le

PERL 4   PERL 5

Syntax   *alphanum1* le *alphanum2*

string1 le *string2*

Usage   The *le* comparison operator tests the arguments passed to see whether the first argument is less than or equal to the second argument. As you would imagine, this operator is also case sensitive, which allows it to distinguish between a string passed with capitalization and the same string passed in mixed case.

As for the result of using this operator, if the first argument is less than the second or the two arguments are the same, the returned result is 1. If the second argument is less than the first, then a *NULL* is returned.

Examples   This example assigns a number to *$num1* and *$num2*. These two variables are then compared and a result based on the comparison is printed:

```
$num1 = "4";
$num2 = "3";

if ($num1 le $num2){
   print('$num1 is less than or equal to $num2'."\n");
}else{

   # this line will be printed to the user's screen
   print('$num2 is less than $num1'."\n");
   }
```

This example shows how the *le* operator can distinguish between strings of various cases:

```
$string1 = "One";
$string2 = "one";

if ($string1 le $string2){

   # this line will be printed to the user's screen
   print('$string1 is less than or equal to $string2'."\n");
```

```
}else{
   print('$string2 is less than $string1'."\n");
}
```

Parameters   alphanumeric
             string

Value   numeric

See Also   Appendix C (Operators), cmp, eq, gt, ne, lt, xor

length

PERL 4   PERL 5

Syntax   length(*EXPRESSION*)

Usage   The *length* function returns the length of *EXPRESSION* in bytes. Note that
           length will not function as implied on arrays.

> **Tip**
>
> *If you wish to return the length of an array, simply assign the array
> to a variable. This can be done as follows:*
> ```
> # define an array
> @array = ("one", "two", "three");
> # evaluate its length by reading it into a variable
> $arrayLength = @array;
> ```

Examples   This example defines two variables, one as a string and the other as a
             numeric value. Each of these two variables are then passed to the *length*
             function with the resulting value stored in other variables. These resulting
             values are then printed to the user's screen:

```
$string = ("This is a string of characters");
$num = 68970;

$stringLength = length($string);
$numLength = length($num);

# prints '30' as answer
print("The length of the string is: $stringLength\n");
```

```
# prints '5' as answer
print("The length of the numeric value is: $numLength\n");
```

Parameters | expression

Value | numeric

link

FUNCTION

PERL 4   PERL 5

Syntax | link(*string1*, *string2*)

Usage | The *link* function creates a file defined by *string2* that is linked to the previously created file *string1*. If the link is successful, then a 1 is returned, while a 0 is returned for an unsuccessful link.
This creates a hard link to the file so that if the previously created file is deleted, the newly created file will still exist; this is unlike the *symlink* command, which creates a symbolic link.

Examples | This example links *linked.txt* to *test.txt*:

```
link("test.txt", "linked.txt");
```

Parameters | string

Value | numeric

See Also | symlink, unlink

listen

SYSTEM CALL

PERL 4   PERL 5

Syntax | listen(*SOCKET_VARIABLE*, *num*)

Usage | The *listen* function causes your script to listen on a certain port for a connection. You use this function when creating your own server. The first argument is the socket handle you created through a call to socket, and the second argument is the maximum number of connections to queue up if the connection is busy.
This function returns True if the listen call succeeded and False otherwise, with the error being placed in the special variable *$!*.

Examples The following example creates a very simple server with no error checking. It accepts a connection to port 2468, prints a message to the client, and then closes. Please see the *Socket* entry in the Perl Modules section for a more detailed example:

```
use Socket;

socket(SERVER, PF_INET, SOCK_STREAM, getprotobyname('tcp'));
bind(SERVER, sockaddr_in(2468, INADDR_ANY));
listen(SERVER, SOMAXCONN);

accept(CLIENT, SERVER);
print CLIENT "Welcome!\n";
print CLIENT "Goodbye!\n";
close CLIENT;
```

Parameters handle
numeric

Value boolean

See Also accept, bind, listen, socket, Socket Module, your system documentation on *listen*

local

FUNCTION

PERL 4 PERL 5

Syntax local(*EXPRESSION*)

Usage The *local* function creates a local instance of the global *EXPRESSION* passed. This is commonly used when passing variables to subroutines. This ensures that the value passed will not be adversely affected by variables in the subroutine.

> **Note**
>
> *All variables are global by default, so you may find* local *to be a very useful function for your implementation.*

Note that there is a difference between this function and the *my* function. The *local* function creates a local instance of the global variable that can then be passed to any subroutine and still maintain the local initialization. The *my* operator creates the local instance in the same manner as the *local* function;

however, the instance created with *my* can not be passed to other subroutines. The global value rather than the local instance is what is passed to the subroutines for evaluation.

Consider this usage example. If you have a global variable counting the number of calls you are making to a specific subroutine, and that subroutine also has a variable of the same name, then it is possible to overwrite the value of your global variable with the subroutine's value. The *local* function could be used to create a local instance of the global variable to ensure that the global value stays intact while the local value has the freedom of changing.

Examples   This example declares a global variable and then, in the body of an *if* loop, declares a *local* instance of this variable. This *local* instance is then reassigned a value of 45 and prints the following loop values to the screen. After exiting the *if* loop, the *local* variable is discarded and the global variable is "reassigned." The trailing *print* statement prints the reassigned global value of 1 to the screen to demonstrate this reassignment.

See the entry for *my* for a function contrasting example:

```
# define a global variable
$global = 1;

# print '1' to screen to verify
print("$global ");

if($global){

    # declare this instance of '$global' local
    local ($global);

    # change the value of the local variable
    for($global = 45; $global < 51; $global++){

        # prints '45 46 47 48 49 50' to screen
        print("$global ");
    }
}

# prints original global '1' to screen
print("$global ");
```

Parameters   expression

Value   expression

See Also   my, package

localtime

Syntax   localtime(*timeFormat*)

Usage   The *localtime* function returns the system
month day, month, year, weekday, year day, and w...
savings time. This time format is in the form of your local time zone.
    Do note that the weekday and the month are zero-based. So the first
month or day of the week is returned as 0.

Examples   This example returns *time* into all the appropriate variables, at which time
the information they contain is printed to the user's screen. An *if* loop is used
to determine if it is daylight savings time:

```
($seconds, $minutes, $hour, $monthDate, $month, $year, $weekDay,
   $yearDate, $dayLightSavings) = localtime(time);

# print the output
print("The time is: $hour:$minutes:$seconds\n\n");
print("It is the $weekDay day of the week,\n");
print("the $monthDate day of month $month,\n");
print("the $yearDate day of the year,\n");

# determine if it is day light savings time
if($dayLightSavings){
   print("and it is daylight savings time.\n");
}else{
   print("and it is not daylight savings time.\n");
}
```

Parameters   timeFormat

Value   properties

See Also   gmtime, time

L

print LocaltimE (time) returns

Syntax	log(*num*)

Usage   The *log* arithmetic function returns the logarithm, base *e*, of *num* passed.

Examples   This example prints the *log* value of 10 concatenated with a newline character to the user's screen:

```
# prints '2.30258509299405'
print(log(10)."\n");
```

Parameters   numeric

Value   numeric

See Also   abs, atan2, cos, exp, sin, sqrt

L

lstat

Syntax   lstat(*FILE_VARIABLE*)
         lstat(*string*)

Usage   The *lstat* function converts the file defined by *FILE_VARIABLE* or *string* into its device number, inode number, file mode, number of links, user ID, group ID, device identifier, total byte size of file, last access time, last modify time, inode change time, preferred blocksize, and the actual number of blocks allocated. It is effectively the same as the *stat* function except that, if implemented on a symbolic link, it will *stat* the link rather than the file it links to.

Examples   This example opens a file under the handle *INFILE* and then passes it to *lstat* for variable processing. The trailing *print* statement prints the values of the variables to the user's screen:

```
open(INFILE, "test.txt") || die("Error: opening file\n");

# read values into variables
($devNum, $inode, $mode, $numLink, $userID, $groupID, $devIDFR, $size,
    $accessTime, $modTime, $createTime, $blockSize, $blocks) =
    lstat(INFILE);

# print variables to screen
print("$devNum $inode $mode $numLink $userID $groupID $devIDFR $size
    $accessTime $modTime $createTime $blockSize $blocks\n");
```

Parameters   handle
             string

Value   properties

See Also   stat

lt
OPERATOR

PERL 4   PERL 5

Syntax   *alphanum1* lt *alphanum2*

string1 lt *string2*

Usage   The *lt* comparison operator tests the arguments passed to see if the first argument is less than the second argument. As you would imagine, this operator is also case sensitive, which allows it to distinguish between a string passed with capitalization and the same string passed with mixed case.

As for the result of using this operator, if the first argument is less than the second, the returned result is 1. If the second argument is less than the first or the two arguments are equal, a *NULL* is returned.

Examples   This example assigns a number to *$num1* and *$num2*. These two variables are then compared and a result based on the comparison is printed:

```
$num1 = "4";
$num2 = "3";

if ($num1 lt $num2){
    print('$num1 is less than $num2'."\n");
}else{

    # this line will be printed to the user's screen
    print('$num2 is less than $num1'."\n");
    }
```

This example shows how the *lt* operator can distinguish between strings of various cases:

```
$string1 = "One";
$string2 = "one";

if ($string1 lt $string2){

    # this line will be printed to the user's screen
    print('$string1 is less than $string2'."\n");

}else{
    print('$string2 is less than $string1'."\n");
}
```

Parameters   alphanumeric
string

Value   numeric

See Also   Appendix C (Operators), cmp, eq, gt, ne, le, xor

m

PERL 4   PERL 5

Syntax   m/*original*/*options*

m/*original*/

Usage   The *m* operator searches the string passed to it for the first instance of a string defined by *original*. The function itself returns a 1 if the string was found and *undef* otherwise. Also note that this operator is the default operator used for // searches, so it will still work even if the *m* is left off.

The *options* field allows you to specify the type of search you would like to perform on the string. The following is a description of the options that you can pass to the *m* operator:

Option	Description
g	Find all instances of original in the string passed.
i	Make the search case insensitive.
m	Treat the string passed as multiple lines.
o	Compile the pattern once.
s	Treat the string passed as a single line.
x	Use the extended regular expressions.

M

Examples   This example opens a file to read data. After the file is successfully opened, a *while* loop is used to iterate through the file. The *m* operator is used to look for the string "Perl" in the file:

```
# open a file to read data out of
open(INFILE, "test.txt") or die("Error: unable to open file");

# iterate through the file
while(<INFILE>){

   # check to see if the current line contains 'Perl'
   if($_ =~ m/Perl/){
      print("I found the string in the file\n");
   }else{
      print("No instances were found\n");
   }
}

# close the file
close(INFILE);
```

Parameters	options
	string

Value	numeric

See Also	s, split, tr, y, Appendix C (Pattern Matching)

map

Syntax	map({*CODE*} @*list*)
	map(*FUNCTION*, @*list*)

Usage   The *map* function applies a list to *FUNCTION* or a set of commands defined in *CODE*. This is used when implementing a function (or set of commands) on an entire list of elements. Notice that when you pass the list directly to *CODE*, you should not have the comma delimiter.

Examples   This example defines a list of hexadecimal values and then passes it to the *hex* function via *map* where the contents of the list are mapped to their decimal value:

```
# define a list of hexadecimal values
@list = ("FFF", "10AB", "345");

# map these characters to their decimal value
@decList = map(hex, @list);

# print original list to screen
print("@list\n");

# print results to screen
print("@decList\n");
```

This second example demonstrates the ability to pass your list straight to code. To show its functionality, I have merely passed this list to the *chr* function.

The example defines a list of decimal values and then passes it to the *chr* function via *map* where the contents of the list are mapped to their ASCII value and changed within the @*list* array instead of the returned value:

```
# define a list of decimal values
@list = ("235", "121", "88");

# print original list to screen
print("@list\n");

# map these characters to their ASCII value
map({$_ = chr;} @list);

# print results to screen
print("@list\n");
```

Parameters   code
function
list

Value   code result
function result

See Also   grep

M

mkdir

SYSTEM CALL

PERL 4   PERL 5

Syntax   mkdir(*string*, *permission*)

Usage   The *mkdir* function creates a directory defined by *string* and defines the rights to the directory by *permission*. If the directory is successfully created, the *mkdir* function returns a 1, while an unsuccessful directory creation returns a 0.

Examples   This example creates a directory named "Test_Directory" with group reading permissions in the current working directory of the executing script:

```
mkdir("Test_Directory", 740);
```

Parameters   permission
string

Value   numeric

See Also   closedir, opendir, your system documentation on *mkdir*

msgctl

Syntax   msgctl(*MSGID*, *COMMAND*, *buffer*)

Usage   The *msgctl* function is part of a set of UNIX System V Interprocess Communi-
         cations (IPC) commands.
             The *msgctl* function allows the programmer to set control options for the
         message queue and send commands. The following commands can be used:
         IPC_STAT, IPC_SET, or IPC_RMID. This function returns an undefined value
         if it fails, 0 if the system call returns 0 (this isn't a failure), or the return value
         from the system call.

Examples See *msgsnd* for an example using all the *msg** commands.

See Also msgget, msgrcv, msgsnd, your system documentation on *msgctl*

msgget

Syntax   msgget(*key*, *flags*);

Usage   The *msgget* function is part of a set of UNIX System V Interprocess Commu-
         nications (IPC) commands. They are generally used on machines that do not
         support sockets but need to have a method of process communication.
             The *msgget* function is used to create a message queue ID that is associ-
         ated with the given *key*. This ID can then be used by the *msgsnd* and *msgrcv*
         functions.

Examples See *msgsnd* for an example using all the *msg** commands.

See Also msgctl, msgrcv, msgsnd, your system documentation on *msgget*

msgrcv

Syntax   msgrcv MSGID, VARIABLE, SIZE, TYPE, FLAGS

Usage   The *msgrcv* function is part of a set of UNIX System V Interprocess Commu-
          nications (IPC) commands.
              The *msgrcv* function is used to pull a message off the message queue
          associated with the message ID. The variable passed is where the message
          will be stored. This message can be up to *SIZE* bytes in length. The TYPE
          determines what type of message to receive. See your system documentation
          and *msgsnd* for more information on the TYPE.

Examples See *msgsnd* for an example using all the *msg** commands.

See Also msgctl, msgget, msgsnd, your system documentation on *msgrcv*

msgsnd

M

Syntax   msgsnd(MSGID, MESSAGE, FLAGS)

Usage   The *msgsnd* function is part of a set of UNIX System V Interprocess Commu-
          nications (IPC) commands.
              The *msgsnd* function is used to place a message on the queue. The mes-
          sage must be a packed variable with the message being specified as a long
          data type, in the first piece of the structure.

Examples The following example shows how to use the *msg** functions to communicate
          between a child and parent process after forking:

```perl
# create a private ID for this process
$id = msgget(IPC_PRIVATE, IPC_CREAT);

if ( $pid = fork() ) {

    # create a message with a type of 1
    $msg = pack('la*', 1, "here's a message" );

    # send the message
    msgsnd($id, $msg, IPC_NOWAIT);
    exit;
```

```
} elsif(defined($pid)){

    # receive the next message with a type of 1
    msgrcv($id, $receive, 50, 1, IPC_NOWAIT);
    print "Received: $receive\n";

    # remove the message ID
    msgctl($id, IPC_RMID, undef);
    exit;
}
```

See Also   msgctl, msgget, msgrcv, your system documentation on *msgsnd*

my
OPERATOR

PERL 5

Syntax   my(*EXPRESSION*)

Usage   The *my* function creates a local instance of the global *EXPRESSION* passed.
This is commonly used when passing variables to subroutines because it
ensures that the value passed will not be adversely affected by variables in
the routine.

Note that there is a difference between this function and the *local* function.
The *local* function creates a local instance of the global variable that can then
be passed to any subroutine and still maintain the local initialization. The *my*
operator creates the local instance in the same manner as the *local* function;
however, the instance created with *my* can not be passed to other subroutines. The global value rather than the local instance is passed to the subroutines for evaluation.

A usage example would involve a global variable being passed to a
specific subroutine. The subroutine would also have a variable of the same
name that performs another task. Since there are now two variables with the
same name, it is possible to overwrite the value of your global variable with
the subroutine's value. In this instance, the *my* function can be used to create
a local instance of the global variable inside the body of the subroutine to
ensure that the global value stayed intact while the local value had the
freedom of changing.

Examples   This example declares a global variable and then passes it to a subroutine
where a local instance of the variable is created using the *my* function. The
following function is used to show the value of the reassigned variable
before calling the second subroutine. This local instance is then reassigned a
value of 100 and a second *print* call is made. The second routine is then

called and again the value is printed. This time the value printed is the original declaration. This demonstrates how a local instance of a variable created with the *my* function can only hold its value while in the body of the initializing routine.

See the entry for *local* for a function-contrasting example:

```
# define a global variable
$global = 1;

# call first subroutine
&localTest;

# print value after routine call is over
print("Current value: $global\n");

# first routine defined: declares local version with my
sub localTest{

    # print initial value
    print("Initial value in localTest subroutine: $global\n");

    # define the variable local to this routine
    my($global);

    # reassign the local variable to a new value
    $global = 100;

    # print the new value
    print("Reassigned value in localTest subroutine: $global\n");

    # call the second subroutine
    &localTest2;
}

# second routine defined: shows local variable not passed
sub localTest2{

    # print the value of the variable passed
    print("The value in the localTest2 subroutine is: $global\n");
}
```

M

Parameters	expression
Value	expression
See Also	local, package

ne

Syntax   *alphanum1* ne *alphanum2*

          string1 ne *string2*

Usage   The *ne* comparison operator tests the arguments passed to see if they are *not* equal. As you would imagine, this operator is also case sensitive. It is able to distinguish between a string passed with capitalization and the same string with all lowercase.

      As for the result of using this operator, if the two strings are the same, the returned result is 0. If they are not equal, a 1 is returned.

Examples   This example assigns numbers to two variables. The two variables are then compared, and the *print* function prints a result based on the comparison. The result of this example prints the "not equal" string to the user's screen:

```
# define 2 variables with numeric values
$num1 = "4";
$num2 = "3";

# test to see if they are equal
if ($num1 ne $num2){

    # this line is printed
    print('$num1 and $num2 are not equal'."\n");

}else{
    print('$num1 and $num2 are equal'."\n");
}
```

      This example shows how the *ne* operator can distinguish between strings of various cases. The result of this example prints the "not equal" string to the user's screen:

```
# define 2 variables with strings
$string1 = "One";
$string2 = "one";

# see if these strings are the same
if ($string1 ne $string2){

    # this line is printed
    print('$string1 and $string2 are not equal'."\n");

}else{
    print('$string1 and $string2 are equal'."\n");
}
```

Parameters	alphanumeric string
Value	numeric
See Also	cmp, eq, gt, le, lt, Appendix C (Operators), xor

new

Syntax	new(*CLASS*)

Usage   Even though this is not a function built into Perl, the *new* subroutine is commonly used to create a new instance of *CLASS*. This will be familiar to the C++ and Java programmers out there, but keep in mind that you must define the *new* subroutine before you call it. Unlike with C++ or Java, *new* is not provided for you—it must be defined in the *CLASS* constructor.

Examples   The following example creates a new instance of an Image object from the GD external module:

```
$image = new GD::Image(100,200);
```

Parameters	class
Value	type of class
See Also	sub

next

Syntax	next(*SECTION*)

Usage   The *next* element of a loop control is called in the body of the loop. It is often used in *while* and *until* loops to return to the start of the loop for another iteration.

Examples   This example shows a *next* implementation on a *while* loop. It initializes *$i* to 0 and then enters the loop. After incrementing the loop variable, the *next* loop control checks to see if the variable is equal to 2 via an *if* statement. If the *next* loop control is not implemented, the script prints the loop number to the screen, but when the loop variable is 2, the print statement is skipped.

The result of this example will skip the printing of the second iteration:

```
# define a variable that will act as a counter
$i = 0;

LOOP: while ($i < 5){
        $i++;

        # skip 2nd iteration
        next LOOP if ($i eq "2");

        print ("Loop number $i\n");
        }
```

Parameters   section

See Also   do, else, elsif, for, foreach, if, last, Appendix C (Loop Control), require, until, use, while

N

no

Syntax   no *MODULE*

no *MODULE @list*

Usage   The *no* declaration is effectively the "undo" of the *use* declaration. If you wish to "uninclude" a module that you have previously included using the *use* declaration, you pass the module name to *no*.

The optional *@list* argument can be the list of features you want removed from your current program's name space.

Examples   This example shows a module being included and then unincluded:

```
# include the module
use MyModule;

# uninclude the module
no MyModule;
```

This example shows a list of features being unincluded from a module:

```
# include the module
use MyModule;

# uninclude the module's feature 'funcs'
no MyModule 'funcs';
```

Parameters   list
              module

See Also   import, require, use

not

Syntax   not(*alphanumeric*)

          not(*string*)

          not(*$list*)

          not(*@array*)

          not(*%array*)

N

Usage   The *not* unary negation operator returns a 1 only if the argument passed is 0.
          If arrays or lists are passed, they must be empty to return a 0. If any other
          value is passed, nothing is returned.
              I have created a truth table that defines the characteristics of the *not* unary
          negation operator. Under the sample argument, I have listed the possible
          cases that could occur, while the right column contains the result of *not*ing
          the argument.

Truth Table	
argument	not *(argument)*
0	1
nonzero	NULL

Examples This example assigns a 0 to *$one*. The variable is then negated using the *not* operator and places the result in *$result*:

```
# define a variable
$one = 0;

# feed the variable to the 'not' function and store the
# value in another variable
$result = not($one);

# prints '1' to screen
print("$result\n");
```

Parameters alphanumeric
array
list
string

Value numeric

See Also cmp, eq, gt, le, lt, ne, Appendix C (Operators), xor

N

oct

Syntax   oct(*num*)

oct

Usage   The *oct* function returns the decimal value of the octal *num* passed. If no
argument is passed to the function, this translation is performed on $_.

   When using this function, note that if you pass a string that starts with 0x,
it will be interpreted as a hexadecimal value. This can be useful if you want
to write a subroutine that has the ability to handle hexadecimal or octal
numbers and you do not want to explicitly determine what type of values
are to be passed.

Examples This function prints the octal representation of 40 concatenated with a
newline:

```
# prints '32' to the screen
print(oct(40)."\n");
```

Parameters numeric

Value   numeric

See Also hex

O

open

Syntax   open(*FILE_VARIABLE*, *string*)

Usage   The *open* function opens the file specified in *string* as the handle,
FILE_VARIABLE. This allows you to make any further reference and manipulation by calling the handle rather than the explicit path and file. The result
of opening a file with this function returns a *TRUE*, nonzero, if successful
and an undefined if unsuccessful.

   As you will see in the next paragraph, it is possible to "pipe" the opened
file. If this method is used, the process ID is returned by *open*. Since *open*
returns a numeric value on a successful implementation, then it is easy to
verify that the file was opened correctly by *oring open* with *die*.

In conjunction with the *open* function, a programmer can use a variety of "methods" to open files in their scripts. These methods represent the type of manipulation you plan to perform after the file is opened. Represented by a series of symbols at the beginning or the end of the file string, these methods tell the script if the files will be used for reading, writing, or various other tasks such as piping. Do note that it is possible to contain shell metacharacters in piped opens, which allows you to take a piped input executed by the shell, "/bin/sh," and pipe it again in your script. See the second example for this type of usage.

The following is a table of methods that can be used when opening a file into a script.

Method	Location	Description
<	Beginning	Opened for input (default if none specified).
>	Beginning	Opened for output.
>>	Beginning	Opened for appending.
+	Beginning	Located before < or > to specify that your script is to have read and write access to the file opened.
|	Beginning	Command on your system to which output is piped.
|	Ending	Command on your system to which input is piped.
-	By itself	Refers to STDIN.
>-	By itself	Refers to STOUT.
>&	Beginning	Signifies that the string that follows is a handle, not a specific filename. Can be used in conjunction with and after the following methods: >, >>, +>, <, <<, +<

Examples   This example shows how easy it is to open a file in your script. If the file you are opening is in your working directory, then no path needs to be specified. In this example, I have opened a file that is not in the working directory to show how to specify the path to the file. The *die* function call verifies that the file was opened correctly:

```
open(TESTFILE, '/etc/passwd') or die("Error: file unopened!\n");
```

This example takes the result of a piped input, from the Sed-to-Perl program, and opens it for another pipe:

```
$sedFile = "test";
open(PERLFILE, "s2p <$sedFile |") or die(Error: opening file\n");
```

Parameters   handle
methods
string

Value   numeric

See Also   close, closedir, die, opendir, sysopen

opendir

Syntax   `opendir(DIR_VARIABLE, string)`

Usage   The *opendir* function opens the directory specified in *string* under the handle *DIR_VARIABLE*. This allows you to make any further reference and manipulation by calling the handle, rather than the explicit path and directory. Opening a directory with this function returns a *TRUE*, nonzero, if successful and an undefined if unsuccessful. Since *opendir* returns a numeric value on a successful implementation, it is easy to verify that the file was opened correctly by "oring" *opendir* with *die*.

Examples   This example opens the /bin directory under the handle *BINDIR*. After a successful implementation, the file is then closed using *closedir*:

```
opendir(BINDIR, '/bin') or die("Error: opening directory\n");
closedir(BINDIR);
```

Parameters   handle
string

Value   numeric

See Also   close, closedir, open

O

or

Syntax   `element1 or element2`

Usage   The *or* logical operator returns *element1* if either element exists, or *element2* if *element1* does not exist. If neither exists, then a NULL is returned. Perl's *or* is not a bitwise operator but rather a low precedence version of the " | | " operator. It could be commonly used to verify the existence of variables in your script as well as to return the second argument based on this existence.

For those of you who are unfamiliar with logical operations, a "truth table" can be constructed based on the possible arguments passed. By looking at a truth table of the possible results, the result of an *or* operation can be determined.

I have created a truth table that takes *element1* and *element2* as the arguments passed to it. Under each column, I have listed all possible cases the two elements could encounter, while the right column contains the result of *or*ing the two together. As you can see, the *or* operator only returns a *FALSE* (zero in a Perl implementation) result when both of the arguments are *FALSE*. A NULL assignment would be used for any *FALSE* results.

Truth Table		
element1	element2	element1 or element2
FALSE	FALSE	FALSE
FALSE	TRUE	TRUE
TRUE	FALSE	TRUE
TRUE	TRUE	TRUE

Examples   This example assigns a number to *$j* and then compares this variable to an undefined *$i*. Since *$i* is undefined, the nonexistent string will be printed:

```
# but there is no '$i' or '$j'!
if ($i or $j){
   print('$i exists!'."\n");
}else{

   # this line will be printed
   print('$i does not exist!'."\n");
}
```

Parameters alphanumeric

Value boolean
numeric

See Also Appendix C (Operators), and, cmp, eq, not, undef, xor

ord

Syntax ord

Usage The *ord* function returns the unsigned ASCII value of the first character passed.

Examples This example returns and prints the ASCII value of *a* since it is the first character passed to the *ord* function. The printed *a* is concatenated with a newline character:

```
$example = "abc";

# prints '97' to screen
print(ord($example)."\n");
```

Parameters string

Value numeric

See Also Appendix C (ASCII Character Set), hex, oct

O

pack

Syntax   pack(*FORMAT*, *@list*)

Usage   The *pack* function converts a list of values passed into a binary structure and returns it as a string. The *FORMAT* passed should account for all characters to be *pack*ed. When implementing on a list that has multiple similar entries, pass an integer value after each *FORMAT* to specify the number of that type to be packed. If, for instance, you wish to pack two signed character items, you should use the following method:

```
$packed = pack('i6', 9, 90);
```

This is the same as passing 'iiiiii' as the format but the code is shorter. For the types a, A, b, B, h, H, and P, the number following the option indicates the length to be packed. If you use a * instead of a number, then the rest of the list will be packed according to the preceding type.

The following table lists the *pack* options followed by a brief description. These options will occupy the *FORMAT* field that is passed.

Option	Definition
A	Space-buffered ASCII string
a	NULL-buffered ASCII string
B	High-to-low bit string
b	Low-to-high bit string
C	Unsigned character
c	Signed character
d	Double-precision float number
f	Single-precision float number
H	High-to-low hexadecimal string
h	Low-to-high hexadecimal string
I	Unsigned integer
i	Signed integer
L	Unsigned long integer
l	Signed long integer
N	Long in big-endian network order
n	Short in big-endian network order
P	Pointer to a fixed-length string
p	Pointer to a string

Option	Definition
S	Unsigned short value
s	Signed short value
V	Long in little-endian VAX order
v	Short in little-endian VAX order
u	uuencoded string
X	Back one byte
x	NULL byte
@	Fill with NULL

Examples The following script simply packs and unpacks a list of arguments. You can see how pack affects the list as the arguments change:

```
$format = 'i3cc';
@list = ( 1, 2, 3, 89, 95 );
$packed = pack ($format, @list);
print length($packed), "\n";
print $packed, "\n";
@ret = unpack ($format, $packed);
print "@ret\n";
# This will print:
# 14        (4 bytes for each int and one for each char)
# Y_        (The character representation of the chars)
# 1 2 3 89 95  (the list pulled back out)

# $format = 'A15A5';
# @list = ( "Howdy", "Partner" );
# would print:
# 20        (then length of the strings)
# Howdy           Partn
# Howdy Partn

# $format = 'A15A*';
# list remains the same as above:
# 22
# Howdy           Partner (to fill in the 15 length string)
# Howdy Partner

# $format = 'a15a*';
# list is the same
# 22
# HowdyPartner    (filled with nulls)
# Howdy Partner
```

```
# $format = "aa";
# list is the same
# 2
# HP
# H P

# $format = 'a2';
# list is the same
# 2
# Ho     (it just pulls in the first 2 chars from the
# Ho      first argument)
```

Parameters   format
            list

Value   string

See Also   unpack

package

DECLARATION

PERL 5

Syntax   package NAME;

Usage   The *package* command declares the enclosing block to use the named namespace. Any unqualified variables that are used will belong in this namespace. This command is generally used at the beginning of a file that will be used by another script with the *require* or *use* functions. You can access variables within a package by $PackageName::variable. The default package is main, thus in a standard program $var is the same as $::var and $main::var.

        The package command has the same scope as local and has no effect on the usage of variables declared using my.

Examples   The following example shows the effect of the package command:

```
$var = "0th value";
package One;
```

```
      # it's undefined
      print "$var\n";
      $var = "1st value";
      my ($var2) = "new value";
      {
         package Two;
         $var = "2nd value";

         # 0th value
         print "$main::var\n";

         # 1st value
         print "$One::var\n";

         # new value
         print "$var2\n";
      }

      # 1st value
      print "$var\n";
```

Parameters string

See Also my, local

pipe

Syntax pipe(*FILE_VARIABLE1, FILE_VARIABLE2*)

Usage The *pipe* function opens a pair of connections that are often used to allow a parent and child process to communicate. *FILE_VARIABLE1* represents a file from which to read, while *FILE_VARIABLE2* represents a file to write. This function returns true if it succeeds and false otherwise. See your system documentation on *pipe* for more information.

Examples The following example creates a pipe and then forks. The child process can then communicate with the parent via the pipe:

```
pipe(ONE, TWO);
if ($pid = fork()) {
  close ( TWO );
  while ( <ONE> ) {
     print;
  }
} elsif (defined($pid)) {
  close ( ONE );
  print TWO "Test\n";
  print TWO "Test2\n";
}
```

Parameters   handle

Value   numeric

See Also   your system documentation on *pipe*

pop
FUNCTION

PERL 4   PERL 5

Syntax   pop(*@array*)

pop

Usage   The *pop* function "pops" off and returns the last element in *@array*. Note that by popping off this element, the size of the array is reduced by 1. For those of you who are familiar with stacks and queues, it effectively mimics popping an element off a stack.

When *pop* is used with no arguments passed, it is executed on *@ARGV* if in your main script or on *@_* if in a subroutine.

Examples   This example defines *@array* and prints its contents to the screen. The *pop* function is then called and its return value is printed on a newline. The final *print* statement demonstrates how the *pop* function actually removes the item popped:

```perl
# define an array
@array = ("one", "two");

# prints 'one two'
print("@array\n");

# prints 'two'
print(pop(@array)."\n");

# prints 'one'
print("@array\n");
```

Parameters   array

Value   string

See Also   push, shift, splice, unshift

pos

Syntax   pos(*string*)

Usage   The *pos* function returns the offset of the last m//g regular expression on the variable. If no variable is passed, then $_ is used. If it is modified, then the next time the expression is evaluated, it will begin at the new offset.

Examples   The following script displays where the last search was found and what is left of the string to search on:

```perl
$var = "123123123123123123";
while ( $var =~ m/231/g ) {
    print "Found at: ", pos($var), "\n";
    print substr($var, pos($var)), " left to search.\n";
}
```

Parameters   string

Value   offset

See Also   m

print

Syntax
```
print(EXPRESSION)
print(FILE_VARIABLE EXPRESSION)
print(FUNCTION)
```

Usage   The *print* function is used to display or write information to a specific location; it returns a 1 if successful and a 0 if unsuccessful. When *EXPRESSION* is the only argument passed, as in the first syntactical definition, its value will be printed by default to *STDOUT*.

The second definition demonstrates *print*'s ability to write information to a file defined by the handle *FILE_VARIABLE*. In this implementation, *EXPRESSION* is written to the handle passed.

The *print* function can also be used in conjunction with other functions, as in the third syntactical definition. This gives the programmer the ability to immediately display the results of a function implementation rather than storing the value in a variable and then printing it to the screen or file.

> **Tip**
>
> *It is important to properly format the* EXPRESSION *you passed. If the information passed is contained in beginning and ending double quotes (" "), then the value of* EXPRESSION *will be printed. If it is contained in single quotes (' '), then the actual expression will be printed. See the third example for a better understanding of this rule.*

Examples   This is the classic first program for all programmers—the "Hello World" program simply prints a string to the screen. I added in the concatenation operator to demonstrate how strings and variables can be assembled to print a single string to the screen:

```
# define 'World!' in variable
$world = "World!";

# print 'Hello Perl World!'
print("Hello Perl" . $world . "\n");
```

This example demonstrates how the *print* function can write information to a file. I open a file in write mode and then write the "Hello Perl World" string to this file. To do this, you passed the opened file's handle as the first argument to *print*:

```
# open file for writing
open(OUT, ">test.txt") || die("Error: unable to open file\n");

# print 'Hello Perl World' to "test.txt" via its handle
print(OUT "Hello Perl World!\n");
```

This example shows how you can pass the results of a function call straight to *print*. Here I declare a list of four items. I then use the *join* function to join these items, separated by a space, together to create a single string, which is then printed to the screen:

```
# define a list to pass to the 'join' function
@list = ("Hello", "Perl", "World!", "\n");

# print results of 'join' function
print(join(" ", @list));
```

This example shows the various methods to print information. Notice that this information is different depending on what surrounds the information to be printed:

```
# define the string
$string = ("Hello Perl World!\n");

# prints 'Hello Perl World!'
print($string);

# prints 'Hello Perl World!' as well
print("$string");

# prints '$string'
print('$string');
```

Parameters	handle
	expression
Value	numeric
See Also	open, printf, write

printf

Syntax   `printf(string, EXPRESSION)`

`printf(FILE_VARIABLE, string, EXPRESSION)`

Usage   The *printf* function has many of the same properties as the *print* function; however, it lets you better format your output. This is simply done by placing a field specifier in your string passed followed by a comma-separated *EXPRESSION*. When the statement is printed to the screen or file, it will replace the field specifier with *EXPRESSION* in the specified format.

The following is a table of the formatting options along with a brief description of each:

Option	Description
%c	Character
%d	Decimal number
%e	Scientific notation float
%f	Fixed-point float
%g	Compact float
%ld	Long decimal number
%lo	Long octal number
%lu	Long unsigned number
%lx	Long hexadecimal number
%o	Octal number
%s	String
%u	Unsigned decimal number
%X	Uppercase hexadecimal number
%x	Hexadecimal number

Examples   This example defines a string and a numeric value in two variables. The *printf* function call passes a string and the field specifiers where the variables are then inserted to their locations before the string is printed:

```
# define the number and string
$num = 3456.4;
$string = ("Hello Perl World");

# prints 'The cost is $ 3456.40 and the
# string is Hello Perl World'
printf("The cost is \$%8.2f and the string is %s", $num, $string);
```

This example demonstrates how the *printf* function can write information to a file. Here I open a file in write mode and assign the string "Hello Perl World" to a variable. The *printf* function then takes the passed information and writes the information to the file. The "string" field specifier, *%s*, is replaced with the value of *$text* when the information is written:

```
# open file for writing
open(OUT, ">test.txt") || die("Error: unable to open file\n");

#define the string
$text = ("Hello Perl World!\n");

# print text to that file via its handle
printf(OUT "The string is: %s", $text);
```

Parameters   expression
             handle
             string

Value   numeric

See Also   open, print, sprintf, write

push

FUNCTION

PERL 4   PERL 5

Syntax   push(*@array, @list*)

Usage   The *push* function "pushes" the elements of *@list* onto *@array*, increasing the size of *@array* by the number of items pushed. This function returns the size of *@array* after all items have been pushed.

Examples This example defines a list and an array for processing. It prints the original contents of *@array* and then passes it to the *push* function, where the new array is stored. The final print statement prints the size of the new array to the user's screen:

```
# define an array and a list
@array = ("One", "Two");
@list = ("Three", "Four", "Five");

# print the original contents of the array
print("The original contents are: @array\n");
```

```
# push the elements in
@newArray = push(@array, @list);

# print the new size
print ("The size is now: @newArray\n");
```

Parameters   array
              list

Value   numeric

See Also   pop, shift, splice, unshift

P

quotemeta

Syntax   quotemeta(*string*)

Usage   The *quotemeta* function takes a string and returns it with a backslash placed before all regular expression metacharacters. Metacharacters are commonly found in Perl to represent, or to be part of a representation of, other pre-defined variables, functions, or operators. The following is a list of metacharacters common to Perl:

      $ ^   *   (   )   + | \   [{   ?   .

Examples   This example defines a string, *$list*. The result of passing it to the *quotemeta* function is then printed concatenated with a newline character. Since a space is considered a metacharacter by Perl, a backslash is returned before each space in the sentence as well as before the metacharacters:

```
$list = ('These are metacharacters: $~');

# prints 'These\ are\ metacharacters\:\ \$\~' to screen
print(quotemeta($list)."\n");
```

Parameters   string

Value   string

See Also   split

Q

qw

Syntax   qw(*string*)

qw/*string*/

Usage   The *qw* function takes the contents of *string* and returns a list. This allows
you to create a list in much the same way you do with the *split* function.
Either syntactical definition can be used with the *qw* function; it is left
entirely up to the programmer.

It is also possible to return the number of entries in the created list by
assigning the list to a scalar variable, as shown in the second example.

Examples   This example uses the *qw* function to define @*list*. The eighth entry in the list
is then printed and concatenated with a newline character:

```
@list = qw(Each of these will be put in a list entry);

# prints 'list'
print(@list[8]."\n");
```

This example assigns the total number of entries in @*list* to $*numEntries*
and then prints it to the user's screen:

```
@list = qw/Each of these will be put in a list entry/;
$numEntries = @list;

# prints '10'
print($numEntries."\n");
```

Parameters   string

Value   string

See Also   split

rand

PERL 4   PERL 5

Syntax rand(*num*)

rand

Usage The *rand* function returns a fractional random number from 0 to *num*. If *num* is omitted, as in the second syntactical definition, a value from 0 to 1 is returned. Do note that *num* should be a positive number.

> ### Tip
>
> *Since this function returns a fractional value, you might want to use the* int *function to return an integer from 0 to* num. *Note that* num *will never be returned since* int *only uses the integer portion and doesn't round off the number.*

Examples This example returns the random value to a variable and then prints it to the screen. The second *print* call multiplies the random number by 10 to return a value between 0 and 35:

```
# pass a number to the function
$random = rand(35);

# value of the random number
print($random."\n");

# value x 10
print(($random*100)."\n");
```

Parameters numeric

Value numeric

See Also srand

R

read

Syntax   read(*FILE_VARIABLE*, *$scalar*, *num*)

read(*FILE_VARIABLE*, *$scalar*, *num*, *num2*)

Usage   The *read* function reads *num* bytes from the handle *FILE_VARIABLE* into the scalar variable *$scalar*. The function returns the number of bytes that were actually read.

> ### Tip
>
> *If you wish to read the same file, but you want to read it into different variables, you will have to close the file and reopen it for the second variable. Once a byte has been* read *in, the only way you can access it again is to close, open, and re*read *the file.*

When a second numeric value is passed, as in the second definition, the resultant *$scalar* is buffed with *num2* bytes before any data is written to it. See the example for a better understanding of this implementation.

Examples   This example opens a file to read data. Let's suppose the following line of text is in the opened file:

Hello Perl World!

The *read* function is then called and reads 17 bytes of information. After the file is closed, the 17 bytes are printed to the user's screen.

To demonstrate the buffering that occurs, I reopen the file and again *read* data. This is done after the second numeric value is passed *read*. This buffer of 4 bytes is passed to the variable before the data, which is very apparent when the variable is printed to the screen:

```
# open a file for reading
open(TEST, 'test.txt') or die("Error: opening file");

# read info from 'TEST'
read(TEST, $data, 17);
close(TEST);
```

```
# re-open the file for reading
open(TEST, 'test.txt') or die("Error: opening file");

# again read info the 'TEST'
read(TEST, $data2, 17 , 4);
close(TEST);

# prints 'Hello Perl World!'
print("$data\n");

# prints '   Hello Perl World!'
print("$data2\n");
```

Parameters   handle
numeric
scalar

Value   numeric

See Also   getc, sysread

readdir

FUNCTION

PERL 4   PERL 5

Syntax   readdir(*DIR_VARIABLE*)

Usage   The *readdir* function returns the contents the directory defined in the handle passed.

> **Tip**
>
> *Read the results of this function into an array so that all the contents can be accessed individually.*

Examples   This example opens your current directory, reads its contents into an array, and prints the contents to the user's screen. I used the *join* function to add newline characters to each of the entries so they would be placed on individual lines for easier reading:

```
# open your current working directory
opendir(CURRDIR, ".") || die("Error: unable to open directory");

# print the contents of the directory on a newline
print(join("\n", readdir(CURRDIR))."\n");

# close your directory
closedir(CURRDIR);
```

Parameters   handle

Value   string

See Also   closedir, opendir

readlink

FUNCTION

PERL 4   PERL 5

Syntax   readlink(*symbolic_link*)

Usage   The *readlink* function returns the filename to which the *symbolic_link* points. Do note that the returned string may be relative to the link you are evaluating, not the location of the script that evaluates the link. This will become apparent when you execute this function on a link that is not in your current directory.

Examples   This example returns the path to my HTML directory and prints it to the screen:

```
# returns '/pub/users/awyke/html'
$linkPath = readlink("/allen");

# print results to screen
print("$linkPath\n");
```

Parameters   linked filename

Value   filename

See Also   link

recv

PERL 4   PERL 5

Syntax   recv(*SOCK_VARIABLE*, $scalar, num, flag)

Usage   The *recv* function attempts to receive a message, according to the *flag* passed, on the socket defined by *SOCK_VARIABLE*. The message size is defined by length *num* and will be stored in *$scalar*. The function itself returns the address of the sending connection if successful or a *NULL* if unsuccessful. To determine the *flag*s that can be passed to this function, see your system documentation on *recv* (type **man recv** at the command line if you're using UNIX), which takes the same flags as Perl's *recv*.

Examples   The following example creates a simple server, which accepts connections, reads 8 bytes of data from the client, and then closes the connection:

```
use Socket;
socket(SERVER, AF_INET, SOCK_STREAM, getprotobyname('tcp'));
bind(SERVER, sockaddr_in(3456, INADDR_ANY));
listen(SERVER, SOMAXCONN);
accept(CLIENT, SERVER);
recv(CLIENT, $data, 8, undef);
print CLIENT "You said: $data\n";
close (CLIENT);
```

Parameters   flag
handle
numeric
scalar

Value   socket address

See Also   accept, Bundled modules: Socket , connect, listen, socket, your system documentation on *recv*

R

redo

FUNCTION

PERL 4 PERL 5

Syntax   redo(*SECTION*)

redo

Usage   The *redo* function continues the executing loop without evaluating the condition binding the loop. When *SECTION* is not passed, as in the second syntactical definition, the function is implemented on the innermost executing loop.

You will want to note that when this function is contained in a loop with a *continue* implementation, the *continue* section will not be implemented in the occurrence immediately after the execution of the *redo* function.

Examples   This example implements a *for* loop that will normally print only values until $i = 2. In this example, however, when $i = 2, a second loop is entered. Here the value of $i is incremented to 3 and the *redo* function is called. Under normal circumstances, the *for* loop would not execute, but the *redo* function forces the loop to execute one more instance:

```
LOOP: for($i = 0; $i < 3; $i++){
        print("$i\n");
        if ($i == 2){
            $i++;
            redo(LOOP);
        }
    }
```

Parameters   section

See Also   next

ref

FUNCTION

PERL 5

Syntax   ref(*EXPRESSION*)

Usage   The *ref* function returns the reference type of the variable passed to it. If *EXPRESSION* cannot be evaluated, a *NULL* is returned. The type of built-in return values are defined in the following table:

Value	Description
ARRAY	An array reference
CODE	A subroutine reference
GLOB	A glob reference
HASH	An associative array reference
SCALAR	A scalar reference
REF	A reference to a reference

Examples The following example creates a scalar reference and then prints the output of the ref command:

```
$scalar = "one";
$ref = \$scalar;
print ref($ref), "\n";  # displays "SCALAR\n"
```

Parameters expression

Value boolean
string

rename

FUNCTION

PERL 4   PERL 5

Syntax rename(*filename1*, *filename2*)

Usage The *rename* function renames *filename1* to *filename2*. If the renaming is successful, a 1 is returned; otherwise, a 0 is returned.

Examples This example renames the file *test.txt* to *newfilename.txt*:

```
rename("test.txt", "newfilename.txt");
```

Parameters filename

Value numeric

R

require

Syntax   `require(EXPRESSION)`

`require(package)`

Usage   The *require* function creates a dependency of the *EXPRESSION* passed, returning a 1 if successful. It can be used to include a set of functions defined in a secondary file. Do note that the result of the required file must be nonzero for the inclusion to be permitted. This can be done by simply having the last line in your included file be as follows:

`1;`

This assignment will force a nonzero return value when the file is included, hence a successful *require*.

In the second syntactical definition, the require function is used to require subpackages stored in the package passed.

Examples   This example uses the *require* function call to execute the contents of a second script in the middle of the current script. For this example, suppose that *test2.txt* has the following line of code:

`print("This is the second file\n");`

Since we *require* this file in the original script, this *print* function is executed:

```
# this script will print the following:
#
# This is the first file
# This is the second file
# This is the first file again

print("This is the first file\n");

# execute the contents of 'test2.pl'
require("test2.pl");

print("This is the first file again\n");
```

This example uses a function that is defined in the file that has been *required*. The contents of the *required* file, myfunc.pl, is as follows:

```
# subroutine that returns the result of a division
sub divide{
   $result = $a/$b;
   return($result);
}

# forces a true value when required but has
# no functionality
1;
```

Now that the *required* file has been written, it can be included for use in other scripts. The following is an example of using the subroutine we just defined in our myfunc.pl script. This example prompts the user for two numbers, that will be passed to the *divide* function in the *required* file. The result of the implementation is then printed to the user's screen:

```
# require the file with the subroutines
require("myfunc.pl");

# prompt the user for a numerator
print("Enter the numerator: ");
$a = (<STDIN>);
chop($a);

# prompt the user for a denominator
print("Enter the denominator: ");
$b = (<STDIN>);
chop($b);

# implement a function that is included by require
&divide;

# print the result of the subroutine
print('The value of $a/$b is: '.$result);
```

R

Parameters   expression

Value   boolean

See Also   do, use

reset

Syntax   `reset(`*`characters`*`)`

`reset`

Usage   The *reset* function reinitializes all variables (to an undefined value) that start with one of the *characters* passed. When no arguments are passed, as in the second definition, *reset* will reinitialize ?REGEXP? searches. ?REGEXP? searches are the same as /REGEXP/ searches except that a ?REGEXP? search only matches the first occurrence of the expression and multiple searches won't find it again unless reset is called.

You also have the ability to define a range of characters to *reset* by using a hyphen between the first and last character of the range you wish to clear. For example, if you wish to clear all variables that begin with the characters *a* through *c*, then you would use the following line of code:

```
reset("a-c");
```

Be careful when implementing this technique or passing capital letters because there are various special variables (such as ARGV) that you may *reset* unknowingly.

> **Tip**
>
> *Use the* reset *function just before a loop to clear any unwanted global variables that might have the same name as your loop control variables. Be careful though—you do not want to clear variables that you will be using again. Also note that variables created with* my *will not be affected by the* reset *function.*

R

Examples   This example initializes a scalar variable and an array and then prints their value to the screen. The *reset* function is called, passing *t*, which resets both variables since they both begin with this character. The final call to the *print* function then prints the reset values.

```
# declare some variables
$test = 5;
@testArray = ("This", "is", "an", "array");

# print original value of variables
print('$test is: '.$test."\n");
print('@testArray is: '.@testArray."\n");
```

```
# call reset, passing 't'. both variables are cleared
reset("t");

# print values after reset is called - both are NULL
print('$test is: '.$test."\n");
print('@testArray is: '.@testArray."\n");
```

Parameters   characters

Value   numeric

return

FUNCTION

PERL 4   PERL 5

Syntax   return(*EXPRESSION*)

return

Usage   The *return* function returns the value of *EXPRESSION*. Used in subroutines and with *eval*, *return* returns the results of these implementations. If *EXPRESSION* is not passed, then the value of the last expression is returned. Be careful that you do not use this function outside of *eval* or a subroutine because it will cause a fatal error.

Examples   This example prompts the user for two variables that are passed to a subroutine, where the variables are multiplied. The result is returned and printed to the user's screen:

```
# prompt user for a constant
print("Please enter a number: ");
$const = (<STDIN>);
chop($const);

# prompt user to multiply by
print("Please enter a number to multiply by: ");
$mult = (<STDIN>);
chop($mult);

# print result of passing variables to multiply routine
print("The result is: ".&multiply."\n");
```

R

```
# define subroutine
sub multiply{
    $result = $const * $mult;

    # use 'return' to return the result
    return($result);
}
```

Parameters   expression

Value   expression

See Also   eval

reverse

Syntax   reverse(*@list*)

reverse(*%array*)

Usage   The *reverse* function returns in reverse order the list passed. The actual list is not changed, but the results of this function can be returned into another list for future manipulation.

The second definition shows *reverse*'s ability to handle an associative array. Keep in mind, though, that when the contents of an associative array are returned, they are generally not in the order that you entered. Using the *reverse* function will reverse the order that the array is in, but remember that the results you desire might not be obtained.

Examples   This example defines a list and prints its contents to the screen. The *reverse* function is called and its results are stored in *@newList*, which is then printed to the screen:

```
# define a list
@list = ("one", "two", "three");

# print the original list to the screen
print("@list\n");

# reverse the list using the 'reverse' function
@newList = reverse(@list);

# print the reversed list to the screen
print("@newList\n");
```

This example demonstrates *reverse*'s ability to reverse the order of an associative array. As in the previous example, the original contents are printed to the user's screen and then passed to *reverse*. The *join* function is used to put the contents on new lines. Without using this method, the contents are printed as a single string:

```
# define an array
%list = ("one", 1, "two", 2, "three", 3);

# print the original array to the screen. use 'join'
# to put the entries on new lines
print(join("\t", %list)."\n");

# reverse the array using the 'reverse' function
%newList = reverse(%list);

# print the new array to the screen. use 'join'
# to put the entries on new lines
print(join("\t", %newList)."\n");
```

Parameters   array
              list

Value   string

See Also   sort

rewinddir

FUNCTION

PERL 4   PERL 5

R

Syntax   `rewinddir(DIR_HANDLE)`

Usage   The *rewinddir* function rewinds the given directory handle so that the next call to readdir will return the first file (or an array beginning with the first file) in the directory. You can use this function if you wish to cycle through the directory entries more than once.

Examples   The following example reads in the current directory and prints the directories and files in separate lists:

```
format STDOUT_TOP =
Directories                         Other
----------                          ----
.
```

```
format STDOUT =
@<<<<<<<<<<<<<<<<<<<<<<<<<<   @<<<<<<<<<<<<<<<<<<<<<<<<<<<
$dirs[$i],                          $other[$i]
.
opendir(HERE, ".");
@dirs = grep ( -d, readdir(HERE) );
rewinddir(HERE);
@other = grep ( !-d, readdir(HERE) );
foreach $i ( 0..($#dirs > $#other ? $#dirs : $#other) ) {
    write;
}
```

Parameters	handle
Value	numeric
See Also	closedir, opendir, readdir

rindex

FUNCTION

PERL 5

Syntax rindex(*string, character, index*)

rindex(*string, searchString, index*)

rindex(*string, character*)

rindex(*string, searchString*)

Usage The *rindex* function returns the last location of *character* in *string*. If a string is passed, as in the second and last syntactical definition, then the position of the first character of the string is returned. Passing *index* allows you to specify an end location for your search. You can tell your script to only search up to a certain position for a string or character. See the second example for a better understanding of this usage.

As with the *index* function, the return value of *rindex* is zero based, meaning that the first character of the *string* passed is in location 0. This function returns a -1 if no instance is found.

Examples This example defines a string and then prompts the user for a character or string to search. The results of the *rindex* call is then stored in a variable and printed to the user's screen. If, for instance, the user enters an *i* to search for, this example will return 14:

```
# store a string in a variable
$string = ("This is my string");

# prompt the user for a character or string
print("Enter a character or string to search for: ");
$search = (<STDIN>);
chop($search);

# return the characters index location
$found = rindex($string, $search);

# print the results to the screen
print("Your string was found at position $found\n");
```

This example is a similar implementation to the first example; however the user is asked to provide an index to end the search. In this type of implementation, *rindex* will find the last occurrence before the index passed. If the user entered *i* to search for, as in the first example, and then entered 10 as the ending index, the *rindex* function would return 5. This type of implementation should help you understand the passing of an index:

```
# store a string in a variable
$string = ("This is my string");

# prompt the user for a character or string
print("Enter a character or string to search for: ");
$search = (<STDIN>);
chop($search);

# prompt the user for an end location
print("Enter an end location: ");
$index = (<STDIN>);
chop($index);

# return the characters index location
$found = rindex($string, $search, $index);

# print the results to the screen
print("Your string was found at position $found");
```

Parameters   character
                numeric
                string

Value   numeric

See Also   index

R

rmdir

Syntax   rmdir(*string*)

rmdir

Usage   The *rmdir* function deletes the directory specified by *string*. If the deletion is successful, a 1 is returned, while a 0 is returned if unsuccessful. Do note that the directory you wish to remove must be empty before you can remove it.

It is also possible to use this function without any arguments as in the second syntactical definition. In this type of implementation, *rmdir* will delete the directory contained in $_.

Examples   This example deletes the directory specified by the user. If the directory does not exist or the directory is not empty, then the *die* function warns the user that the directory was unable to be removed:

```
# prompt the user for a directory to delete
print("What directory would you like to delete? ");
$delDIR = (<STDIN>);
chop($delDIR);

# delete the directory entered
rmdir($delDIR) or die("Error: unable to delete directory");
```

Parameters   directory

Value   numeric

See Also   mkdir

R

S

Syntax *s/original/replacement/*

s/original/replacement/option

Usage The *s* operator searches the string passed to it for items matching the regular expression defined by *original* and then replaces all instances with *replacement*.

The *option* field allows you to specify the type of search and replace you would like to perform on the string. The following is a description and list of the options that you can pass to the *s* operator:

Option	Description
e	Tells Perl to evaluate the right side as an expression.
g	Finds all occurrences in the string passed.
i	Performs a case-insensitive search.
m	Tells Perl to treat the string being parsed as multiple lines.
o	Tells Perl to compile the pattern only once.
s	Tells Perl to treat the string being parsed as a single line.
x	Uses Perl's extended regular expressions. See the Pattern Matching entry in Appendix C for a list of these.

Examples This example defines a string and then passes it to the *s* operator. In this example, all the *i*'s in the string are replaced with *o* and the results are printed to the screen:

```
# define a string
$string = ("This is my string\n");

# replace all the 'i' characters with 'o'
$string =~ s/i/o/g;

# prints 'Thos os my strong' to screen
print("$string\n");
```

This example demonstrates the use of the *s* operator with the *i* and *g* option. Without *g*, only the first instance would be replaced:

```
# define a string
$string = ("Let's delElte some charactErs\n");
```

```
# replace all the 'e' characters with 'p'
$string =~ s/e/p/ig;

# prints 'Lpt's dplpltp somp charactprs' to screen
print("$string\n");
```

Parameters   alphanumeric

Value   numeric

See Also   Appendix C (Pattern Matching), m, tr, y

scalar

Syntax   scalar(*EXPRESSION*)

Usage   The *scalar* declaration forces *EXPRESSION* to be evaluated in scalar context. When evaluated in scalar context, the expression passed is evaluated as a single value. When implemented on an array, the length of the array is returned.

Examples   This example defines an array and then prints its contents to the screen. The array is again printed to the screen, but this time it is done in scalar context. This is done to demonstrate how *scalar* forces the array to be evaluated in scalar context:

```
# define and array
@array = (1, 2, 3, 4);

# print the contents of the array = 1234
print @array;
print("\n");

# print the array in scalar context = 4
print scalar(@array);
print("\n");
```

Parameters   expression

Value   scalar

See Also   int

seek

Syntax seek(*FILE_VARIABLE*, *num*, *index*)

Usage The *seek* function allows you to move forward and backward in a given file. The file to be implemented is defined by *FILE_VARIABLE*, while *num* specifies the offset to begin the *seek*. The final argument, *index*, specifies the relative position of your offset. The returned result of this function is 1 if successful and 0 otherwise.

The following table defines the various *index* values you can pass to this function:

Index	Description
0	Beginning of the file.
1	Current position of the file.
2	End of the file.

Examples The following example opens a file for reading and then skips the first 10 bytes:

```
# open a file for reading
open(INFILE, "test.txt") or die("Error: unable to open file");

# skip 10 bytes from the beginning of the file
seek(INFILE, 10, 1);
```

Parameters handle
numeric

Value numeric

See Also read, readdir, seekdir

S

seekdir

Syntax   seekdir(*DIR_VARIABLE*, *num*)

Usage   The *seekdir* function works in much the same manner as *seek* except that it allows you to skip backward and forward in a directory defined by the *DIR_VARIABLE* handle rather than in a file. *Num* is the location, returned by *telldir*, that you wish to skip to. This function is used to reposition *readdir* calls to the location defined by *num*.

Examples   The following script reads the current directory and cycles through all the files. When it finds a directory, it saves the directory location using the *telldir* function. After it loops through all the files, it uses *seekdir* to go back to the first file after the last directory and prints it:

```
opendir(HERE, ".");
while ( $file = readdir(HERE) ) {
   if ( -d $file ) {
      $lastdir = telldir(HERE);
   }
}
seekdir(HERE, $lastdir);
$file = readdir(HERE);
print "$file\n";
```

Parameters   handle
numeric

Value   numeric

See Also   closedir, opendir, readdir, seek, tell, telldir

S

select

PERL 4   PERL 5

Syntax
```
select(FILE_VARIABLE)
select(READBITS, WRITEBITS, ERRORBITS, timeout);
```

Usage
The *select* operator has two distinct sets of functionality. The first definition shows the syntax for implementing this function on a file handle. In this type of implementation, the file handle passed is "selected" to be the default handle for various types of operations, such as *print* and *write*.

In the second definition, *select* is used to determine which of your file handles are ready to perform I/O functions or have an error condition. It is an interface to the select system call. You can create bitmasks to be passed to it using the *vec* function, as follows:

```
$readbits = "";
vec($readbits, fileno(STDOUT), 1) = 1;
```

You can then use $readbits as the *READBITS* argument to select. The IO::Select module provides a much nicer interface to this function.

Examples
This example opens a file for writing and then uses *select* to assign the handle for all default operations. The final *print* function is implemented to show that the statement will be written to the file rather than written to the default STDOUT:

```
# open a file for writing
open(OUTFILE, ">test.txt") or die("Error: unable to open file");

# select the opened file for default operations
select(OUTFILE);

# print the following string to the file without
# explicitly declaring a handle to write to
print("Hello Perl World!\n");
```

Parameters
handle

See Also
Optional Module: IO::Select

S

semctl

Syntax   semctl(*semID, semNum, semCommand, semArgument*)

Usage   The *semctl* function calls the UNIX System V Interprocess Communications
(IPC) command to implement various control operations. This function can
only be implemented on machines that support this type of communication.
You must include the following lines in your code to implement this function
in your script:

```
require("ipc.ph");
require("sem.ph");
```

As for the function itself, *semID* can be returned by calling the *semget*
function; a list of the *semCommand*s can be found in your /usr/include/sys/
ipc.h header file.

An example and a more detailed description on semaphores is beyond the
scope of this book. You should check your system's documentation for
additional information on this function.

Parameters   numeric

Value   numeric

See Also   semget, semop, your system documentation for *semctl*

semget

Syntax   semget(*KEY, num, semflag*)

Usage   The *semget* function calls the UNIX System V Interprocess Communications
(IPC) command to create a semaphore and return its ID. This function can
only be implemented on machines that support this type of communication.
You must include the following lines in your code to implement this function
in your script:

```
require("ipc.ph");
require("sem.ph");
```

As for the function itself, *KEY* is IPC_PRIVATE or a constant, and *num* is the number of semaphores created. You will need to see your system's documentation on *semget* for a description of the *semflag* argument passed to this function.

An example and a more detailed description on semaphores is beyond the scope of this book. You should check your system's documentation for additional information on this function.

Parameters numeric

Value numeric

See Also semctl, semop, your system documentation for *semget*

semop

PERL 4   PERL 5

Syntax semop(*semID*, *@array*)

Usage The *semop* function calls the UNIX System V Interprocess Communications (IPC) command to perform a semaphore operation. This function can only be implemented on machines that support this type of communication. You must include the following lines in your code to implement this function in your script:

```
require("ipc.ph");
require("sem.ph");
```

As for the function itself, *semID* can be returned by calling the *semget* function, and *@array* is a packed array of semaphore structures consisting of various components. Please see your system's documentation on *semop* for a description of these components.

An example and a more detailed description on semaphores is beyond the scope of this book. You should check your system's documentation for additional information on this function.

Parameters numeric

Value numeric

See Also semctl, semget, your system documentation for *semop*

S

send

PERL 4   PERL 5

Syntax   send(*SOC_VARIABLE*, *socMessage*, *socFlags*)

send(*SOC_VARIABLE*, *socMessage*, *socFlags*, TO)

Usage   The *send* function sends a message to the specified socket, *SOC_VARIABLE*.
You will need to see your system's documentation on *send* for a description
of the arguments and flags passed to this function. If the socket you're using
isn't currently connected, you need to supply the *TO* filehandle and then
send works like the *sendto* system call. It is generally easier to use the normal
IO functions (like *print*) instead of *send*, but some systems only allow *send*
and *recv* when used with sockets.

Examples The following example creates a simple server and uses the send function to
send a message to the client:

```
use Socket;
socket(SERVER, AF_INET, SOCK_STREAM, getprotobyname('tcp'));
bind(SERVER, sockaddr_in(3456, INADDR_ANY));
listen(SERVER, SOMAXCONN);
accept(CLIENT, SERVER);
send (CLIENT, "Welcome\n", undef);
close (CLIENT);
```

Parameters handle
string
flags

Value   numeric

See Also accept, bind, listen, recv

S

setpgrp

Syntax   setpgrp(*processID*, *groupID*)

Usage   The *setpgrp* function sets the process group ID for the specified process. Note
         that you will get a fatal error if the system you are running doesn't support
         setpgrp. Passing 0 as the *processID* will change the process group on the
         current process. On some systems, *setpgrp* will be phased out and *setsid* will
         be used. See the POSIX module for information on using the *setsid* function.

Parameters   numeric

Value   numeric

See Also   getpgrp, your system documentation on *setpgrp*

setpriority

Syntax   setpriority(*type*, *processID*, *priority*)

Usage   The *setpriority* function changes the current priority for a process, process
         group, a user ID, or your program. The *type* argument signifies the type,
         while *processID* is the ID for the process you wish to change. The final
         argument, *priority*, is the new priority you wish to suppress on the process.
         Note that you will get a fatal error if the system you are running doesn't
         support *setpriority*.

Examples   The following code fragment will up the priority on the current process,
           possibly making it run faster on a busy system:

         setpriority(0, 0, 10);

Parameters   numeric

Value   numeric

See Also   getpriority, your system documentation on *setpriority*

S

setsockopt

FUNCTION

PERL 4   PERL 5

Syntax   setsockopt(*SOC_VARIABLE*, *optionLevel*, *optionName*, *optionValue*)

Usage   The *setsockopt* function allows you to set a socket option on the passed socket. This option is defined by the level of the option, its name, and its value.

The most common option level you'll use is at the socket level, SOL_SOCKET. If you want the option you're setting to be interpreted at any other level, you should use the protocol number of that level (by using *getprotobyname*). The option value will most often be 0 or 1 to turn the option off or on. The possible option names are:

- **SO_BROADCAST.** Enables the ability to send broadcast messages.
- **SO_DEBUG.** Enables recording of debug information.
- **SO_DONTROUTE.** Enables the routing bypass for outgoing messages.
- **SO_KEEPALIVE.** Enables the keep connections alive option.
- **SO_LINGER.** Keeps the socket open if data is still present when the socket closes. The socket will close when the data is read.
- **SO_OOBINLINE.** Enables the ability to receive out-of-band data.
- **SO_RCVBUF.** Sets the input buffer size.
- **SO_REUSEADDR.** Enables the reuse of a local address.
- **SO_SNDBUF.** Set the output buffer size.
- **SO_ERROR.** Gets and clears the current error on the socket (this is only for *getsockopt*).
- **SO_TYPE.** Gets the type of the socket (this is only for *getsockopt*).

You should check your system's documentation on *setsockopt* for additional information on this function.

S

Examples   This example enables the SO_REUSEADDR option to make sure the port can be reused for the connection:

```
use Socket;
socket(SERVER, AF_INET, SOCK_STREAM, getprotobyname('tcp'));
setsockopt(SERVER, SOL_SOCKET, SO_REUSEADDR, 1);
bind(SERVER, sockaddr_in(3456, INADDR_ANY));
listen(SERVER, SOMAXCONN);
accept(CLIENT, SERVER);
print CLIENT "Welcome\n";
close (CLIENT);
```

Parameters   handle
              numeric
              string

Value   numeric

See Also   getsockopt, your system documentation on *setsockopt*

shift

Syntax   `shift(@array)`

Usage   The *shift* function shifts off and returns the first element in an array.

Examples   This example defines an array and then prints it to the screen. The results of
              a *shift* function call are held in a variable. The variable and array are again
              printed to the screen:

```
# define array
@array = ("A", "B", "C");

# print the contents of the array
print(join(" ", @array)."\n");

# shift off first entry
$first = shift(@array);

# print results
print("The entry shifted off was: $first\n");
print("The array is now: ".join(" ", @array));
```

Parameters   array

Value   element

See Also   pop, push, unshift

shmctl

SYSTEM CALL

PERL 4   PERL 5

Syntax   shmctl(*shmID, shmCommand, shmArgument*)

Usage   The *shmctl* function calls the UNIX System V Interprocess Communications
           (IPC) command to set options and send commands to shared memory
           segments. This function can only be implemented on machines that support
           this type of communication. You must include the following lines in your
           code to implement this function in your script:

```
require("ipc.ph");
require("sem.ph");
```

           An example and a more detailed description on shared memory segments
           is beyond the scope of this book. You should check your system's documen-
           tation for additional information on this function.

Parameters numeric

Value   numeric

See Also   shmget, shmread, shmwrite, your system documentation on *shmctl*

shmget

SYSTEM CALL

PERL 4   PERL 5

Syntax   shmget(*key, num, flag*)

Usage   The *shmget* function calls the UNIX System V Interprocess Communications
           (IPC) command and is used to create shared memory segments. This func-
           tion can only be implemented on machines that support this type of commu-
           nication. You must include the following lines in your code to implement
           this function in your script:

```
require("ipc.ph");
require("sem.ph");
```

An example and a more detailed description on shared memory segments is beyond the scope of this book. You should check your system's documentation for additional information on this function.

Parameters   flag
               numeric

Value   numeric

See Also   shmctl, shmread, shmwrite, your system documentation on *shmget*

shmread

Syntax   shmread(*shmID, variable, index, num*)

Usage   The *shmread* function calls the UNIX System V Interprocess Communications (IPC) command, which is used to read from the shared memory segments. This function can only be implemented on machines that support this type of communication. You must include the following lines in your code to implement this function in your script:

```
require("ipc.ph");
require("sem.ph");
```

As for the function itself, *shmID* can be returned by calling the *shmget* function, and *variable* holds the returned data. The final two arguments, *index* and *num*, specify the index location to start reading from and the *num* of bytes to read.

An example and a more detailed description on shared memory segments is beyond the scope of this book. You should check additional specific documentation for more information on this function.

Parameters   numeric
               variable

Value   numeric

See Also   shmctl, shmget, shmwrite

shmwrite

FUNCTION

PERL 4   PERL 5

Syntax   shmwrite(*shmID, string, index, num*)

Usage   The *shmwrite* function calls the UNIX System V Interprocess Communications (IPC) command to send data to shared memory segments. This function can only be implemented on machines that support this type of communication. You must include the following lines in your code to implement this function in your script:

```
require("ipc.ph");
require("sem.ph");
```

As for the function itself, *shmID* can be returned by calling the *shmget* function, and *string* holds the string of data to write. The final two arguments, *index* and *num*, specify the index location to start writing to and the *num* of bytes to write.

An example and a more detailed description on shared memory segments is beyond the scope of this book. You should check additional specific documentation for more information on this function.

Parameters numeric
string

Value   numeric

See Also shmctl, shmget, shmread

shutdown

FUNCTION

PERL 4   PERL 5

Syntax   shutdown(*SOC_VARIABLE, num*)

Usage   The *shutdown* function shuts downs a socket connection defined by *SOC_VARIABLE*. The shutdown is performed by the method defined by *num*. The following table defines the methods that can be passed:

Method	Description
0	No more receives are permitted.
1	No more sends are permitted.
2	Nothing is permitted.

Examples   The following example creates a simple server and then shuts down the connection completely:

```
use Socket;
socket(SERVER, AF_INET, SOCK_STREAM, getprotobyname('tcp'));
bind(SERVER, sockaddr_in(3456, INADDR_ANY));
listen(SERVER, SOMAXCONN);
accept(CLIENT, SERVER);
send (CLIENT, "Welcome\n", undef);
shutdown(SERVER, 2);
```

Parameters   handle
             numeric

See Also   accept, bind, listen, recv, send, socket

sin

OPERATOR

PERL 4   PERL 5

Syntax   sin(*num*)

Usage   The *sin* arithmetic function returns, in radians, the sine of a *num*.

Examples   The following example assigns the sine of a number:

```
# execute the function
$sinVar = sin(55);

# prints '-0.99975517335862'
print("$sinVar\n");
```

Parameters   numeric

Value   numeric

See Also   abs, atan2, cos, exp, log, sqrt

S

sleep

FUNCTION

PERL 4   PERL 5

Syntax   sleep(*num*)

sleep

Usage   The *sleep* function causes your script to enter a pause state for *num* seconds. After the pause has completed, *num* is returned.

> ### Tip
>
> *If you do not pass any arguments to* sleep, *your script will pause indefinitely. To restart the script, send it to a SIGALARM.*

Examples   The following example pauses for 15 seconds when run. Since the *sleep* function is called in the body of a *print* function, the number of seconds paused will be printed to the screen:

```
# print '15' to screen
print(sleep(15)."\n");
```

Parameters   numeric

Value   numeric

See Also   times

socket

FUNCTION

PERL 4   PERL 5

Syntax   socket(*SOC_VARIABLE, DOMAIN_FLAG, connectionType, num*)

Usage   The *socket* function creates a socket connection under the handle *SOC_VARIABLE*; the socket connection is based on the *DOMAIN_FLAG, connectionType,* and *num* passed.

DOMAIN_FLAG defines the protocol family you wish to use. Information on the types of flags you can pass is generally contained in your /usr/include/sys/socket.h file and can be imported by using the Socket module. You should also be able to find information on the various *connectionType*s within this same file.

The final argument is the number of the protocol you wish to use. This protocol information can be retrieved via a *getprotobyname* call and placed into a variable before being passed to *socket*. If the socket is created successfully, *TRUE* is returned.

Examples The following example creates a simple client that will connect to a server, read any output, and print it:

```
use Socket;
$serverIP = inet_aton('localhost');
$serverAddr = sockaddr_in(3456, $serverIP);

socket(CLIENT, AF_INET, SOCK_STREAM, getprotobyname('tcp'));
connect(CLIENT, $serverAddr);

while ( <CLIENT> ) {
    print;
}
```

Parameters flags
handle
numeric

Value boolean

See Also accept, bind, getprotobyname, listen, recv, send, shutdown, socketpair

socketpair

FUNCTION

PERL 4 PERL 5

Syntax socketpair(*SOC_VARIABLE1*, *SOC_VARIABLE2*, *DOMAIN_FLAG*, *connectionType*, *num*)

Usage The *socketpair* function creates a pair of socket connections under the handles *SOC_VARIABLE1* and *SOC_VARIABLE2*; the socket connection will be based on the *DOMAIN_FLAG*, *connectionType*, and *num* passed.

DOMAIN_FLAG defines the protocol family you wish to use. Currently, socketpair can only be used with the AF_UNIX protocol family. Information on the types of flags you can pass is generally contained in your /usr/include/sys/socket.h file, which can be imported via the Socket module. You should also be able to find information on the various *connectionTypes* within this same file.

The final argument is the number of the protocol you wish to use. This information can be retrieved via a *getprotobyname* call and placed into a variable before being passed to *socket*. If the socket is created successfully, *TRUE* is returned.

Examples The following example creates a pair of sockets to communicate between a parent and child after forking:

```
use Socket;
socketpair(SOCK1, SOCK2, AF_UNIX, SOCK_STREAM, getprotobyname('ip'));
if ( $pid = fork() ) {
    close (SOCK1);
    $read = <SOCK2>;
    print "Got '$read' from child.\n";
    exit;
} elsif ( defined($pid) ) {
    close (SOCK2);
    print SOCK1 "Hi from child.";
    exit;
}
```

Parameters flags
handle
numeric

Value boolean

See Also accept, bind, getprotobyname, listen, recv, send, shutdown, socket

sort

FUNCTION

PERL 4   PERL 5

Syntax sort(*@list*)

sort(*subroutine @list*)

Usage The *sort* function orders the list passed to it. The newly ordered list is returned and can be read into a list variable.

You can also change the default ordering of ascending order by passing the list to a *subroutine,* as in the second definition. In this type of implementation, you would first create a subroutine to process the sorting (i.e., : >=). The values of the list are passed to the routine in the special variables $a and $b, which allow you to perform your sorts. Be sure not to modify these variables because they are passed by reference and modifying them will change their values.

Examples   This example defines a numeric list and then passes it to the *sort* function where the sorted list is stored in a new list. The result is then printed to the screen:

```
# define a numeric list
@numericList = (1, 5, ,7, 2, 8, 3, 9, 4, 6);

# sort the list
@newList = sort(@numericList);

# print the results to the screen
print(join(" ", @newList)."\n");
```

This example defines a numeric list and then passes it to the *sort* function where the list is sorted via your subroutine. The result is then printed to the screen:

```
# define a numeric list
@numericList = (1, 5, ,7, 2, 8, 3, 9, 4, 6);

# sort the list
@newList = sort(greaterOrEqual @numericList);

# print the results to the screen
print(join(" ", @newList)."\n");

# define your subroutine
sub greaterOrEqual{
   $a >= $b;
}
```

Parameters   list
subroutine

Value   list

splice

Syntax
```
splice(@array, num)
splice(@array, num, num2)
splice(@array, num, num2, @list)
```

Usage
The *splice* function removes all entries following *num* from @*array*. If *num2* is passed, as in the second and third definition, then only *num2* consecutive entries will be removed. This function returns the removed element.

The final definition demonstrates *splice*'s ability to replace the removed entries with the contents of @*list*. See the second example for this type of implementation.

Examples
This example defines an array and then passes it to the *splice* function. Only the second entry, indexed by 1, is removed. The result is printed to the screen:

```
# define and array
@array = ("A", "B", "C");

# remove 'B' only
splice(@array, 1, 1);

# print the results to the screen
print(join(" ", @array)."\n");
```

This example defines an array and list. The array is then passed to the *splice* function where only the second entry, indexed by 1, is removed. Since a list is passed to the function as well, the removed entry is replaced with the entire contents of the list. The result is printed to the screen:

```
# define and array and list
@array = ("A", "B", "C");
@list = ("2", "3 4");

# remove 'B' only and replace it with '2 3 4'
splice(@array, 1, 1, @list);

# print 'A 2 3 4 C'
print(join(" ", @array)."\n");
```

S

Parameters	array
	list
	numeric

Value	list

See Also	pop, push, shift, unshift

split

Syntax	`split/`*separator*`/, `*string*
	`split/`*separator*`/, `*string*`, `*num*

Usage   The *split* function separates *string* based on occurrences of *separator*. This function returns a list based on this separation.

If *num* is passed, as in the second definition, then the number of returned values in the list is limited to *num*. In this type of implementation, each entry will be read into a new list position until *num* - 1 positions are filled. If this criteria has been met, then the remaining contents of *string* will be placed into entry *num*. See Appendix C for additional pattern matching information.

Examples   This example defines a string and then performs a *split* based on any occurrences of spaces. The result of this function is returned into an array and printed to the screen:

```
# define a string
$string = ("Hello Perl World");

# split the string on occurrences of spaces
@list = split/ /, $string;

# print the results with each entry on a new line
print(join("\n", @list)."\n");
```

Parameters	numeric
	separator characteristics
	string

Value	list

See Also	Appendix C (Pattern Matching), m, s, tr, y

sprintf

Syntax   sprintf(*format*, *@list*)

Usage   The *sprintf* function takes *@list* and returns a formatted string based on the *format* passed. The following is a table of the formatting options along with a brief description of each:

Option	Description
%c	Character
%d	Decimal number
%e	Scientific notation float
%f	Fixed point float
%g	Compact float
%ld	Long decimal number
%lo	Long octal number
%lu	Long unsigned number
%lx	Long hexadecimal number
%o	Octal Number
%s	String
%u	Unsigned decimal number
%X	Uppercase hexadecimal number
%x	Hexadecimal number

Examples   The following example formats a float to two decimal places so that it can be used to represent currency:

```
$yearlySalary = 130000;
$payPeriods = 24;
$grossPerPeriod = sprinf("%.2f", $yearlySalary/$payPeriod);
print "\$$grossPerPeriod twice a month.\n";
```

Parameters   formatting information
list

Value   string

See Also   format, printf

sqrt

Syntax	sqrt(*num*)
Usage	The *sqrt* arithmetic function returns the square root of the *num* passed.
Examples	This example returns and prints the square root of 144:

```
# print '12' to screen
print(sqrt(144)."\n");
```

Parameters	numeric
Value	numeric
See Also	abs, atan2, cos, exp, log, sin

srand

Syntax	srand(*EXPRESSION*)
Usage	The *srand* function is used to seed all calls to *rand*. This is necessary since *rand* will always return the same random number if passed the same argument. *Srand* allows the programmer to add an additional "variable" into the equation that will offset the random number generated by *rand*.

> **Tip**
>
> *Pass an ever-changing value to* srand *to ensure that your seed is not static. If it is, then* rand *will once again return the same random numbers.*

Examples	This example passes *srand* the scripts process ID and system *time*. These two expressions have a bitwise exclusive OR performed on them within the function. This ensures that the data passed to *srand* will be constantly changing. The final *print* statement demonstrates how *rand* changes dynamically after the seed:

S

```
# seed rand function calls with a bitwise XOR  between
# the scripts process ID and time
srand($$^time);

# print a random number based on 10 - this is done
# twice to demonstrate how it changes after the seed
print(rand(10)."\n");
print(rand(10)."\n");
```

Parameters expression

Value seed

See Also rand

stat

FUNCTION

PERL 4   PERL 5

Syntax stat(*FILE_VARIABLE*)
stat(*filename*)

Usage The *stat* function returns 13 numeric properties of the file defined by
FILE_VARIABLE or explicitly defined by *filename*. Do note that not all of the
properties are supported on all systems.
The following is a table with the order and description of these properties;
the Order column denotes the order that the properties are returned (i.e., 1
signifies that this item was the first returned element from the *stat* function)
and the Property column defines the type of property:

Order	Property	Description
1	Device	Contains the device on which the file is located.
2	Inode	Internal reference number for the file.
3	File Information	Permissions and type of file.
4	Links	Number of hard links to the file.
5	User ID	ID of the file owner.
6	Group ID	ID of the group of the file owner.
7	Device Identifier	Returns the device type if the file is a device.
8	Size	Size of the file in bytes.

Order	Property	Description
9	Last Access	Returns the time the file was last accessed.
10	Last Modify	Returns the time the file was last modified.
11	Last Inode Change	Returns the time the file's status was last changed.
12	Preferred Block Size	Returns the preferred block size for all input/output operations for the file system on which the file resides.
13	Block Allocated	Returns the actual block size for all input/output operations for the file.

Examples   This example opens a file and passes its handle to the *stat* function. Each of the properties is then printed to the screen:

```
# open a file to evaluate
open(INFILE, "test.txt") or die("Error: unable to open file");

# get the status of the file
($device, $irn, $fileInfo, $links, $userID, $groupID, $deviceID, $size,
  $access, $modify, $inrChange, $preferredIO, $IO) = stat(INFILE);

# close the file
close(INFILE);

# print the results
print('$device is: '.$device."\n");
print('$irn is: '.$irn."\n");
print('$fileInfo is: '.$fileInfo."\n");
print('$links is: '.$links."\n");
print('$userID is: '.$userID."\n");
print('$groupID is: '.$groupID."\n");
print('$deviceID is: '.$deviceID."\n");
print('$size is: '.$size."\n");
print('$access is: '.$access."\n");
print('$modify is: '.$modify."\n");
print('$inrChange is: '.$inrChange."\n");
print('$preferredIO is: '.$preferredIO."\n");
print('$IO is: '.$IO."\n");
```

Parameters   handle
string

Value   properties

S

study

Syntax   study(*string*)

Usage   The *study* function tells Perl that you wish to perform several searches on the *string* passed. Calling this function stores the contents of *string* in a format for faster searching. This increase in speed may not be apparent for smaller searches, so you should only implement *study* on large searching.

> **Note**
>
> *Any successive calls to* study *supersede previous calls, so be sure you are implementing it as you wish.*

Examples   This example opens a file for reading and then iterates through the file using a *while* loop. In the body of the loop we have asked Perl to "study" $_. Below this function call would be multiple statements that iterate through $_ until the entire file is read:

```
# open a file for reading
open(INFILE, "test.txt") or die("Error: unable to open file");

# iterate through the file
while(<INFILE>){

   # sets up $_ to be studied
   study($_);

   if($_ =~ /Perl/){
     print($_);
     }

   # other multiple if statements would go here
}
```

Parameters   string

Value   numeric

See Also   m, s, tr, y

S

sub

DECLARATION, OPERATOR

PERL 4   PERL 5

Syntax

```
sub subroutine [prototype] {
    CODE
}

sub [prototype] subroutine;

sub [prototype] {
    CODE
}
```

Usage

The *sub* command can act as a declaration as well as an operator. When implemented as a declaration, it defines *subroutine* as a self-contained "function" that executes *CODE*. A subroutine is called by using any of the following syntax:

```
# calls the subroutine defined by 'myroutine'
&myroutine;
require &myroutine;
do &myroutine;
```

You can pass arguments to and from the subroutine in much the same manner as you pass arguments to and from your functions in C or C++ or to and from methods in Java. When these items are passed, they are manipulated by the code inside.

The second syntactical definition demonstrates *sub*'s ability to predefine the routine early in your script. This function, which is new to Perl 5, allows you to make calls to routines without the preceding &.

The third definition creates an anonymous subroutine.

Whichever way you define your subroutine, you can give a prototype to define the arguments that it is expecting. The prototype list can be composed of $ (scalar), @ (array), % (hash), * (filehandle), or & (subroutine). If one of these characters is preceded by a \, then it will expect a variable of that type. If the list has an @ or %, then any following prototype definitions will be ignored since the @ or % will take up the rest of the arguments passed. If you have a semicolon in the list, then any following characters represent optional arguments.

S

Examples   This example prompts the user for two numbers. These numbers are then passed to my *divide* subroutine where they are divided. The result of the division is returned and printed to the screen:

```perl
# prompt the user for a number
print("Please enter a number: ");
chop($numerator = (<STDIN>));

# prompt the user for a denominator
print("Please enter a number to divide the original by: ");
chop($denominator = (<STDIN>));

# call the 'divide' subroutine
&divide;

# print the result of the division
print("The result was: $result\n");

# define the subroutine
sub divide{
   $result = $numerator / $denominator;
   return($result);
}
```

The following example creates a subroutine with a prototype:

```perl
&mySub($var1, 'data', 'data');
sub mySub (\$@) {
   ($first, @rest) = @_;
   print "First is: $first\n";
   print "Rest are: @rest\n";
}
```

Parameters   code
prototype

See Also   do, require, use

S

substr

Syntax   substr(*string*, *index*)

substr(*string*, *index*, *num*)

Usage   The *substr* function searches *string* and returns all the information after the numerically declared *index*. *Index* signifies the byte with which you wish to start your extraction. If *num* is passed, as in the third syntactical definition, the amount of data returned will be limited to *num* bytes.

Examples   This example defines a string and then passes it to the *substr* function. It then prints two characters starting at location 8:

```
# define a string
$string = ("This is my string!");

# print 'my' to screen
print(substr($string, 8, 2)."\n");
```

Parameters   numeric
string

Value   string

symlink

Syntax   symlink(*filename1*, *filename2*)

Usage   The *symlink* function creates a symbolic link from *filename2* to the previously created file *filename1*. If the link is successful, then a 1 is returned, while a 0 is returned for an unsuccessful link.

Examples   This example creates a symbolic link named *linked.txt* to *test.txt*:

```
symlink("test.txt", "linked.txt");
```

Parameters   string

Value   numeric

See Also   link, readlink

syscall

SYSTEM CALL

PERL 4   PERL 5

Syntax	`syscall(@list)`

Usage   The *syscall* function makes a system call to the program named in the first entry of *@list* and passes the arguments that are contained in the successive *@list* entries. This function will cause a fatal error if your system does not support it.

An example and a more detailed description on the values passed to this function is beyond the scope of this book. You should check your system's documentation for additional information on this function.

Parameters   list

See Also   your system documentation for *syscall*

sysopen

FUNCTION, SYSTEM CALL

PERL 5

Syntax   `sysopen(FILE_VARIABLE, filename, flag)`
`sysopen(FILE_VARIABLE, filename, flag, num)`

Usage   The *sysopen* function opens *filename* under the handle *FILE_VARIABLE*. At this point, your system's *open* function is called passing the filename, the mode (*flag*), and the permissions (*num*). Do note that the flags can vary from system to system and that you should consult your *fcntl* library module for a list of *flags*. If you wish to use this function without explicitly declaring a permission, a default value of 0666 will be used.

Examples   The following script uses the sysopen function to open a filehandle and then read all the data from it:

```
sysopen MYFILE, "/tmp/myFile.txt", O_RDWR;

while ( <MYFILE> ) {
   print;
}
```

S

Parameters	handle
	numeric
	string

Value	boolean

See Also	open, your system documentation on *open*

sysread

FUNCTION, SYSTEM CALL

PERL 4   PERL 5

Syntax	sysread(*FILE_VARIABLE*, *$scalar*, *num*)
	sysread(*FILE_VARIABLE*, *$scalar*, *num*, *index*)

Usage   The *sysread* function reads *num* bytes to *$scalar* from *FILE_VARIABLE* using your system's *read* function.

You can also specify a numeric *index* point at which the system will start writing your data to *$scalar*, as in the second definition. This length will act as a buffer between the start of the string and the first bytes written.

If *sysread* is successful in either of these implementations, the number of bytes read is returned. If it is at the end of a file, then 0 is returned.

Examples   This example opens a file for reading and then passes it to the *sysread* function where the first two bytes are read into the *$scalar* variable. The final statement prints the value of *$scalar* to the screen:

```
# open a file for reading
open(INFILE, "test.txt") or die("Error: unable to open file");

# read the first 2 bytes into a variable
sysread(INFILE, $scalar, 2);

# print the bytes read to the screen
print($scalar);
```

Parameters	handle
	numeric
	variable

Value	numeric

See Also	read, your system documentation on *read*

system

Syntax   system(*@list*)

Usage   The *system* function executes a program that is specified in the first entry of *@list* passed and executes it with the additional arguments following the first entry.

     Unlike *exec, system* creates a separate fork for the program and then launches it. *System* then stands by and waits for the program to finish execution, at which time it will resume its own execution. By allowing you to pass arguments to the programs you wish to execute, *system* can, for example, open files in programs or open specific instances of programs.

Examples   This example defines a list that has the program's name in the first entry followed by the options you wish to pass to it:

```
# define the list
@progArg = ("netscape","-mail");

# opens Netscape Mail on a Windows machine when Netscape
# is in your path
system(@progArg);
```

Parameters   list

See Also   eval, exec, flock

syswrite

Syntax   syswrite(*FILE_VARIABLE, $scalar, num*)

         syswrite(*FILE_VARIABLE, $scalar, num, index*)

Usage   The *syswrite* function writes *num* bytes from *$scalar* to *FILE_VARIABLE* using your system's *write* function. You can also specify a numeric *index* point to start your writing, as in the second definition. If *syswrite* is successful in either implementation, the number of bytes written is returned.

Examples The following example opens a file for writing and then uses the *syswrite* function to add data to it:

```
open MYFILE, ">myFile.txt";
$bytes_added = syswrite(MYFILE, "new data\n", 9);
print "$bytes_added written to myFile.txt\n";
```

Parameters handle
numeric
scalar

Value numeric

See Also print, printf, write, your system documentation on *write*

S

tell

Syntax   tell(*FILE_VARIABLE*)

Usage   The *tell* function returns the distance, in bytes, from the current position to the beginning of a file. This position, as with many other Perl functions, is zero based. So if you try to determine the position before any bytes are read, the function will return 0.

Examples   This example opens a file for reading, and then a *while* loop is used to iterate through the file one line at a time. During each iteration, the *tell* function is used to store the current location of the iteration. The result is then printed to the user's screen.
    In this particular example, the *print* statement will be implemented once for each line:

```
# open a file for reading
open(INFILE, "test.txt") or die("Error: unable to open file");

# iterate through the file one line at a time
while(<INFILE>){

    # store the current position of the file in a variable
    $currPosition = tell(INFILE);

    # print the current position to the screen
    print("The current position is $currPosition\n");
}
```

Parameters   handle

Value   numeric

See Also   seek, seekdir, telldir

telldir

FUNCTION

PERL 4   PERL 5

Syntax   `telldir(DIR_VARIABLE)`

Usage   The *telldir* function works in much the same manner as *tell*. It returns the current numeric location in the directory in which you invoke the function. The directory on which this function is implemented is defined by the *DIR_VARIABLE* handle and is iterated through using the *readdir* function. See the example for a better understanding of this function.

Examples   This example opens the current working directory and then iterates through its contents using a *while* loop. The argument passed to the *while* loop reads the current file into a variable for later use. In the body of the loop, the *telldir* function is called to return the current location with a trailing *print* statement that prints the current file and location to the user's screen:

```
# open a directory for reading
opendir(CURRDIR, " ") or die("Error: unable to open directory");

# iterate through the directory one entry at a time. read
# current file into variable to print later
while($file = readdir(CURRDIR)){

    # read the current location into a variable
    $currDir = telldir(CURRDIR);

    # print file and location to screen
    print("The current file is $file and it is at $currDir\n");
}
```

Parameters   handle

Value   numeric

See Also   readdir, seek, seekdir, tell

T

tie

Syntax   `tie VARIABLE, PACKAGE, @list`

Usage   The *tie* function ties a variable to a package (or class). This is most often used with the *DBM_File modules to tie an associative array to a DBM file. This function returns a reference to the instance of the class that was created. The *@list* depends on the class you are tying.

Examples   The following example ties an associative array to a GDBM_File class and then iterates through the database printing every key/value pair:

```
use GDBM_File;
tie %data, "GDBM_File", "mydbm", GDBM_WRCREAT, 0644;
while ( ($key, $val) = each %data ) {
    print "$key = $val\n"
}
untie %data;
```

Parameters   variable
class
list

Value   reference

See Also   require, tied, untie, use

tied

Syntax   `tied(variable)`

Usage   The *tied* function returns a reference to the package name to which *variable* has been bound. If *variable* is not bound to a package, then a *NULL* is returned. See the entry for *tie* to understand how a variable can be bound to a package. You can use the *ref* function to determine the name of the package if for some reason you don't know what it is.

Examples   The following example ties an associative array to a GDBM_File and then prints the name of the package it's tied to:

```
use GDBM_File;
tie %data, "GDBM_File", "mydbm", GDBM_WRCREAT, 0644;
print "Tied to: ", ref(tied(%data)), "\n";
untie %data;
```

Parameters   variable

Value   reference

See Also   tie, untie

time

FUNCTION

PERL 4   PERL 5

Syntax   time

Usage   The *time* function returns the number of seconds since January 1, 1970.

> **Tip**
>
> *Pass this function as an argument to* gmtime *to assign* time's *results to appropriate, predefined properties (day of the week, day of the month, month, and so on). This removes the task of organizing the return value of* time *into usable information.*

Examples   This example uses the *time* function to determine the approximate number of minutes since January 1, 1970. After this result has been read into a variable, it is passed to other equations to determine the number of hours, days, and years as well:

```
# determine minutes, hours, days, and years since 1/1/70
$minutes = time / 60;
$hours = $minutes / 60;
$days = $hours / 24;
$years = $days / 365;
```

T

```
# print results to screen
print("There have been $minutes minutes\n");
print("There have been $hours hours\n");
print("There have been $days days\n");
print("There have been $years years\n");
```

Value   numeric

See Also   gmtime, localtime, stat, utime

times

FUNCTION

PERL 4   PERL 5

Syntax   `times`

Usage   The *times* function returns the amount of time used by the currently executing script and any child processes it may contain. The returned format contains the following four properties in this order:

- User time elapsed for this script
- System time elapsed for this script
- User time elapsed for a child process
- System time elapsed for a child process

Examples   The following example prints the amount of user time your code takes up. You can replace the while loop with your own code:

```
$beginning = (times)[0];
$i = 1000;
while ( $i-- ) {
    $num += $i;
}
print "$num\n";
$ending = (times)[0];
print "Took: ", $ending - $beginning, " seconds of CPU time.\n";
```

Value   array

See Also   Bundled modules: Benchmark

tr

Syntax   `tr/original/replacement/`

`tr/original/replacement/option`

Usage   The *tr* function searches the string passed to it for items defined by *original* and then replaces all instances with *replacement*. The function itself returns the number of instances that were replaced.

> **Tip**
>
> *Want to replace a whole field of sequential characters or numbers without creating a list of each alphanumeric character? The* tr *function allows you to pass a specified field to search for and/or replace by inserting a "-" to represent the beginning and ending alphanumeric characters. You will also want to enclose the field in [] to ensure that the* tr *function understands that you wish to treat this as an entire field. See the third example for a better understanding of this type of implementation.*

The *option* field allows you to specify the type of search and replace you would like to perform on the string. The following is a description and list of the options you can pass to the *tr* function:

Option	Description
c	Replaces all non*original* characters with *replacement*. See the second example of *y* for this type of implementation.
d	Deletes all *original* instances found. After the deletion, the blank space is removed rather than leaving a blank. See the second example for this type of implementation.
s	Replaces any sequential *original* occurrences with only one *replacement*. For instance, if you replaced all the *o*'s in "look" with *i*, then the resultant string would be "lik."

Examples   This example defines a string and then passes it to the *tr* function. In this example, all the *i*'s in the string are replaced with *o* and the results are printed to the screen:

```
# define a string
$string = ("This is my string\n");
```

```
# replace all the 'i' characters with 'o'
$string =~ tr/i/o/;

# prints 'Thos os my strong' to screen
print("$string\n");
```

This example demonstrates the use of the *tr* function with the *d* option. Since no replacement is passed (if a replacement was passed, it would be the same without the *d* option), all occurrences of *e* are removed:

```
# define a string
$string = ("Let's delete some characters\n");

# delete all the 'e' characters
$string =~ tr/e//d;

# prints 'Lt's dlt som charactrs' to screen
print("$string\n");
```

This example defines a lowercase version of the alphabet in a string and then passes it to the *tr* function to convert to uppercase. The "-" is used to specify an entire field of sequential characters, which, in this example, represents all characters from *a* to *z*. The results of this implementation are printed to the user's screen:

```
# define lowercase alphabet
$alphabet = ("abcdefghijklmnopqrstuvwxyz\n");

# change lowercase to uppercase
$alphabet =~ tr/[a-z]/[A-Z]/;

# print uppercase alphabet to screen
print("$alphabet\n");
```

Parameters   alphanumeric

Value   numeric

See Also   m, s, y, Appendix C (Pattern Matching)

truncate

Syntax   truncate(*FILE_VARIABLE*, *num*)

truncate(*string*, *num*)

Usage   The *truncate* function truncates the file defined under the *FILE_VARIABLE* handle to the length specified by *num*. If you wish to truncate a specific file without assigning it a handle first, as in the second definition, then the name of the file should be contained in *string*. You must be sure in either case that the file to be truncated is opened in write mode rather than the default read mode for this function to work.

> **Tip**
>
> *When you open the file, use '+<' to place it in read and write mode. If you just use '>', it deletes the file and creates a new one.*

Examples   This example opens a file in write mode and then passes it to the *truncate* function. The second argument passed to this function tells it to truncate the file to the first 1000 bytes. The final line in the script closes the opened file:

```
# open a file in write mode
open(INFILE, "+<data.txt") or die("Error: unable to open file");

# truncate the file to 1000 bytes
truncate(INFILE, 1000);

# close the file
close(INFILE);
```

Parameters   handle
numeric
string

Value   numeric

uc

Syntax   uc(*string*)

Usage   The *uc* function converts and returns the uppercase version of the *string* passed.

Examples   This example defines a string of mixed case in *$string*. The string is then passed to *uc* and its output is printed to the user's screen. A concatenated newline character is added to return the user's prompt to a new line:

```
# define a string of mixed case
$string = ("This IS A strING of MIXed CaSe");

# print 'THIS IS A STRING OF MIXED CASE'
print(uc($string)."\n");
```

Parameters   string

Value   string

See Also   lc, lcfirst, m, s, tr, ucfirst, y

ucfirst

Syntax   ucfirst(*string*)

Usage   The *ucfirst* function works in much the same manner as the *uc* function. It creates an uppercase conversion on the string passed. This function, however, converts only the first character of *string* to uppercase.

U

Examples This example defines a string of mixed case in *$string*. Since *ucfirst* only changes the first character to uppercase, the rest of the string is left intact. A concatenated newline character is added to the output to return the user's prompt to a new line:

```
# define a string of all lowercase
$string = ("this is a lowercase string");

# print 'This is a lowercase string'
print(ucfirst($string)."\n");
```

Parameters string

Value string

See Also lc, lcfirst, m, s, tr, uc, y

umask

Syntax umask(*num*)

Usage The *umask* function defines the umask (defined by *num*) for the current process and returns the previous one. The umask determines how permissions are set on a new file. The default permission is 0666 and the default umask is 022. This will make any new files read/write for the owner of the file and read-only for the group and others.

Examples This example sets the umask so that newly created files are accessible by anyone in the same group as the user running the script:

```
umask 002;
open ( FILE, ">group.txt" );
close ( FILE );
```

Parameters numeric

Value numeric

U

undef

Syntax   undef(*EXPRESSION*)

Usage   The *undef* operator sets the passed *EXPRESSION* to *NULL*.

Examples   This example defines several expressions and prints their values to the screen. The *undef* operator is then used on these variables, after which their new values are again printed to the screen. Notice that I only removed certain instances in the array implementations:

```
# define some variables
$string = ("Hello Perl World!");
$numeric = 568;
@array = ("One", "Two", "Three");
%assocArray = ("A", 1, "B", 2, "C", 3);

# print their values to the screen
print("The string is: $string\n");
print("The numeric value is: $numeric\n");
print("The array is: ".join(" ", @array)."\n");
print ("The associative array is: ".join(" ", %assocArray)."\n\n");

# undef the variables
undef($string);
undef($numeric);
undef(@array[1]);  # removes only 'Two'
undef(%assocArray);

# print their undef values to the screen
print("The string is: $string\n");
print("The numeric value is: $numeric\n");
print("The array is: ".join(" ", @array)."\n");
print ("The associative array is: ".join(" ", %assocArray)."\n");
```

Parameters   expression

Value   null

See Also   delete

unless

PERL 4   PERL 5

Syntax
```
unless(CONDITION){
    CODE
}
```

Usage
The *unless* loop control command is used in the same manner as when you are negating the *CONDITION* of an *if* statement. In an *unless* implementation, you specify code that will be executed when the condition is not met. See the example for a better understanding of this concept.

Examples
This example prompts the user to enter a number less than 10. If the user follows these directions, then the statement contained in the body of the *unless* condition will be printed:

```
# prompt user for number
print("Please enter a number less than 10: ");
$input = (<STDIN>);
chop($input);

# use the 'unless' command to verify entry
unless($input >= 10){
    print("Thank you for following instructions!\n");
}
```

Parameters
condition

Value
numeric

See Also
if

U

unlink

Syntax unlink(<*string*>)

unlink(*string*)

unlink(@*list*)

Usage The *unlink* function removes the file (or files) specified by the argument passed. The first definition shows how the function can remove files with similar names. Note that a * can be used to signify any series of characters for this type of implementation. Be sure to use <> to enclose the string when using this definition or the function will not operate properly. See the first example for this type of implementation.

The second syntactical definition is used when removing a single file defined by *string*. If you wish to remove a set of files, you can do so by passing them in a list, as in the last definition.

Examples This example shows how a set of files with the same extension can be removed. The number of successfully removed files is stored in a variable and printed to the screen:

```
# remove all files ending in '.txt'
# store number removed in variable
$removed = unlink(<*.txt>);

# print the number removed to screen
print("There were $removed files removed\n");
```

In this example, the file to be removed is explicitly passed:

```
# remove the file 'test.txt' store number removed in
# variable
$removed = unlink("test.txt");

# print the number removed to screen
print("There were $removed files removed\n");
```

U

This example defines a list of files to be removed and then passes it to the *unlink* function:

```
# define a list of files to be removed
@list = ("test.txt", "test2.txt");

# remove all files in '@list' and
# store number removed in variable
$removed = unlink(@list);

# print the number removed to screen
print("There were $removed files removed\n");
```

Parameters	list
	string

Value	numeric

See Also	rmdir

unpack

Syntax   unpack(*FORMAT*, *string*)

Usage   The *unpack* function converts a binary string into a list of values. The *FOR-MAT* passed should account for all characters to be *unpack*ed. This is the converse of the pack function. It is most often used to retrieve data from system calls that return a data structure (like *ioctl*) and for socket functions. When retrieving a list that has multiple similar entries, pass an integer value after each *FORMAT* to specify the number of that type to be packed. If, for instance, you wish to unpack two signed integer items, you should use the following method:

```
@list = unpack('i6', $packedString);
```

This is the same as passing 'iiiiii' as the format but the code is shorter. For the types a, A, b, B, h, H, and P, a number following the option indicates the length to be packed. If you use a * instead of a number, then the rest of the list will be packed according to the preceding type.

U

The following table lists each *unpack* option followed by a brief description. These options will occupy the *FORMAT* field that is passed.

Option	Definition
A	Space-buffed ASCII string
a	NULL-character-buffed ASCII string
B	High-to-low bit string
b	Low-to-high bit string
C	Unsigned character
c	Signed character
d	Double-precision float number
f	Single-precision float number
H	High-to-low hexadecimal string
h	Low-to-high hexadecimal string
I	Unsigned integer
i	Signed integer
L	Unsigned long integer
l	Signed long integer
N	Long in big-endian network order
n	Short in big-endian network order
P	Pointer to a fixed-length string
p	Pointer to a string
S	Unsigned short value
s	Signed short value
V	Long in little-endian VAX order
v	Short in little-endian VAX order
u	uuencoded string
X	Back one byte
x	NULL byte
@	Fill with NULL

Examples   The following example creates a simple TCP/IP server that prints the IP address of the client back to the client. It uses unpack to determine the Internet address of the client:

```
use Socket;
socket(SOCK, AF_INET, SOCK_STREAM, getprotobyname('tcp'));
$sockaddr = sockaddr_in(7777, INADDR_ANY);
bind(SOCK, $sockaddr);
listne(SOCK, SOMAXCONN);
$peer = accept(CLIENT, SOCK);
($port, $iaddr) = sockaddr_in($peer);
@ip = unpack("C4", $iaddr);
```

```
print CLIENT "Welcome from ", join ( '.', @ip ), "\n";
close ( CLIENT );
close ( SOCK );
```

Parameters   format
packed string

Value   list

See Also   pack

unshift

Syntax   unshift(*@array*, *@list*)

Usage   The *unshift* functions adds the contents of *@list* to the front of *@array*. The function returns the new size of *@array*.

Examples   This example defines an array and a list and then passes them to *unshift*. The return value of this function is the new size of the array and is stored in a variable. The trailing *print* statements print out the new size of the array and its contents:

```
# define a list and an array
@list = ("one", "two");
@array[0] = ("three");
@array[1] = ("four");

# append the list to the array and return the new
# array size to a variable
$size = unshift(@array, @list);

# print the new array and its size
print("The new array is of size: $size\n");
print("The elements in the array are as follows:\n");
print(join("\n", @array)."\n");
```

Parameters   array
list

Value   numeric

See Also   shift

U

untie

FUNCTION

PERL 5

Syntax   untie(*variable*)

Usage   The *untie* function breaks the association between *variable* and the package to which it is *tie*d. See the entry for *tie* for more information on creating this association.

Examples   This example ties an associative array to a GDBM_File package and then unties it:

```
tie %data, "GDBM_File", "myGDBM", GDBM_WRCREAT, 0664;

# perform data access with the associative array
untie %data;
```

Parameters   variable

See Also   tie, tied

until

LOOP CONTROL

PERL 4   PERL 5

Syntax
```
until(CONDITION){
    CODE
}
```
```
until(CONDITION){
    CODE
}continue{
    CODE
}
```

U

Usage   The *until* loop is used to perform a series of tasks until *CONDITION* is met. This function also allows you to specify a *continue* block of *CODE*, as the second syntactical definition defines.

Examples   This example defines a variable and then enters an *until* loop. In the body of the *until* loop, the current loop iteration number is printed to the screen and is incremented. This continues until the fifth iteration, when the loop fails its condition and exits:

```
# define a variable
$loop = 0;

# loop until the loop variable is 5
until($loop == 5){
   print("We are on loop $loop\n");
   $loop++;
}
```

Parameters   condition

See Also   Appendix C (Loop Control), continue, else, elsif, if, unless, while

use

Syntax   use *MODULE*

use *MODULE @list*

Usage   The *use* declaration allows you to "include" a module in your currently executing script. If you wish to remove the module after implementing the *use* declaration, you should pass the module to *no*. The list following the module name is a list of symbols (methods or variables) to be imported into your namespace. If you don't specify a list, the default list of symbols from the package will be imported. Any symbols that aren't exported can be accessed via the fully qualified name, that is, MyModule::symbol.

The package will be imported at compile time and is the same as having the following definition for a BEGIN subroutine:

```
BEGIN { require MyModule; import MyModule @list; }
```

Examples   This example shows the syntax for including a module named MyModule.pm into your script. The inclusion will allow you access to the components contained in the module:

```
# modules to include
use MyModule;
```

U

The following example shows how you can import only specific symbols. It will import the methods inet_ntoa and inet_aton from the Socket module:

```
use Socket qw('inet_ntoa', 'inet_aton');
```

Parameters	list
	module
See Also	import, no, require

utime

Syntax utime(*num1*, *num2*, *@list*)

Usage The *utime* function allows you to change the access (*num1*) and modification (*num2*) times on the list of files passed. The function returns the number of successful changes upon completion.

Examples The following script updates all the files in the current directory so that their access and modification times are set to the current time:

```
opendir( HERE, "." );
$now = time;
@files = readdir(HERE);
$numfiles = @files;
$changed = utime( $now, $now, @files );
closedir( HERE );
print "$changed of $numfiles files updated\n";
```

Parameters	list
	numeric
Value	numeric
See Also	stat, time

U

values

Syntax   `values(%array)`

Usage   The *values* function returns all the values of the associative array, *%array*. They are returned in no specific order, but each value is listed.

Examples   This example defines an associative array, *%array*, and then prints out all the values in the array on a new line. Notice that the *join* function had to be used to insert newline characters between each value. Without it, one continuous string prints to the screen:

```
# define an associative array
%array = ('one', "1", 'two', "2", 'three', "3");

# print the values on new lines
print (join("\n", values(%array))."\n");
```

Parameters   array

Value   string

See Also   each, keys

vec

Syntax   `vec(EXPRESSION, numIndex, numBits)`

            `vec(EXPRESSION, numIndex, numBits) = num`

Usage   In the first syntactical definition, *vec* splits the passed expression into grouped bit segments. The segments are of length *numBits*. Since splitting up *EXPRESSION* creates smaller sections, there may be a need to access each individual section. This is done by "indexing" the sections in the same manner arrays are indexed, with *numIndex* defining the section you wish to access. In short, this function returns the *numIndex* of size *numBits* of *EXPRESSION*. Note that *numBits* should be of the power 2^N, where *N* is a number from 1 to 5. This gives you the numbers from 1 to 32 to use as the bit assignment.

V

The second definition allows you to assign the *numBits* at *numIndex* of *EXPRESSION* to *num*. In short, it allows you to assign the bits located at the index to the binary representation of *num*.

Examples This example shows a string of bits being passed to *vec*. The *pack* function is called to ensure that the bits are ordered from high to low (*B option) for proper processing. To ensure proper implementation, this function is called before the *vec* function is called:

```
# put the bits in the proper order
$string = pack("*B", "11010011");
$index = 0;
$bits = 2;

print(vec($string, $index, $bits)."\n");
```

This example assigns the last four bits of *$vector* to '0011':

```
# assigns '0011' to end of $vector
vec($vector, 0, 4) = 3;
```

Parameters expression
numeric

Value numeric

See Also pack, split, unpack

V

wait

Syntax   wait

Usage   The *wait* function waits for a child process to end and then returns the process identification, ID, of a terminated child process. If the child process you are checking for termination does not exist, -1 is returned.

Examples   The following example forks a new process. The parent process prints a message and then waits for the child to exit before continuing:

```
# parent process
if ( $pid = fork ) {
   print ("parent: Not waiting.\n");
   wait;
   print ("parent: Child is done.\n");

# child process
} elsif ( defined $pid ) {
   print ("child: I'm sleeping");
   $cnt = 5;
   while ( $cnt-- ) {
      sleep 1;
      print (".");
   }
   print ("\n");
} else {
   die ("No fork! $!\n");
}
```

Value   numeric

See Also   waitpid

W

waitpid

Syntax   `waitpid(numID, num)`

Usage   The *waitpid* function waits for process *numID* to terminate based on the flag (*num*) passed to it.

> **Tip**
>
> *On a UNIX system, you can check out the manual page for more information about the flags that can be passed to* waitpid. *To do this, simply type* **man waitpid** *at your shell prompt.*

Upon completion of the termination, a 1 is returned by the function. If the process does not exist, then the function returns 0. If you wish to have access to flags other than 0, then you need to insert one of the following lines into your script:

```
# if you are using Perl 4
require "sys/wait.ph";

# if you are using Perl 5
use POSIX qw(waitpid);
```

Taking a quick look at these files will show you the various types of flags you have access to and can pass.

Examples   This example waits for the predefined *$process* to terminate on the normal wait:

```
waitpid($process, 0);
```

Parameters   process
numeric

Value   numeric

See Also   wait, your system documentation on *waitpid*

W

wantarray

FUNCTION

PERL 4   PERL 5

Syntax   `wantarray`

Usage   The *wantarray* function tests whether the subroutine currently executing is
looking for a list or a scalar value. If the routine is looking for a list, then
TRUE is returned; if a scalar value is sought, a *FALSE* is returned.

Examples This example has a subroutine that returns the array passed to it if it's in an
array context and returns the first element of the array if it's in a scalar
context:

```
@test = ( "one", "two", "three" );
$var1 = &sub1(@test);
@arr1 = &sub1(@test);

# will display 'one'
print ("$var1\n");

# will display 'one two three'
print ("@arr1\n");

sub sub1 {
   return wantarray ? @_ : $_[0];
}
```

Value   boolean

See Also caller

warn

FUNCTION

PERL 4   PERL 5

Syntax   `warn(@list)`

`warn(string)`

Usage   The *warn* function returns a statement contained in *string* or *@list* to alert a
user that a specified event has occurred. This "event," determined by the
programmer, can serve multiple purposes. It can let the user know that an
error has occurred, or it can simply be used to print a message to the screen
when a certain part of the script has executed.

Used as a debugging tool, *warn* commonly serves the purpose of alerting a user when an error has occurred. Unlike *die* however, the *warn* function will not stop the execution of your script, which can be very beneficial when you are performing recursive tasks on multiple directories and want your script to continue running even if an error occurs.

Examples   This example attempts to open multiple files in the same directory. If a file is missing, *warn* will alert the user then proceed opening the files:

```
for($i = 1; $i < 11; $i++){
    open(FILE, "test$i.txt") || warn("Error opening test$i.txt\n");
}
```

Parameters   list
string

Value   string

See Also   die, exit

while

PERL 4   PERL 5

Syntax
```
while(CONDITION){
    CODE
}
```
```
while(CONDITION){
    CODE
}continue{
    CODE
}
```

Usage   The *while* loop is used to perform a series of tasks while *CONDITION* is met. This function also allows you to specify a *continue* block of *CODE*, as the second syntactical definition defines, that will be executed after each iteration through the loop.

Examples   This example opens a file for reading and iterates through the file one line at a time using a *while* loop. The contents of the currently read string is printed to the user's screen via $_:

```
# open a file to read data out of
open(INFILE, "test.txt") or die("Error: unable to open file");

# iterate through the file
while(<INFILE>){

    # print the current line of the file to the screen
    print("$_\n");
}

# close the file
close(INFILE);
```

Parameters   condition

See Also   continue, else, elsif, if, unless, until

write

Syntax   `write(FILE_VARIALBLE)`

`write`

Usage   The *write* function writes a declared format to *FILE_VARIABLE*. It gives you the ability to assign a specified format to a handle, which eases the implementation of the various formats you have defined.

You can also use *write* without any arguments, which is usually done when writing multiple lines. Commonly found in the body of *while* loops, the *write* function follows the format declaration. Since the type of format you wish to implement is contained in the preceding line, it is only necessary to tell Perl to *write* the data. To better understand this concept, see the following example.

Examples   This example opens an information file that contains a person's *name, age,* and *social security number* on each line. For example:

`Allen 24 555555555`

After the file is opened, each line is read, splitting the information and assigning it to the appropriate variable.

W

As you can see, there are two different format declarations, *NAME_FIRST* and *AGE_FIRST*. Each declaration instructs the output to be printed with a seven-character name, a three-character age, and an eight-character social security number. However, the order in which this information is printed to the user's screen is different. The "$~" assignment is used to select the format desired. After this format is chosen, the *write* function is called to write the formatted output to the user's screen:

```perl
# open a file for reading input
open(FILE1, 'students.txt') || die ("Error: opening file\n");

# define a format that is 'name first'
format NAME_FIRST =
@<<<<<< @<<   @<<<<<<<<
$name,     $age, $ssn
    # be sure to include this period, "."!

# define a format that is 'age first'
format AGE_FIRST =
@<<< @<<<<<< @<<<<<<<<<
$age, $name,     $ssn
.    # be sure to include this period, "."!

while(<FILE1>){
   ($name, $age, $ssn) = split;

   # use 'Age First' format
   $~ = "AGE_FIRST";

   # here is the 'write' function call
   write;
   }
```

Parameters   handle

Value   string

See Also   Appendix C (Formatting), format, formline, print

X

OPERATOR

PERL 4 PERL 5

Syntax   *string* x *num*

Usage   Commonly referred to as the "repeat" string operator, *x* generates the string passed to it *num* times.

Examples   This example prints the string defined in *$list* to the user's screen five times:

```
$list = ("I love Perl!\n");
$rep = 5;

print($list x $rep);
```

Parameters   string

See Also   Appendix C (Operators)

xor

OPERATOR

PERL 5

Syntax   *num1* xor *num2*

           string1 xor *string2*

Usage   The *xor* logical operator returns a 1 or 0 result based on its assessment of the elements passed to it. If one, and only one, of the strings or numbers passed contains a value not equal to zero, then a 1 is returned. If both have nonzero values or both are zero, then 0 is returned. Note that an empty string constitutes a zero value.

      Those of you who are unfamiliar with logical operations should note that each argument passed is tested and a result is returned based on the assessment of the operator invoked. The following truth table defines the characteristics of the *xor* operator. Under each sample argument, I have listed all possible cases that could occur, while the far right column contains the result of *xor*ing the arguments together.

X

For simplicity, I have assigned a *TRUE* value for any entry that is nonzero, and *FALSE* for any entry that equals zero. As you can see, the *xor* operator returns a *TRUE* result only when one of the arguments is *TRUE*. In short, only one of the arguments passed can have a value for this operator to return a *TRUE*.

Truth Table		
num1	*num2*	*element1* xor *element2*
FALSE	FALSE	FALSE
FALSE	TRUE	TRUE
TRUE	FALSE	TRUE
TRUE	TRUE	FALSE

Examples This example assigns a number to *$one* and *$two*. The two variables are then compared and the *print* statement prints a result to the user's screen. The result of running this example is *TRUE*, so it would print the "Success" statement to the user's screen:

```
# define 2 numeric variables
$one = 1;
$two = 0;

# determine if only one has a value via the xor operator
if ($one xor $two){
   print("Success\n");
}else{
   print("Failure\n");
   }
```

Parameters alphanumeric
string

Value numeric

See Also Appendix C (Operators), cmp, eq, gt, le, lt, ne, not

X

y

Syntax   `y/original/replacement/`

`y/original/replacement/option`

Usage   The *y* function, which is identical to the Perl *tr* function, searches the string passed to it for alphanumeric characters defined by *original* and then replaces all instances with *replacement*. The function itself returns the number of instances that were replaced. The *y* function is contained in Perl for those programmers who are familiar with the *sed* programming syntax.

> **Tip**
>
> *Want to replace a whole field of sequential characters or numbers without creating a list of each alphanumeric character? The* y *function allows you to pass a specified field to search for and/or replace by inserting a "-" to represent the beginning and ending alphanumeric characters. You will also want to enclose the field in [] to ensure that the* y *function understands that you wish to treat this as an entire field. See the third example of the* tr *function for a better understanding of this type of implementation.*

The *option* field allows you to specify the type of search and replace you would like to perform on the string. The following is a description of the options that you can pass to the *y* function:

Option	Description
c	Replaces all non-*original* characters with *replacement*. See the second example for this type of implementation.
d	Deletes all *original* instances found. After the deletion, the blank space is removed rather than leaving a space. See the second example for *tr* for this type of implementation.
s	Replaces any sequential *original* occurrences with only one *replacement*. For instance, if you replaced all the *o*'s in "look" with *i*, then the resultant string would be "lik."

Y

Examples This example defines a string and then passes it to the *y* function. In this example, all the *i*'s in the string are replaced with *o* and the results are printed to the screen:

```
# define a string
$string = ("This is my string\n");

# replace all the 'i' characters with 'o'
$string =~ y/i/o/;

# prints 'Thos os my strong' to screen
print("$string\n");
```

This example demonstrates the use of the *y* function with the *c* option. Since I am invoking the compliment, all occurrences of *e* remain and all other characters are converted to 1:

```
# define a string
$string = ("Let's compliment\n");

# leave all the 'e' characters and turn the rest to '1'
$string =~ y/e/1/c;

# prints '1e11111111111e111' to screen
print("$string\n");
```

Parameters alphanumeric

Value numeric

See Also Appendix C (Pattern Matching), m, s, tr,

Y

Perl Modules

II

Modules Bundled With Perl

Perl modules are a way to provide extra functionality to your scripts. There are modules that provide access to a database or let you create CGI (Common Gateway Interface) scripts a lot easier. Modules are only available for Perl 5. Sometimes modules simply provide access to new functions that you can call from your script and others provide an object interface with methods and variables that you can access.

To access a module from your script, you call the *use* function with the module name. You then have access to the exported functions from that module.

AnyDBM_File

Syntax   use AnyDBM_File;

Usage   The *AnyDBM_File* module doesn't have anything built in to itself; it is merely there to inherit from the other DBM modules. It defaults to inheriting from NDBM_File. If that module isn't installed, it then checks for DB_File, GDBM_File, SDBM_File, or ODBM_File. SDBM_File will always be there because it is bundled with the Perl installation. See the specific DBM modules for more information.

    If you use the dbmopen function, it will simply call tie to bind the associative array to the DBM class from which AnyDBM_File inherits. You can change what DBM module dbmopen will bind to by modifying the @ISA array in the AnyDBM_File module:

```
@AnyDBM_File::ISA = ("SDBM_File");
```

    Or you can simply use the DBM module you wish and it will be tied to the associative array when dbmopen is called:

```
use SDBM_File;
```
    You can also call the tie function to bind your associative array without using AnyDBM_File or dbmopen. You can also use this method to open multiple databases of different types:

```
use SDBM_File;
tie %data, "SDBM_File", "dbfile", O_RDWR, 0644;
```

Examples   The following example shows how to create a simple database file and write some data to it:

```
use AnyDBM_File;
@AnyDBM_File::ISA = ("SDBM_File");
dbmopen(%data, "phone", 0644);
$data{'Terry} = "555-1234";
$data{'Nancy'} = "555-4321";
$data{'Fred'} = "555-5858";
dbmclose (data);
```

An alternate way to create the same database would be:

```
use SDBM_File;
tie %data, "SDBM_File", "phone", O_CREAT|O_RDWR, 0644;
$data{'Terry} = "555-1234";
$data{'Nancy'} = "555-4321";
$data{'Fred'} = "555-5858";
untie %data;
```

See Also   Modules: DB_File, GDBM_File, NDBM_File, ODBM_File, SDBM_File
Functions: dbmopen, tie

AutoLoader

Syntax   use AutoLoader;

Usage   When you're creating your own modules, you can use the *AutoLoader* module to cause your functions to only be loaded when needed. These functions must be stored in a separate file that has the same name as the function and the suffix .al. If you wanted to have the function func1 in MyModule load only when necessary, you would store the function in a file named auto/MyModule/func1.al, where auto is a directory at the same level as the MyModule.pm file.

Any module using the AutoLoader should have the marker __END__ before the subroutine definitions. When Perl is compiling, it will stop parsing the file when it reaches __END__.

The AutoLoader module is similar to the SelfLoader module except the SelfLoader stores the subroutines in the module file instead of in separate files. A disadvantage of using the SelfLoader is that is must parse the lines after __DATA__ to cache the routines. The AutoLoader is generally faster but requires that you use a utility like AutoSplit to create the function files.

If your system has a limited filename length and the function name exceeds that length, you may run into problems with conflicting file names.

See Also   Bundled Modules: AutoSplit, SelfLoader

AutoSplit

Functions   autosplit, autosplit_lib_modules

Syntax   use AutoSplit;

autosplit(*file*, *directory*, *keepOld*, *checkAutoLoad*, *checkTime*);

autosplit_lib_modules(*array*);

Usage   The *AutoSplit* module will split up a module you've created into the files that are necessary for use with the AutoLoader module. The autosplit method splits *file* into the appropriate files in *directory*. It also creates a file named autosplit.ix, which declares all the routines and keeps a timestamp for when the module was last split.

The *keepOld* parameter is a flag to determine whether any .al files in the split hierarchy should remain if they're no longer in the module. The *checkAutoLoad* parameter is a flag to determine if the AutoSplit module should check the module it's splitting to be sure the AutoLoader is being used in it. If this flag is set to true, the AutoSplit module will skip the file. The *checkTime* parameter is a flag to determine whether the files should be created if the module file hasn't been updated since the split files have been created.

The autosplit_lib_modules method takes a list of modules that are expected to be in the lib directory relative to the current directory. Each of these modules is then set to be split.

Only subroutines following the __END__ marker are split into distinct files; all the others are loaded when the module is loaded.

The AutoSplit module will warn the user if there are subroutines that may cause naming problems on machines with limited filename length. AutoSplit will also cause warnings if there is not an __END__ marker in the file, if there's no package declaration in the file, or if it can't create the necessary directories or files it needs.

Example   The following script splits the module MyModule into the appropriate files for the AutoLoader module:

```
Use AutoSplit;
autosplit("MyModule.pm", "/usr/local/lib/perl", 0, 1, 0);
```

This script creates the necessary files to be auto loaded from the MyModule module. It first checks to make sure the module uses the AutoLoader and deletes any functions that are no longer part of the module.

See Also   Bundled Modules: AutoLoader

Benchmark

MODULE

Functions   clearallcache, clearcache, debug, disablecache, enablecache, new, timediff, timeit, timestr, timethese, timethis

Syntax
```
use Benchmark;

clearallcache();

clearcache($count);

Benchmark->debug($flag);

disablecache();

enablecache();

$time1 = new Benchmark;

$time = timediff($time1, $time2);

$time = timeit($count, 'CODE');

timestr($time);

@times = timethese($count, {'time1' => 'CODE1',
    'time2' => 'CODE2'
        } );

$time = timethis($count, 'CODE');
```

Usage The *Benchmark* module allows you to determine how efficient a section of code is. When you use the timeit method, first a null loop is run $count times, and then your CODE is executed $count times. The difference between the two is returned by the method. This time can be read in a more friendly output by using the timestr method. The timestr method returns a string in the following format:

```
N secs ( X.xx usr  X.xx sys =  X.xx cpu)
```

The timethis method is similar to the timeit method except that it prints a header of 'timethis $count: ' followed by the output of timestr to STDOUT.

```
timethis($count, 'CODE');
```

is equivalent to:

```
print "timethis $count: " . timestr(timeit($count, 'CODE')) . "\n";
```

The timethese method is similar to timethis except it takes multiple pieces of CODE and displays the results based on the name associated with the code. See the example for more information.

The new method of the Benchmark module simply returns the current time. You can assign the current time to a variable, run a section of your code, and then assign a second variable to the current time and use the timediff method to determine how much time has passed.

You can enable debugging by passing a 1 to the debug method and turn it off by passing a 0.

The timeit, timethis, timethese, timediff, and timestr functions are automatically imported when you use the Benchmark module. The caching modules are only imported if you request them.

When the timeit method is called and the null loop is run $count times, the time is stored in a cache associated with the $count. The clearcache method will remove the $count value from the cache when called. The clearallcache method will remove all the caches that have been created. The enablecache and disablecache method will enable or disable caching, respectively.

Example The following example uses the various Benchmark functions to compare two different implementations of a factorial subroutine:

```
use Benchmark;
use Benchmark ('disablecache');
disablecache(); # turn off caching
@t = timethese(1000, {
   'fact1' => '&fact1(25)',
   'fact2' => '&fact2(25)',
} );
```

```
$t = timeit(1000, '&fact1(25)');
print "fact1: " . timestr($t) . "\n";
timethis(1000, '&fact2(25)');
$i = 1000;
$t1 = new Benchmark;
while ( $i-- ) {
   &fact1(25);
}
$t2 = new Benchmark;
print "fact1: " . timestr(timediff($t2, $t1)) . "\n";
# a recursive factorial
sub fact1 {
   local($num) = $_[0];
   if ( $num == 1 ) {
     return 1;
   } else {
     return $num * &fact1($num-1);
   }
}

# a factorial loop
sub fact2 {
   local($num) = $_[0];
   $ret = $num;
   while ( --$num ) {
     $ret *= $num;
   }
   return $ret;
}
```

The output of this script on my machine was:

```
Benchmark: timing 1000 iterations of fact1, fact2...
fact1:  3 secs ( 3.18 usr  0.00 sys =  3.18 cpu)
fact2:  1 secs ( 0.45 usr  0.00 sys =  0.45 cpu)
fact1:  3 secs ( 3.16 usr  0.00 sys =  3.16 cpu)
timethis 1000:  0 secs ( 0.45 usr  0.00 sys =  0.45 cpu)
fact1:  4 secs ( 3.18 usr  0.00 sys =  3.18 cpu)
```

Yours should appear similar with the numbers differing. In this test, recursion isn't always the best method of doing things.

Carp

Functions   carp, croak, confess

Syntax   `use Carp;`

`carp` *string*;

`croak` *string*;

`confess` *string*;

Usage   The *Carp* functions are useful when reporting errors from within a module or subroutine. They are similar to the warn and die functions except they report where the subroutine was called from in the code.

The carp function prints the message *string*, prints the line number it was called from to STDERR, and then continues execution of the script. The croak function prints the message string, prints the line number it was called from to STDERR, and then halts the execution of the script. The confess function is similar to croak except it traces all subroutine calls.

Examples   The first example has a subroutine psub that prints the arguments passed to it, but it will print a warning if there is only one argument passed to it and it will die if there are no arguments passed to it:

```
use Carp;
&psub("one", "two", "three");
&psub("one");
&psub;
print "End of script\n";

sub psub {
  if ( $#_ < 0 ) {
    croak "Not enough arguments";
  } elsif ( $#_ == 0 ) {
    carp "Only one argument";
  }
  print "@_\n";
}
```

This script produces the following output when run (the line numbers reported here may be slightly different than what you get):

```
one two three
Only one argument at ./carp.pl line 13
main::psub called at ./carp.pl line 6
one
Not enough arguments at ./carp.pl line 11
main::psub called at ./carp.pl line 7
```

The following example is similar to the first, only the definition of psub has been changed and a second subroutine has been added:

```
sub psub {
if ( $#_ < 0 ) {
    &ssub("Not enough arguments");
  } elsif ( $#_ == 0 ) {
    carp "Only one argument";
  }
  print "@_\n";
}
sub ssub {
  confess $_[0];
}
```

This script produces the following output when run:

```
one two three
Only one argument at ./carp.pl line 13
main::psub called at ./carp.pl line 6
one
Not enough arguments at ./carp.pl line 20
main::ssub called at ./carp.pl line 11
main::psub called at ./carp.pl line 7
```

Parameters   string

See Also   Functions: die, warn

Config

Functions   config_sh, config_vars, myconfig

Variables   %Config

Syntax
```
use Config qw(config_sh config_vars myconfig);
config_sh();
config_vars(array);
myconfig();
```

Usage   The *Config* module holds all the configuration variables set by the Configure
         script when Perl was installed on the machine. If you just type **use Config** at
         the beginning of your script, you can access the %Config associative array,
         which holds all of the variables and their values. The first example shows
         you how to use this array.

         The config_sh function returns the configuration information in the form
         of a shell script. The config_vars function prints to STDOUT the requested
         configuration variables that are named in the array passed to this function.
         The variables are printed in the following format:

```
name='value';
```

         The myconfig function returns a more readable summary of the configu-
         ration information.

         This configuration isn't stored in the Perl executable so there may be some
         discrepancies between the information and the actual configuration of the
         Perl binary. The Config module checks the version number of the binary
         against the version from the configuration information to prevent this as
         much as is possible.

Examples The first example loops through all the variables stored in the %Config
         associative array and displays them to STDOUT:

```
use Config;
while ( ( $var, $val ) = each %Config ) {
   print "$var = $val\n";
}
```

         The next example shows how you can use the functions included in the
         Config module:

```
use Config qw(config_sh config_vars myconfig);
print config_sh();
print myconfig();
config_vars("cc", "ld");
```

         This prints out quite a bit of data. The output of the config_vars command
         on my system is:

```
cc='gcc';
ld='gcc';
```

Parameters array

Cwd

Functions   chdir, cwd, fastgetcwd, getcwd

Syntax
```
use Cwd;
$currentDir = cwd
chdir $newDir;
$currentDir = fastgetcwd;
$currentDir = getcwd;
```

Usage   The *Cwd* module gives you functions to retrieve the current working directory of your program. The cwd function is the safest function to use for your
current system. On most operating systems, cwd is the same as 'pwd', but
using cwd makes your scripts more portable. The getcwd function is the
same as the getcwd system call. The fastcwd function is the fastest of the
three, but it is also the most dangerous because you could conceivably
change out of a directory that you can't change back in to.
   The chdir function overrides the default Perl chdir function. You must
import this function explicitly:

```
Use Cwd 'chdir';
```

   The chdir function will keep the PWD environment variable up to date
when you change directories.

Examples   The following example shows how you can use the Cwd module. You can
replace the cwd function call with getcwd or fastgetcwd and get the same
results. Assume the starting directory is /tmp.

```
use Cwd;
chdir "/etc";# this is Perl's default chdir
$curDir = cwd;
print "$curDir\n"; # prints "/etc"
print $ENV{'PWD'}, "\n";  # prints "/tmp"

use Cwd 'chdir';
chdir "/etc";# the module's chdir
$curDir = cwd;
print "$curDir\n"; # prints "/etc"
print $ENV{'PWD'}, "\n";  # prints "/etc"
```

Parameters   string

See Also   Functions: chdir

diagnostics

Functions   disable, enable

Variables   PRETTY

Syntax

```
use diagnostics;
use diagnostics -verbose;
diagnostics::disable();
diagnostics::enable();
$diagnostics::PRETTY = 1;
```

Usage   The *diagnostics* pragma adds more diagnostic messages when compiling and running your programs. When you use the diagnostics pragma, the -w flag is automatically set and any diagnostic messages are sent to STDERR.

      You can't unload the diagnostics program with the no function since diagnostics works at compile time as well as run time. You can use the enable and disable functions to turn diagnostics on and off in your program at run time, though.

      The -verbose flag causes the perldiag main page introduction to be displayed before the rest of the diagnostic information. If you set the PRETTY variable in a BEGIN block (before you load the module), you will see nicer escape sequences for pagers.

Examples   The follow program gives you a few compile time and run time error messages just to give you an idea of what diagnostics does:

```
use diagnostics;
print TEST "one\n";
$test = $a + $b;
local $c, $d = @test;
```

DirHandle

Functions   new, read, rewind

Syntax

```
use DirHandle;
$dirh = new DirHandle directory;
$file = $dirh->read();
$dirh->rewind();
```

Usage   The *DirHandle* module is an object-oriented alternative to the built-in
          functions opendir, readdir, rewinddir, and closedir. The DirHandle is
          automatically closed when the last reference to it goes out of scope. The read
          method can be interpreted in either a scalar or array context. In an array
          context, it will return all the files in the directory, and in scalar context, it will
          return the next file. It is useful to access read in scalar context to loop
          through the contents of a directory.

Examples The following script reads in all the contents of the current directory. It will
          first read them into an array and print that array; then it will rewind the
          directory and use a while loop to process each item. If it's a directory, it will
          print the directory name followed by a '/'. If it's a symbolic link, it will print
          the file name followed by an @. A symbolic link to a directory will be
          followed by both. Other files are printed normally:

```
use DirHandle;
$dirh = new DirHandle ".";
@files = $dirh->read();
print "@files\n";
$dirh->rewind();
while ( $file = $dirh->read() ) {
   print "$file";
   print "/" if -d $file;
   print "\@" if -l $file;
   print "\n";
}
```

See Also Functions: closedir, opendir, readdir, rewinddir

DynaLoader   MODULE

Functions   bootstrap, dl_error, dl_expandspec, dl_findfile, dl_find_symbol,
            dl_install_xsub, dl_load_file, dl_undef_symbols

Variables $dl_debug, @dl_library_path, @dl_resolve_symbols, @dl_resolve_using

Syntax   package *MyModule*;

            require DynaLoader;

            push (@ISA, "DynaLoader");

            bootstrap *MyModule*;

            $errmsg = dl_error;

```
$path = dl_expandspec($spec);

@filepaths = dl_findfile(@librarylist);

$symbol_ref = dl_find_symbol($library_ref, $symbol);

dl_install_xsub($subname, $symbol_ref[, $filename]);

$library_ref = dl_load_file($filename);

@symbol_list = dl_undef_symbols();
```

Usage The *DynaLoader* module is an interface to allow your modules to be dynamically loaded by Perl. The bootstrap method will either call the bootstrap method from your module or call the bootstrap method from DynaLoader, which will then load your module and call its bootstrap method. You only need the first four lines listed in the Syntax section to use the DynaLoader in your module.

The rest of the variables and functions are used when implementing DynaLoader on a new platform.

The @dl_library_path array is a list of all the directories that dl_findfile should search through to find a library file. The directories are searched in the order they appear in the array. The @dl_library_path array will be initialized to a default set of directories (such as /usr/lib). This array is used to determine the path of a library file when the dl_findfile method is called.

The @dl_resolve_using array is a list of libraries that can be used to resolve any undefined symbols. This array might not be used on some platforms.

The @dl_require_symbols array contains a list of symbol names that are in the library file being dynamically loaded. This isn't required on all platforms.

The $dl_debug variable is used to turn on internal debugging messages. It is set to the PERL_DL_DEBUG environment variable if it exists, or you can set it within your program. The higher the number set to $dl_debug, the more information you will see.

The dl_error method returns the last error message from a failed call to a DynaLoader method. This message will remain even through subsequent successful method calls.

The dl_findfile method determines the absolute path names for the list of library names passed to it. It uses the @dl_library_path array to search. The list of library names is generally in the format *'name'*, which is converted to the filename libname.*x*, where *x* is a platform-specific file suffix. You can include directories in the list of library names by using the -L prefix. Those directories will be searched before @dl_library_path. The following example shows how you can use this method:

```
@dl_resolve_using = dl_findfile("-L/usr/local/lib", "-lmylib");
```

The dl_expandspec method is used for peculiar systems that need special filename handling when dealing with symbolic names for files. The dl_expandspec method can be implemented to expand the symbolic name to the necessary filename.

The dl_load_file method is used to dynamically load the file passed to it and return a library reference to it.

The dl_find_symbol method returns the address of the symbol passed to it in the library passed to it. This address is handled as a symbol reference.

The dl_undef_symbols method is a list of symbol names that were undefined after a call to dl_load_file. Most platforms return an empty list for this method.

The dl_install_xsub creates a Perl subroutine with the assigned *subname* associated with the symbol reference passed to it. If a filename isn't passed to this method, then DynaLoader will be used to find the symbol.

The bootstrap method is the entry point to dynamically load modules in Perl. It locates the module by searching through the @INC array. It then uses dl_findfile to determine the filename to load. It sets @dl_require_symbols to include boot_*MyModule* and executes the file auto/*MyModule*/*MyModule*.bs if it exists. This file is generally used to add any necessary files for the platform to @dl_resolve_using. It then calls dl_load_file and dl_undef_symbols to warn if any symbols remain undefined. It calls dl_find_symbol to find the boot_*MyModule* symbol and then installs it as *MyModule*::bootstrap using dl_install_xsub. It then calls *MyModule*::bootstrap.

See Also   Bundled Modules: SelfLoader

English

MODULE

Variables   See the table in the Usage section for a listing of the English module variables.

Syntax   use English;

Usage

English Module Variable	Equivalent Perl Variable
$ACCUMULATOR	$^A
@ARG	@_
$ARG	$_
$BASETIME	$^T
$CHILD_ERROR	$?
$DEBUGGING	$^D
$EFFECTIVE_GROUP_ID	$)
$EFFECTIVE_USER_ID	$>
$EGID	$)

English Module Variable	Equivalent Perl Variable
$ERRNO	$!
$EUID	$>
$EVAL_ERROR	$@
$EXECUTABLE_NAME	$^X
$FORMAT_LINE_BREAK_CHARACTERS	$:
$FORMAT_LINEFEED	$^L
$FORMAT_LINES_LEFT	$-
$FORMAT_LINES_PER_PAGE	$=
$FORMAT_NAME	$~
$FORMAT_PAGE_NUMBER	$%
$FORMAT_TOP_NAME	$^
$GID	$(
$INPLACE_EDIT	$^I
$INPUT_LINE_NUMBER	$.
$INPUT_RECORD_SEPARATOR	$/
$LAST_PAREN_MATCH	$+
$LIST_SEPARATOR	$î
$MATCH	$&
$NR	$.
$ORS	$\
$OS_ERROR	$!
$OSNAME	$^O
$OUTPUT_AUTOFLUSH	$l
$OUTPUT_FIELD_SEPARATOR	$\
$PERL_VERSION	$]
$PERLDB	$^P
$PID	$$
$POSTMATCH	$'
$PREMATCH	$`
$PROCESS_ID	$$
$PROGRAM_NAME	$0
$REAL_GROUP_ID	$(
$REAL_USER_ID	$<
$RS	$/
$SUBSCRIPT_SEPARATOR	$;
$SUBSEP	$;
$SYSTEM_FD_MAX	$^F
$UID	$<
$WARNING	$^W

Examples
This example simply uses the $ERRNO variable instead of the $! to make the script more readable if an error occurs:

```
use English;
open ( MYFILE, "<myfile.txt") or die $ERRNO;
```

See Also
Appendix B, " Perl Special Variables"

Env

Functions   import

Variables   See the Usage section.

Syntax
```
use Env;
use Env (array);
Env::import();
```

Usage
The *Env* module ties environment variables to Perl variables of the same name. If you pass an array of variable names when you import the module, only those variables will be tied to Perl variables. If you call the import method in your script, then all the environment variables will be tied, for example:

```
use Env (array);
Env::import();
```

is the same as:

```
use Env;
```

To remove the tied variable, simply undef it:

```
undef $VAR;
```

Examples
The following example can be used to modify the PATH environment variable an alternate way than using the %ENV associative array. This generally doesn't give much benefit unless you modify environment variables often in your script.

```
use Env ("path");
$PATH .= "/bin/test";
```

Exporter

Functions   export_fail, export_tags, export_ok_tags, require_version

Variables   @EXPORT, @EXPORT_FAIL, @EXPORT_OK, %EXPORT_TAGS

Syntax
```
require Exporter;
Exporter::export_tags($name);
Exporter::export_ok_tags($name);
$module->require_version($number);
$module->export_fail(@array);
```

Usage   The *Exporter* module is used when you are creating your own module. It defines which functions will be exported when your module is imported by another script. The symbols listed in the @EXPORT array will automatically be exported when your module is used. The symbols listed in the @EXPORT_OK array will be exported if the importing script requests them. The %EXPORT_TAGS associative array contains aliases for a list of symbols to be imported.

The @EXPORT_FAIL array is used to keep symbols from being imported by other scripts. If a script attempts to import one of these symbols, the export_fail method is called with the list of symbols in the @EXPORT_FAIL array that are being imported. If you implement this method in your module, then the list of symbols it returns will cause an error for each symbol. If it returns an empty list, the symbols will be imported without any errors. The default method from the Exporter module will return the list passed to export_fail.

The symbols listed in the %EXPORT_TAGS array must also be listed in either the @EXPORT or @EXPORT_OK arrays. The export_tags and export_ok_tags functions will add the symbols associated with the tag to the @EXPORT or @EXPORT_TAGS arrays, respectively. For example:

```
%EXPORT_TAGS = ( 'list1' => ['a', 'b', 'c'],
    'list2' => ['d', 'e', 'f'] );
Exporter::export_tags('list1');
Exporter::export_ok_tags('list2');
```

At this point, the @EXPORT array would consist of 'a', 'b', and 'c' and the @EXPORT_OK array would consist of 'd', 'e', and 'f'. Note that the values of the associative array are stored as array references. The tagged names can be imported into a script.

The require_version method can be called from a script importing your module to make sure the version of the module is valid for that script. You can implement this in your module or use the Exporter module default, which will check the value passed to require_version against the $VERSION variable of the module.

Examples The following example creates a module named MyModule with a list of symbols that are exported or can be exported. Below the module is a list of import commands that can be used in files importing MyModule.

```
package MyModule;
require Exporter;
# this is so that the default modules from Exporter
# can be accessed from your module
@ISA = ("Exporter");
@EXPORT = ( 'one' );
@EXPORT_OK = ( 'one', 'two', 'three' );
$EXPORT_TAGS = ( 'tag1' => ['four', 'five', 'six'],
    'tag2' => ['seven', 'eight'],
    'tag3' => ['four', 'nine'] );
Exporter::export_ok_tags('tag1');
Exporter::export_ok_tags('tag2');
Exporter::export_ok_tags('tag3');
# the following commands can be used when importing
# MyModule:
use MyModule;# one will be imported
use MyModule ( 'one', 'two', 'four' );
# one, two, and four will be imported
use MyModule ( ':tag1', ':tag3', '!four' );
# five, six and nine will be imported
```

See Also Functions: no, use

Fcntl

Syntax use Fcntl;

Usage   When you load the *Fcntl* module, the following definitions are created, which can be passed to the fcntl function to send commands to a file handle:

- **F_DUPFD.** The function returns a new file descriptor that is the same as the file handle. The descriptor will be numbered with the lowest available file descriptor greater than the argument passed as the third argument.

- **F_FREESP.** The function frees disk space from a section of the file referred to by the file handle. The section is specified by the third argument and must be a packed variable. Please see your system documentation on fcntl for more information on this argument.

- **F_GETFD.** The function returns the close-on-exec flag associated with the file handle.

- **F_GETFL.** The function returns the file handle status flags.

- **F_GETLK.** The function is locked as requested in the packed variable passed as the third argument. See your system documentation for more information on this variable.
- **F_SETFD.** The function sets the close-on-exec flag associated with the file handle to the third argument. It can be either 0 or 1.
- **F_SETFL.** The function sets the status flag associated with the file handle to the third argument.
- **F_SETLK.** The function sets or clears a file section lock described by the packed variable passed as the third argument.
- **F_SETLKW.** This is the same as F_SETLK except that if a read or write lock is blocked by other locks, it will wait until the section is available to be locked.

Examples   This example returns the status flag of the file handle and sets it to the scalar $ret:

```
use Fcntl;
$ret = fcntl(FILE1, F_GETFL);
```

See Also   Functions: fcntl

FileCache

Functions   Cacheout

Properties   maxopen

Syntax
```
use FileCache;
$filename = pathToFile;
cacheout $filename;

$FileCache::maxopen = num;
```

Usage   The *FileCache* module allows you to keep more files open than the operating system permits. When you use the cacheout method, it will open the file named $filename with the filehandle of the same name. When you want to write to a file, you must invoke the cacheout method to be sure that it's open. You can have multiple writes to the currently open file without having to call cacheout again.

     When you first call cacheout on a filename it hasn't seen before, it will create the file if it doesn't exist and make it zero length if it does. Subsequent calls to cacheout will append data to that file.

The cacheout method uses the value of NOFILE in sys/param.h to find out how many files are allowed to be open. If this value is incorrect (which it is on some systems), you'll need to set $FileCache::maxopen to the correct value of NOFILE minus four.

Examples The following script takes a filename as an argument with the following format:

num: *data*

This script will read in that file and create a file named *num* and print *data* to that file. It uses FileCache if there are more unique numbers in the file than are allowed to be open at the same time. This is faster than opening the file, writing the data, and then closing the file for each line:

```
Use FileCache;
While ( <> ) {
    ( $file, $data ) = /^(\d+): (.+)$/;
    cacheout $file;
    print $file $data;
}
```

Assume we read in a file with the following data:

```
1: testing
2: testing2
3: testing3
2: 2 again
3: 3 again
4: testing4
5: testing5
4: 4 again
1: 1 again
5: 5 again
3: another 3
2: another 2
```

This would create five files named 1 through 5 with the data listed beside the appropriate number.

See Also Functions: open, close

FileHandle

Functions   autoflush, clearerr, close, eof, fileno, fdopen, format_formfeed,
format_line_break_characters, format_lines_left, format_lines_per_page,
format_name, format_page_number, format_top_name, getc, getline,
getlines, gets, getpos, input_line_number, input_record_separator, new,
new_from_fd, open, output_field_separator, output_record_separator, print,
printf, seek, setpos, setvbuf, tell

Syntax   `use FileHandle;`

`$handle = new FileHandle;`

`$handle->autoflush 1;`

`$handle->clearerr;`

`$handle->close;`

`$handle->eof;`

`$handle->fileno;`

`$handle->fdopen(handle, mode);`

`$handle->format_formfeed = value;`

`$handle->format_line_break_characters = value;`

`$handle->format_lines_left;`

`$handle->format_lines_per_page = value;`

`$handle->format_name = value;`

`$handle->format_page_number;`

`$handle->format_top_name = value;`

`$ch = $handle->getc;`

`$line = $handle->getline;`

`@lines = $handle->getlines;`

`$line = $handle->gets;`

`$pos = $handle->getpos;`

`$num = $handle->input_line_number;`

`$handle->input_record_separator = value;`

`$newhandle = new_from_fd FileHandle handle, mode;`

`$handle->open(file, mode);`

`$handle->output_field_separator = value;`

```
$handle->output_record_separator = value;

$handle->print(value);

$handle->printf(format, values);

$handle->seek(offset, start);

$handle->setpos($pos;)

$handle->setvbuf($buffer, policy, value);

$pos = $handle->tell;
```

Usage   The *FileHandle* module is used to create an object-oriented interface to using file handles. You create a file handle object by a call to new. Any arguments you pass to new will be passed to open after the object has been created. The open method takes one or two arguments. It is an interface for the Perl open function so you can use the same special characters in the filename to determine how the file is open, or you can use the POSIX modes as the second argument. The following shows two different ways to open a file for reading:

```
$handle->open "<$filename";
$handle->open $filename, "r";
```

The new_from_fd method does the same as the new method except it passes its two required arguments to fdopen after the object is created. The fdopen method is like open except the first argument is a file handle, a FileHandle object, or a file descriptor number.

The setvbuf method is only available if the corresponding setvbuf C function is available. It is used to set the buffering policy for the file handle. The first argument is a buffer variable to hold the data, the second is how to buffer the data (which you can use with the built-in macros _IOFBF, _IOLBF, or _IONBF), and the third specifies how much data to buffer at a time. You may cause a fatal error if you try to modify the buffer variable before closing the file handle or making another call to servbuf.

The getpos and setpos functions are only available if their corresponding C functions are on the system. It is generally better to use the tell and seek functions instead. The getpos and tell functions return the current position in the file and the setpos and seek functions each take two arguments. The first is the number of bytes to move and the second determines where to start moving from. If the second argument is 0, the current position will be moved from the beginning of the file. If it's 1, it will move from the current position, and if it's 3, it will move from the end of the file. See the function entries for seek and tell for more information.

The following functions are used exactly the same as the corresponding Perl functions:

- **clearerr.** Clears any system errors that have occurred and clears the eof flag.
- **close.** Closes the file handle. (If you undef the FileHandle variable, it will automatically be closed.)

- **eof.** Returns true if you've tried to read past the end of the file.
- **fileno.** Returns the file descriptor associated with the FileHandle object.
- **getc.** Returns the next character in the file and moves the position ahead one.
- **gets.** Returns the next line in the file and moves the current position to the beginning of the next line.
- **print.** Prints the data to the file handle.
- **printf.** Prints to the file using the specified format and variables. See printf for more information.
- **seek.** Moves the current position in the file.
- **tell.** Returns the current position in the file.

The getline method returns the next line in the file just like the <FILE> operator except that if it's called in an array context, it still only returns one line. The getlines method returns an array of remaining lines in the file just like <FILE> in array context. An error will occur if this method is called in a scalar context.

The following table correlates the FileHandle functions with the special variables they correspond to. For example:

```
Select $handle;
$| = 1;
# is the same as
$handle->autoflush 1;
```

See Appendix B, "Perl Special Variables," to find out what these functions do.

autoflush	$!
format_formfeed	$^L
format_line_break_characters	$:
format_lines_left	$-
format_lines_per_page	$=
format_name	$~
format_page_number	$%
format_top_name	$^
input_line_number	$.
input_record_separator	$/
output_field_separator	$,
output_record_separator	$\

The following FileHandle functions affect all file handles, not just the FileHandle object they were invoked on: input_line_number, input_record_separator, and output_record_separator.

Examples   The following example is a simple replacement for a file copy command. It is not meant for speed but to show the various functions of the FileHandle module:

```perl
use FileHandle;
$startFile = $ARGV[0];
$endFile = $ARGV[1];

$sh = new FileHandle $startFile, "r";
$eh = new FileHandle;
$eh->open ($endFile, "w");
$eh->print (<$sh>);
$eh->print ($sh->getline);
foreach $line ( $sh->getlines ) {
   $eh->print ($line);
}
```

See Also   Functions: close, fileno, open, print, printf, seek, tell, Appendix B, "Perl Special Variables"

integer

Syntax   `use integer;`

Usage   When you use the *integer* pragma, it tells the compiler that all mathematical operations should only use integers until the end of the enclosing block. This is mostly useful on machines without floating-point hardware.

Examples   The following code fragment will only do integer math within the enclosing block and normal math outside it:

```perl
{
   use integer;
   # use integer math
   $num = 22/7;
   $num2 = 27/7;
   print "$num $num2\n";
}
# now use normal math
$num = 22/7;
$num2 = 27/7;
print "$num $num2\n";
```

IO

Syntax   `use IO;`

Usage   The *IO* module loads all of the IO modules at once. The current IO modules are IO::File, IO::Handle, IO::Pipe, IO::Seekable, and IO::Socket.

See Also   IO::File, IO::Handle, IO::Pipe, IO::Seekable, IO::Socket

IO::File

Functions   new, new_tmpfile, open

Syntax
```
use IO::File;
$handle = new IO::File;
$handle = new_tmpfile IO::File;
$handle->open(file, [mode, [permissions]]);
```

Usage   The *IO::File* module is an object interface for dealing with filehandles. It inherits from IO::Handle and IO::Seekable. It is very similar to the FileHandle module.

The new method creates a new instance of an IO::File object and returns it. If any arguments are passed to it, they are passed on to a call to open. If this method fails, the IO::File object is destroyed. The new_tmpfile method creates an opened temporary file that is in read/write mode. On systems where it is possible, this is an anonymous temporary file. If the file can't be created or opened, the IO::File object is destroyed.

The open method takes up to three possible arguments. The first argument is the name of the file to open. This can include the Perl special characters that can be used with the Perl open function (<, >, etc.). You can also use the second argument as a mode (w, r, a, and so on). If a third argument is passed, it is set as the permission of the file created. This permission is the same as the chmod function.

Example   The following example uses the IO::File module to create a simple version of the cat command, which prints the contents of a file to STDOUT.

```
use IO::File;
$file = $ARGV[0];
$fh = new FileHandle $file, "r";
while ( <$fh> ) {
   print;
}
```

See Also   FileHandle, IO::Handle, IO::Seekable

IO::Handle

Functions
Autoflush, close, eof, fdopen, fileno, format_formfeed, format_line_break_characters, format_lines_left, format_lines_per_page, format_name, format_page_number, format_top_name, format_write, getc, getline, getlines, input_line_number, input_record_separator, new, new_from_fd, opened, output_field_separator, output_record_separator, print, printf, read, setvbuf, stat, sysread, syswrite, truncate, untaint, write

Syntax
```
use IO::Handle;

$handle = new IO::Handle;

$handle = new_from_fd IO::Handle FileDescriptor, mode;

$handle->close;

$handle->eof;

$handle->fileno;

$handle->fdopen(handle, mode);

$handle->format_formfeed = value;

$handle->format_line_break_characters = value;

$handle->format_lines_left;

$handle->format_lines_per_page = value;

$handle->format_name = value;

$handle->format_page_number;

$handle->format_top_name = value;

$ch = $handle->getc;

$line = $handle->getline;

@lines = $handle->getlines;

$num = $handle->input_line_number;

$handle->input_record_separator = value;

$handle->output_field_separator = value;

$handle->output_record_separator = value;

$handle->print(value);

$handle->printf(format, values);
```

```
$handle->read(buffer, length[, offset])

$handle->setvbuf($buffer, policy, value);

@fileinfo = $handle->stat();

$handle->sysread(buffer, length[, offset]);

$handle->syswrite(data, length[, offset]);

$handle->truncate(length);

$handle->write(data, length[, offset]);
```

Usage   The *IO::Handle* module is the base class for any other IO handle classes. You probably won't want to create an instance of this object unless you're creating a class that inherits from it.

The new method creates a new instance of an IO::Handle object. The new_from_fd method creates a new instance and then calls the fdopen method.

The following IO::Handle functions correspond to the Perl functions of the same name:

- **close.** Closes the file handle. (If you undef the IO::Handle variable, it will automatically be closed.)
- **eof.** Returns true if you've tried to read past the end of the handle.
- **fileno.** Returns the file descriptor associated with the IO::Handle object.
- **getc.** Returns the next character in the handle and moves the position ahead one.
- **print.** Prints the data to the handle.
- **printf.** Prints to the handle using the specified format and variables. See printf for more information.
- **read.** Reads data from the handle.
- **stat.** Returns information about the handle.
- **truncate.** Truncates the handle to the specified length.
- **sysread.** Does a system read from the handle.
- **syswrite.** Does a system write to the handle.

The following table correlates the IO::Handle functions with the special variables they correspond to. For example:

```
select $handle;
$| = 1;
# is the same as
$handle->autoflush 1;
```

See Appendix B, "Perl Special Variables," to find out what these functions do.

autoflush	$!
format_formfeed	$^L
format_line_break_characters	$:
format_lines_left	$-
format_lines_per_page	$=
format_name	$~
format_page_number	$%
format_top_name	$^
input_line_number	$.
input_record_separator	$/
output_field_separator	$,
output_record_separator	$\

The following IO::Handle functions affect all handles, not just the IO::Handle object they were invoked on: input_line_number, input_record_separator and output_record_separator.

The setvbuf method is only available if the corresponding setvbuf C function is available. It is used to set the buffering policy for the file handle. The first argument is a buffer variable to hold the data, the second is how to buffer the data (you can use the built-in macros _IOFBF, _IOLBF, or _IONBF), and the third specifies much data to buffer at a time. You may cause a fatal error if you try to modify the buffer variable before closing the file handle or making another call to servbuf.

The getline method returns the next line from the handle in scalar context. If this method is accessed in array context, it still only returns one line of the handle. The getlines method returns the remaining lines of the handle in an array. If this method is invoked in scalar context, an error occurs.

The fdopen method is similar to the open Perl function except it takes a filehandle, IO::Handle object, or a file descriptor as an argument. The write method writes the *data* of *length* size starting at an optional *offset* to the handle.

The opened method returns true if the IO::Handle object is a valid file descriptor.

The untaint method marks the object as being taint-clean. This means any data read from the handle will be considered taint-clean. You should be sure you want to mark the object as taint-clean since it can be a security hole if the object isn't really safe when invoking this method.

See Also   FileHandle, IO::File

IO::Pipe

Functions   handles, new, reader, writer

Syntax
```
use IO::Pipe;

$pipe = new IO::Pipe [reader, writer];

$pipe->handles([exec]);

$pipe->reader([exec]);

$pipe->write();
```

Usage   The *IO::Pipe* module provides an object interface for using pipes between processes. The new method creates a new instance of an IO::Pipe object. Any arguments passed to new will be blessed into IO::Handle or one of its subclasses. Those two arguments will be passed to the pipe system call. If no arguments are passed, then the handles method is called after the IO::Pipe object is created.

    The reader method causes the object to be re-blessed into IO::Handle and it becomes the handle at the reading end of the PIPE. If any arguments are passed to this method, then a fork is called and the arguments are passed to exec. The writer method is similar to reader except the object becomes the handle at the writing end of the pipe.

    The handles method is called when an IO::Pipe object is created without any arguments. It returns an array of two blessed objects.

Example   The following example forks and then communicates between the parent and child:

```
use IO;
$pipe = new IO::Pipe;
if ($pid = fork()) {
   $pipe->reader();
   while ( <$pipe> ) {
      print "Parent: $_";
   }
} elsif (defined $pid) {
   $pipe->writer();
   print $pipe "Here's a message from the child.";
}
```

See Also   IO::Handle
Functions: pipe, fork

IO::Seekable

Functions   getpos, seek, setpos, tell

Syntax
```
use IO::Seekable;

$pos = $handle->getpos;

$handle->seek(offset, start);

$handle->setpos(offset, start);

$pos = $handle->tell;
```

Usage   The *IO::Seekable* module is intended to be inherited by other IO::Handle-based objects. It provides functions for moving through a handle. If the C functions fsetpos and fgetpos are available, then the getpos and setpos functions are available.

The getpos and tell functions both return the current position in the handle. The setpos and seek functions change the current position based on the *offset* and the *start* location. If *start* is 0, the offset will move from the beginning of the file; if it's 1, from the current position; and if it's 2, from the end of the file.

See Also   IO::Handle

IO::Socket

Functions   accept, bind, listen, new, peername, protocol, recv, send, socket, socketpair, sockdomain, sockname, sockopt, socktype, timeout

Syntax
```
use IO::Socket;

$socket = new IO::Socket [%args];

$client = $socket->accept([Package]);

$socket->bind(address);

$socket->listen(queue);

$addr = $socket->peername();

$proto = $socket->protocol();

$socket->recv(buffer, length, flags);
```

```
$socket->send(data, length[, flags]);

$socket->socket(domain, type, protocol)

$socket->socketpair(domain, type, protocol);

$domain = $socket->sockdomain();

$addr = $socket->sockname();

$socket->sockopt(option[, value]);

$type = $socket->socktype();

$socket->timeout([num]);
```

Usage The *IO::Socket* module provides an object-oriented interface for using sockets. It inherits all the functions from IO::Handle class. IO::Socket has two subclasses specific to a particular domain: IO::Socket::INET and IO::Socket::Unix.

The new method creates a new instance of an IO::Socket object. It takes an optional argument of a set of key/value pairs. The only key that new reads is Domain, which it used to pass the rest of the pairs to a subclass of IO::Socket (i.e., IO::Socket::INET).

The following functions correspond to the Perl functions of the same name:

- **accept.** Accepts an incoming connection to a server from a client. (The arguments to this method have been modified from the Perl function.)
- **bind.** Binds an address to an open socket.
- **listen.** Listens on the address this socket is bound to.
- **[get]peername.** Returns the socket address at the other end of the socket connection.
- **recv.** Receives a message on the socket.
- **send.** Sends a message to the connected socket.
- **socket.** Opens a socket of the given *domain, type,* and *protocol.*
- **socketpair.** Opens a pair of sockets of the given *domain, type,* and *protocol* and returns them.
- **[get]sockname.** Returns the socket address at this end of the connection.

The accept method has been slightly modified from the Perl function. It accepts the incoming connection and returns an IO::Socket object corresponding to the connected socket. If this method is called in scalar context, it simply returns the created object; if it is called in array context, it returns an array of the object and the address of the peer. If the accept fails, it will return undef or an empty array. If the optional package is passed to accept, the object will be created within that package.

The timeout method sets the timeout amount for the socket. If you don't pass any arguments, then it returns the current timeout value. If you do pass an argument, then it sets the timeout and returns the old value.

The sockopt method is an interface for the getsockopt and setsockopt Perl functions at the SOL_SOCKET level. If it's called with only an option, then it behaves like getsockopt and returns the value for that option. If it's called with an option and a value, it behaves like setsockopt and sets that option to that value.

The sockdomain, socktype, and protocol functions return the domain, type, and protocol of the socket, respectively. If the protocol isn't known, the protocol function returns 0.

Example   The following script is a simple server that can answer for your Web server while you're doing maintenance. It will answer requests on the port you specify or port 8080 if you don't specify one. Any clients that connect will be sent a standard message and then the connection will close. This could be used for any type of stateless messaging server.

The INT, QUIT, and KILL signals have handlers to make sure the client and server sockets close before exiting. In the interest of space, this script doesn't do any error checking:

```
Use Socket;
Use IO;

$SIG{INT} = \&closeall;
$SIG{QUIT} = \&closeall;
$SIG{KILL} = \&closeall;
$SIG{CHDL} = \&childclose;

$port = 8080;
$port = $ARGV[0] if defined($ARGV[0]);
$msg = <<"EOF";
<html>
<head>
<title>System Maintenance</title>
</head>
<body>
<h1>Maintenance</h1>
Sorry.  Our web server is currently down for maintenance.
Please try back soon.
</body>
</html>
EOF
```

```perl
$server = new IO::Socket;
$proto = getprotobyname('tcp');
$server->socket(PF_INET, SOCK_STREAM, $proto);
$server->sockopt(SO_REUSEADDR, pack("l", 1));
$sockaddr = sockaddr_in($port, INADDR_ANY);
$server->bind($sockaddr);
$server->listen(SOMAXCONN);
for($connCount = 1; ; $connCount++) {
   if ($client = $server->accept()) {
      if ( $pid = fork() ) {
         print "$connCount connections handled.\n";
      } elsif (defined($pid)) {
         $client->print($msg);
         $client->close;
         exit(0);
      }
   }
}

sub closeall {
   $client->close if defined($client);
   $server->close if defined($server);
   exit;
}

sub childclose {
wait;
$client->close;
}
```

See Also IO::Handle, IO::Socket::INET, IO::Socket::Unix, Socket

Ioctl

MODULE

Syntax `use Ioctl;`

Usage The *Ioctl* module is used to load the constant and function definitions for input/output control to be used with the Perl ioctl function. It is only useful on UNIX-based machines. You should read your system documentation on ioctl, streamio, and termio for more information on the constants and functions you can access.

See Also Functions: ioctl

lib

Variables   ORIG_INC

Syntax
```
use lib @arr;
no lib @arr;
@INC = @lib::ORIG_INC;
```

Usage   The *lib* module provides an easier way to modify the @INC special variable at compile time. The @INC array is a list of directories where Perl will look when loading external libraries or modules. You'll want to modify this array when you have added your own custom modules or libraries outside the default set of directories.

The following Perl statements are virtually the same:

```
use lib @arr;
BEGIN { unshift(@INC, @arr); }
```

When lib adds a directory to the @INC variable, it also checks to see if *directory*/$archname/auto exists (where $archname is the name for your system architecture) and adds *directory*/$archname to @INC as well. If you specifically add *directory*/$archname to your array list, it will be added twice.

If you wish to remove directories from the @INC variable, you can simply do:

```
no lib @arr;
```

This will delete the first instance of each of the directories in @arr from the @INC variable. You should be careful when doing this and only do it when necessary. If you wish to delete multiple instances of a directory from @INC, you can specify the directory more than once in @arr or have "ALL" as the first element in @arr. In this case, all the instances of those directories will be removed.

When lib is removing directories, it also searches for *directory*/$archname and deletes it as well.

When you first use lib, it saves the current value of @INC in the variable @lib::ORIG_INC. You can use this variable to restore the original value of @INC if you need to.

Examples   The following code fragment adds the current directory to the library search path:

```
use lib ".";
```

See Also   Functions: no, require, use
The special variable @INC

Opcode

Functions
define_optag, empty_opset, full_opset, invert_opset, opcodes, opdesc, opdump, opmask, opmask_add, opset, opset_to_hex, opset_to_ops, verify_opset

Syntax

```
use Opcode;

define_optag(optag, opset);

opset = empty_opset;

opset = full_opset;

opset = invert_opset(opset);

number = opcodes;

desclist = opdesc(oplist);

opdump([pattern]);

opset = opmask;

opmask_add(opset);

opset(oplist);

string = opset_to_hex(opset);

oplist = opset_to_ops(opset)

verify_opset(opset[, croak]);
```

Usage
The *Opcode* module generally isn't used by most programs. You can use the Safe module for an easier interface with the same results. The Opcode module lets you define an operator mask that will be in effect the next time Perl compiles any code. Any code that contains a masked opcode will fail, and the code will not execute.

Most of the Opcode functions take a list of operators for an argument. These lists can be made up of three types of elements: operator names, operator tags, and operator sets. Operator names (opname) are self-explanatory. An operator tag (optag) refers to groups of operators, and the tag names always begin with a colon. There are several operator tags that are defined by the Opcode module. An operator set (opset) is a binary representation of a list of opnames and is generally 43 bytes. Whenever a list of operators is expected, you can use a list of opsets.

The define_optag method takes an optag name and an opset, and it defines optag as a reference to the opset. The optag name must begin with a colon and must not already be defined. Once you define an optag, you can't modify or remove it. Optag names generally start with a capital letter so as not to conflict with the existing optags, which all begin with lowercase letters. If you're using the Opcode module within a package, you should begin the optag name with the package name to make sure there are no conflicts since optag names are always global.

The empty_opset method returns an opset with no operators in it. Conversely, the full_opset method returns an opset containing all the operators. The invert_opset method returns the inverse of the opset passed to it.

The opcodes method returns the number of opcodes available in the current version of Perl. In the future, if you call it in an array context, it will return the list of all the operators. For now you can simply call opset_to_ops and not pass any opset to it.

The opdesc method returns a list of descriptions corresponding to the list of opcodes passed to it. The opdump method will display to STDOUT the list of opcodes and their descriptions. If it's passed an optional pattern, it will only print the opcodes that match the case-insensitive pattern.

The opmask method returns an opset that corresponds to the current opmask of the script. You can add opsets to the opmask by using the opmask_add method. Once you mask an opset, it can't be unmasked.

The opset method takes a list of opcodes and returns a set containing the list. You can do the opposite by using the opset_to_ops method, which takes an opset and returns a list of opcodes. You can use the opset_to_hex method to return a string representation of the opset you pass to it. This is mainly useful for debugging.

The verify_opset method makes sure an opset is valid and returns true if it is, false if it's not. If you pass an optional second argument, then the method will croak (see the Carp module) instead of returning false.

You can pass a negative opname or optag to any of the functions that take an opname or optag by adding a ! to the beginning of it. This will remove those opcodes from the accumulated set.

You can manipulate your opsets by using the bit operators: &, |, ^, or ~. You should always have opsets on each side of these operators since the numerical position of a specific opcode within an opset isn't reliable.

The following table lists the optags provided with the Opcode module and the opcodes they represent.

- **:base_core** — aassign, abs, add, aelem, aelemfast, and, andassign, anoncode, aslice, av2arylen, bit_and, bit_or, bit_xor, chomp, chop, chr, complement, cond_expr, const, defined, delete, die, divide, each, enter, entersub, eq, exists, flip, flop, ge, gt, helem, hex, hslice, i_add, i_divide, i_eq, i_ge, i_gt, i_le, i_lt, i_modulo, i_multiply, i_ncmp, i_ne, i_negate, i_postdec, i_postinc, i_predec, i_preinc, i_subtract, index, int, keys, lc, lcfirst, le, leave, leaveeval, leavesub, left_shift, length, lineseq, list, lslice, lt, match, method, modulo, multiply, ncmp, ne, negate, nextstate, not, null, oct, or, orassign, ord, pop, pos, postdec, postinc, pow, predec, preinc, prototype, push, pushmark, quotemeta, rc2cv, return, reverse, right_shift, rindex, rv2av, rv2hv, rv2sv, sassign, scalar, schomp, schop, scmp, scope, seq, sge, sgt, shift, sle, slt, sne, splice, split, stringify, stub, study, substr, subtract, trans, uc, ucfirst, undef, unshift, unstack, values, vec, wantarray, warn, xor

- **:base_io** — The :base_io ops allow filehandle access but not filename access. This way, only preexisting filehandles can be operated on, but new filehandles can't be created.   enterwrite, eof, formline, getc, leavewrite, print, rcatline, read, readdir, readline, recv, rewinddir, seek, seekdir, send, sysread, syswrite, tell, telldir

- **:base_loop** — The :base_loop ops aren't part of the :base_core tag because they can be used to consume all the CPU time on the system.   enteriter, enterloop, goto, grepstart, grepwhile, iter, last, leaveloop, mapstart, mapwhile, next, redo

- **:base_math** — The :base_math ops aren't part of the :base_core tag because they can be used to cause floating point exceptions or, in the case of rand and srand, have an effect outside the compartment they are executed in.   atan2, cos, exp, log, rand, sin, sqrt, srand

- **:base_mem** — The :base_mem ops aren't part of the :base_core tag because they can be used to take up all the available memory. There are still ways within the :base_core ops to attack memory resources.   anonhasy, anonlist, concat, join, range, repeat

- **:base_orig** — The :base_orig ops are still being considered for placement in a final tag location.   bless, crypt, dbmclose, dbmopen, entertry, gelem, getpgrp, getppid, getpriority, gmtime, gv, gvsv, leavetry, localtime, padany, padav, padhv, padsv, pipe_op, prtf, pushre, ref, refgen, regcmaybe, regcomp, rv2gv, select, setpriority, sockpair, sprintf, srefgen, sselect, subst, substcont, tie, untie

- **:browse** — The :browse tag is a step above the :default tag. It allows file system access but only to read information and not change it. It may change as the Opcode module is developed.   :default, :filesys_read, :sys_db

- **:dangerous** — The :dangerous tag consists of the opcodes that generally wouldn't be part of a tag but are included for completeness.   chroot, dump, syscall

- **:default** — The :default tag is a good set of safe opcodes to allow. The definition of this tag will change as the Opcode module is developed.   :base_core, :base_io, :base_loop, :base_mem, :base_orig

- **:filesys_open** — binmode, close, closedir, open, open_dir, sysopen, umask

- **:filesys_read** — fileno, ftatime, ftbinary, ftblk, ftchr, ftctime, ftdir, fteexec, fteowned, fteread, ftewrite, ftfile, ftis, ftlink, ftmtime, ftpipe, ftrexec, ftrowned, ftrread, ftrwrite, ftsgid, ftsize, ftsock, ftsuid, ftsvtx, fttext, ftty, ftzero, lstat, readlink, stat

- **:filesys_write** — chmod, chown, fcntl, link, mkdir, rename, rmdir, symlink, truncate, unlink, utime

- **:others** — The :others tag is the group of assorted opcodes that don't warrant their own tag.   msgctl, msgget, msgrcv, msgsnd, semctl, semget, semop, shmctl, shmget, shmread, shmwrite

- **:ownprocess** — exec, exit, kill, time, tms
- **:still_to_be_decided** — accept, alarm, bind, caller, chdir, connect, dbstate, dofile, entereval, flock, getpeername, getsockname, gsockopt, ioctl, listen, pack, require, reset, shutdown, sleep, socket, sort, ssockopt, tied, unpack
- **:subprocess** — backtick, fork, glob, system, wait, waitpid
- **:sys_db** — egrent, ehostent, enetent, eprotoent, epwent, eservent, getlogin, ggrent, ggrgid, ggrname, ghbyaddr, ghbyname, ghostent, gnbyaddr, gnbyname, gnetent, gpbyname, gpbynumber, gprotoent, gpwent, gpwnam, gpwuid, gsbyname, gsbynumber, gservent, sgrent, shostent, snetent, sprotoent, spwent, sservent

See Also   Safe

overload

Functions   Method, Overloaded, StrVal

Syntax
```
use overload operation => subroutineRef;
overload::Method(object, operation);
overload::Overloaded(object);
overload::StrVal(object);
```

Usage   The *overload* module allows your custom objects to override various mathematical functions (like +, -, and so on). When you use the overload new method, you pass the list of key/value pairs of operations and subroutine references that will be used for each operation.

The subroutines that overload the normal operators are called with three arguments normally. If the overloaded operation is a binary operation, then the first two arguments are the objects being acted upon. Due to object calling conventions, if you call something like 100+$obj, the $obj object will be the first argument passed instead of 100. You use the third argument to discover this. The third argument will be 0 if the arguments were passed in the correct order, 1 if they were passed in the reverse order, and undefined if the current operation is an assignment operation (i.e., +=). If you're overloading a unary operation, the second argument is always undefined.

The following table lists the operations that can be overloaded.

Operation Type	Operators
Arithmetic	+ - * / % ** << >> x . += -= *= /= %= **= <<= >>= x= .=
Comparison	< > == != <= >= <=> lt gt eq ne le ge cmp
Bit and unary	& ^ | neg ! ~
Transcendental functions	atan2 cos sin exp abs log sqrt
Other	++ — bool ïî 0+
Special	Nomethod fallback =

For the arithmetic operations, the assignment version of the operation can be automatically generated if the nonassignment version is available. The +, - , +=, and -= functions can be used to automatically generate the ++ and ñ operators as well.

For comparison operators, the <=> operator can be used as a substitute for the other numeric comparison operators and cmp can be used as a substitute for the string comparison operators.

The nomethod special operator is called when the module can't find a method for an operation. The method you specify for nomethod takes four arguments, the first three being the same as a normal method and the last being the symbol corresponding to the missing method.

The fallback special operator has three possible values. If it's undefined, Perl will try to automatically generate a method; if that doesn't work, it will call the nomethod method; and if that's not there, it will error. If it's true, Perl will do the same as if it's undefined except it won't cause an error. Instead, Perl will try to do what it would have done if there were no overloading. If it's false yet defined, Perl won't try to automatically generate a method but will call the nomethod method and error if that fails.

The Method method takes an object and an operation and returns the reference to the method that overloads the operation for the object. It returns the undefined value if no method overloads the operation.

The Overloaded method returns true if the object has any overloaded operators.

The StrVal method returns a string value of the object if the ïî operator isn't overloaded.

Examples
The first example creates a very simple Roman numeral package (it only goes up to 10 and only does addition and subtraction) to show how to use the overload module. This file should be named Roman.pm. The second example will then use this module:

```
package Roman;
use overload '+' => \&add,
    '-' => \&subtract,
```

```perl
        '""' => \&myprint;
    %_numeral_to_num = (
        'i' => 1,
        'ii' => 2,
        'iii' => 3,
        'iv' => 4,
        'v' => 5,
        'vi' => 6,
        'vii' => 7,
        'viii' => 8,
        'ix' => 9,
        'x' => 10,
    );

    @_num_to_numeral = ( undef, 'i', 'ii', 'iii', 'iv', 'v', 'vi', 'vii',
        'viii', 'ix', 'x' );
    sub new {
        my $class = shift;
        my $num = shift;
        my $numeral = \$num;
        bless $numeral, $class;
        return $numeral;
    }

    sub add {
        my $numeral = shift;
        my $toadd = shift;
        my $ret = $_num_to_numeral[$_numeral_to_num{$$numeral}
 *      $_numeral_to_num{$$toadd}];
        my $ref = \$ret;
        bless $ref;
    }

    sub subtract {
        my ($numeral, $tosub, $reverse) = @_;
        my ($ret);
        if ( $reverse ) {
            $ret = $_num_to_numeral[$_numeral_to_num{$$tosub} -
```

```
        $_numeral_to_num{$$numeral}];
    } else {
      $ret = $_num_to_numeral[$_numeral_to_num{$$numeral} -
        $_numeral_to_num{$$tosub}];
    }
    my $ref = \$ret;
    bless $ref;
}

sub myprint {
my $numeral = shift;
return $$numeral;
}


1;
```

The second example makes use of the Roman numeral package and performs a few tests with it. I will add the current directory to the include search path (the @INC variable), which is where the Roman.pm file is located:

```
BEGIN { unshift(@INC, "."); }
use Roman;
# create two new Roman numeral objects
$num = new Roman "ii";
$num2 = new Roman "iii";
# add the two numerals to create a third
# and display it.  It should be 'v'
$num3 = $num + $num2;
print "$num3\n";
$num4 = $num3 + $num2;
print "$num4\n";

# now subtract to numerals
# the answer should be 'vi'
$num5 = $num4 - $num;
print "$num5\n";
# let the module automatically generate a method
# for -= based on the - method.
# this answer should be 'iv'
$num5 -= $num;
print "$num5\n";
```

POSIX

Functions   See the table in the Usage section

Variables   See the table in the Usage section

Syntax   `use POSIX;`

`use POSIX ();`

`use POSIX` *symbollist*`;`

`use POSIX` *taglist*`;`

Usage   The *POSIX* module gives you access to almost all of the POSIX 1003.1 standard identifiers. Constants that would be #defines in C are exported into your namespace. The functions are only exported if you explicitly import them (by not passing a list of functions to the use POSIX command). It is generally easier to use the fully qualified package names for these functions.

The functions described in the following table are broken down into three sections: unavailable functions (with alternate functions listed), functions that mimic C or Perl functions, and unique functions that provided extended functionality.

Unavailable POSIX Functions

These functions aren't implemented because for the most part they're specific to C.

Function	Description	Perl Alternative
atexit	C-specific	END { }
atof	C-specific	
atoi	C-specific	
atol	C-specific	
bsearch	Not supplied	associative array (hash table)
calloc	C-specific	
clearerr		FileHandle::clearerr
div	C-specific	
execl	C-specific	exec
execle	C-specific	exec
execlp	C-specific	exec
execv	C-specific	exec
execve	C-specific	exec
fclose		FileHandle::close
fdopen		FileHandle::new_from_fd
feof		FileHandle::eof

Function	Description	Perl Alternative
ferror		FileHandle:error
fflush		FileHandle::flush
fgetc		FileHandle::getc
fgetpos		FileHandle:getpos
fgets		FileHandle:gets
fileno		FileHandle::fileno
fopen		FileHandle::open
fprintf	C-specific	printf
fputc	C-specific	print
fputs	C-specific	print
fread	C-specific	read
free	C-specific	
freopen	C-specific	open
fscanf	C-specific	<> and regular expressions
fseek		FileHandle:seek
fsetpos		FileHandle::setpos
ftell		FileHandle::tell
fwrite	C-specific	print
labs	C-specific	abs
ldiv	C-specific	/ and int
longjmp	C-specific	die
malloc	C-specific	
memchr	C-specific	index
memcmp	C-specific	eq
memcpy	C-specific	=
memmove	C-specific	=
memset	C-specific	x
offsetof	C-specific	
putchar	C-specific	print
puts	C-specific	print
qsort	C-specific	sort
rand	Not portable	rand
realloc	C-specific	
scanf	C-specific	<> and regular expressions
setjmp	C-specific	eval
siglongjmp	C-specific	die
sigsetjmp	C-specific	eval
sscanf	C-specific	regular expressions
strcat	C-specific	.=
strchr	C-specific	index
strcmp	C-specific	eq

Function	Description	Perl Alternative
strcpy	C-specific	=
strcspn	C-specific	regular expressions
strlen	C-specific	length
strncat	C-specific	.= and/or substr
strncmp	C-specific	eq and/or substr
strncpy	C-specific	= and/or substr
strpbrk	C-specific	
strrchr	C-specific	rindex and/or substr
strspn	C-specific	
strtod	C-specific	
strtok	C-specific	
strtol	C-specific	
strtoul	C-specific	
tmpfile		FileHandle::new_tmpfile
ungetc		FileHandle::ungetc
vfprintf	C-specific	
vprintf	C-specific	
vsprintf	C-specific	

Mimic Functions

The mimic functions are identical to Perl or C functions of the same name (if not, the name is specified in the Notes column). See your system documentation or the Perl function description for more information on these functions.

Function	Perl/C	Notes
_exit	C	
abort	C	
abs	Perl	
acos	C	
alarm	Perl	
asctime	C	
asin	C	
assert	C	In C, this is a macro.
atan	C	
atan2	Perl	
ceil	C	
chdir	Perl	
chmod	Perl	
chown	Perl	

Function	Perl/C	Notes
clock	C	
closedir	Perl	
cos	Perl	
cosh	C	
ctime	C	
difftime	C	
dup	C	Uses file descriptors returned from POSIX::open(). Returns undef when it fails.
dub2	C	Uses file descriptors returned from POSIX::open(). Returns undef when it fails.
exit	Perl	
exp	Perl	
fabs	Perl	abs
fcntl	Perl	
floor	C	
fmod	C	
fork	Perl	
fstat	Perl	Uses file descriptors returned from POSIX::open(). The data returned is the same as the data returned from the Perl stat function.
getc	Perl	
getgrid	Perl	
getgrnam	Perl	
getlogin	Perl	
getpgrp	Perl	
getppid	Perl	
getpwnam	Perl	
getpwuid	Perl	
gmtime	Perl	
isalnum	C	Can apply to a single character or an entire string. To return true, all the characters of the string must match the criteria.
isalpha	C	Can apply to a single character or an entire string.
iscntrl	C	Can apply to a single character or an entire string.
isdigit	C	Can apply to a single character or an entire string.
isgraph	C	Can apply to a single character or an entire string.
islower	C	Can apply to a single character or an entire string.
isprint	C	Can apply to a single character or an entire string.
ispunct	C	Can apply to a single character or an entire string.
isspace	C	Can apply to a single character or an entire string.
isupper	C	Can apply to a single character or an entire string.
isxdigit	C	Can apply to a single character or an entire string.

Function	Perl/C	Notes
kill	Perl	
ldexp	C	
link	Perl	
localtime	Perl	
log	Perl	
log10	C	
lseek	Perl	Uses file descriptors returned from POSIX::open(). This function is similar to the Perl seek function. It returns undef when it fails.
mblen	C	
mbstowcs	C	
mbtowc	C	
mkdir	Perl	
mkfifo	C	Returns undef when it fails.
nice	C	Returns undef when it fails.
opendir	Perl	
pause	C	Returns undef when it fails.
perror	C	
pipe	Perl	Returns two file descriptors (like those returned from POSIX::open) instead of file handles.
printf	Perl	
readdir	Perl	
remove	Perl	unlink
rename	Perl	
rewinddir	Perl	
rmdir	Perl	
setpgid	C	Returns undef when it fails.
setsid	C	
sigaction	C	Uses POSIX::SigAction objects for the signal actions passed to this function.
sigset	C	Uses POSIX::SigSet objects for arguments to this function. It returns undef when it fails.
sigprocmask	C	Uses POSIX::SigSet objects for arguments to this function. It returns undef when it fails.
sigsuspend	C	Uses POSIX::SigSet objects for arguments to this function. It returns undef when it fails.
sin	Perl	
sinh	C	
sleep	Perl	
sprintf	Perl	
sqrt	Perl	

Function	Perl/C	Notes
srand	Perl	
stat	Perl	
strcoll	C	
strstr	Perl	index
strxfrm	C	Returns the transformed string instead of taking the destination as an argument.
sysconf	C	
system	Perl	
tan	C	
tanh	C	
tcdrain	C	Returns undef when it fails.
tcflow	C	Returns undef when it fails.
tcflush	C	Returns undef when it fails.
tcgetpgrp	C	
tcsendbreak	C	Returns undef when it fails.
tcsetpgrp	C	Returns undef when it fails.
time	Perl	
tolower	Perl	lc
toupper	Perl	uc
ttyname	C	
tzset	C	
umask	Perl	
unlink	Perl	
utime	Perl	
wait	Perl	
waitpid	Perl	
wcstombs	C	
wctomb	C	

Unique Functions

These functions aren't necessarily unique to the POSIX module, but they have their own description relative to this module.

Function	Syntax/Description
access	POSIX::access(*file, mode*); Determines if the specified mode is accessible on the specified file.
close	POSIX::close(*filedescriptor*); Closes a file. The *filedescriptor* is what was returned from calling POSIX::open. It returns undef when it fails.

➡

Function	Syntax/Description
creat	*filedescriptor* = POSIX::creat(*filename, mode*); Creates a new file and returns an open file descriptor for it. This file descriptor is the same as the file descriptor returned from a POSIX::open call.
ctermid	*path* = POSIX::ctermid(); Returns the path to the controlling terminal of the current process.
cuserid	*usename* = POSIX:cuserid(); Returns the login name of the user running the process.
errno	*errno* = POSIX::errno(); Returns the current value of errno.
fpathconf	*value* = POSIX::fpathconf(*filedescriptor, option*); Returns the value of the current configurable limit or returns the option associated with a file or directory. The *filedescriptor* is one like those returned from POSIX::open. The possible options are (possibly need to be preceded by POSIX::) _PC_LINK_MAX, _PC_MAX_CANNON, _PC_MAX_INPUT, _PC_NAME_MAX, _PC_PATH_MAX, _PC_PIPE_BUF, _PC_CHOWN_RESTRICTED, _PC_NO_TRUNC, _PC_VDISABLE, _PC_ASYNC_IO, _PC_PRIO_IO, and _PC_SYNC_IO. See the fpathconf system call for more information.
frexp	(*mantissa, exponent*) = POSIX::frexp(*float*); Returns the mantissa and exponent of a floating point number in an array context.
getchar	*char* = POSIX::getchar(); Returns the next character available from STDIN.
getcwd	*dir* = POSIX::getcwd(); Returns the current working directory of the process. See also the Cwd bundled module.
getegid	*gid* = POSIX::getegid(); Returns the effective group id of the process running the script.
getenv	*value* = POSIX::getenv(*variable*); Returns the value of the requested environment variable.
geteuid	*uid* = POSIX::geteuid(); Returns the effective user id of the process running the script.
getgid	*gid* = POSIX::getgid(); Returns the group id of the process running the script.
getgroups	*groups* = POSIX::getgroups(); Returns a list of group ids of which the current user is a member.
getpid	*pid* = POSIX::getpid(); Returns the process ID of the current running script.
gets	*line* = POSIX::gets(); Returns the next line available from STDIN.
getuid	*uid* = POSIX::getuid(); Returns the user id of the process running the script.

Function	Syntax/Description
localeconv	*hashref* = POSIX::localeconv(); Returns a reference to an associative array that holds the current locale formatting information. The following keys are available in the array: decimal_point, thousands_sep, grouping, int_curr_symbol, currency_symbol, mon_decimal_point, mon_thousands_sep, mon_grouping, positive_sign, negative_sign, int_frac_digits, frac_digits, p_cs_precedes, p_sep_by_space, n_cs_precedes, n_sep_by_space, p_sign_posn, n_sign_posn. See your system information on localeconv and setlocale.
mktime	*time* = POSIX::mktime(*sec, min, hour, mday, mon, year, wday, yday, isdst*); Takes a list of integers representing a day and time and converts it into seconds since the epoch. The mon, wday, and yday fields all begin at 0 instead of 1. Years are given in years since 1900. See your system information on mktime for more information.
modf	(*fractional, integral*) = POSIX::modf(*float*); Returns the fractional and integral part of a floating point number. It returns an array context.
open	*filedescriptor* = POSIX::open(*filename*[, *flags*[,*mode*]]); Opens a file with the specified flags. The possible flags are listed in the file control constants in the following constants table. You can 'or' these flags together like O_CREATE	O_RDWR to apply multiple flags to the descriptor. The mode can be set like the possible argument to chmod. It returns the file descriptor or undef when it fails.
pathconf	*value* = POSIX::pathconf(*filename, option*); Returns the value of the current configurable limit or option associated with a file or directory. The possible options are listed in the Pathname constants section of the following constants table. See the pathconf system call for more information.
pow	*value* = pow(*num, exponent*); Returns *num* to the power of *exponent*.
read	*length* = POSIX::read(*filedescriptor, buffer, size*); Reads *size* bytes into *buffer* from the *filedescriptor*. The file descriptor is like those returned from a POSIX::open call. If the buffer isn't big enough, Perl will extend it. It returns the number of bytes read when it succeeds and undef when it fails.
setlocale	*locale* = POSIX::setlocale(*category, locale*); Modifies and queries the program's locale. See your system documentation for more information.
setuid	POSIX::setuid(*uid*); Sets the real user id of the current process.
strftime	POSIX::strftime(*format, sec, min, hour, mday, mon, year*[, *wday, yday, isdst*]); Converts date and time information into a readable string. See also the mktime function. Read your system information on strftime to find out about the possible formats for this function.

Function	Syntax/Description
times	(*realtime, usertime, systemtime, childusertime, childsystemtime*) = POSIX::times(); Returns the elapsed times since some point in the past (usually the system startup).The times returned are real-time, user time for this process, system time for this process, user time for child processes, and system time for child processes. Perl's times function only returns four values (it doesn't include real-time).
tmpnam	*tmpfile* = POSIX::tmpnam(); Returns a name for a temporary file.
tzname	(*standard, daylight_savings*) = POSIX::tzname(); Returns the current time conversion information in an array context.
uname	(*systemname, nodename, release, version, machine*) = POSIX::uname(): Returns information about the operating system.
write	*bytes* = POSIX::write(*filedescriptor, buffer, length*); Writes the *buffer* of *length* bytes to filedescriptor (which was opened by a call like POSIX::open) and returns the number of bytes written. It returns undef when it fails.

The following table lists in logical groups the constants included with the POSIX module.

Grouping	Constants
Error	E2BIG, EACCESS, EAGAIN, EBADF, EBUSY, ECHILD, EDEADLK, EDOM, EEXIST, EFAUL, EFBIG, EINTR, EINVAL, EIO, EISDIR, EMFILE, EMLINK, ENAMETOOLONG, ENFILE, ENODE, ENOENT, ENOEXEC, ENOLCK, ENOMEM, ENOSPC, ENOSYS, ENOTDIR, ENOTEMPTY, ENOTTY, ENXIO, EPERM, EPIPE, ERANGE, EROFS, ESPIPE, ESRCH, EXDEV
File Control	FD_CLOEXEC, F_DUPFD, F_GETFD, F_GETFL, F_GETLK, F_OK, F_RDLCK, F_SETFD, F_SETFL, F_SETLK, F_SETLKW, F_UNLCK, F_WRLCK, O_ACCMODE, O_APPEND, O_CREAT, O_EXCL, O_NOCTTY, O_NONBLOCK, O_RDONLY, O_RDWR, O_TRUNC, O_WRONLY
Floating-Point	DBL_DIG, DBL_EPSILON, DBL_MANT_DIG, DBL_MAX, DBL_MAX_10_EXP, DBL_MAX_EXP, DBL_MIN, DBM_MIN_10_EXP, DBL_MIN_EXP, FLT_DIG, DLT_EPISILON, FLT_MANT_DIG, FLT_MAX, FLT_MAX_10_EXP, FLT_MAX_EXP, FLT_MIN, FLT_MIN_10_EXP, FLT_MIN_EXP, FLT_RADIX, FLT_ROUNDS, LDBL_DIG, LDBL_EPSILON, LDBL_MANT_DIG, LDBL_MAX, LDBL_MAX_10_EXP, LDBL_MAX_EXP, LDBL_MIN, LDBL_MIN_10_EXP, LDBL_MIN_EXP

Grouping	Constants
Limit	ARG_MAX, CHAR_BIT, CHAR_MAX, CHAR_MIN, CHILD_MAX, INT_MAX, INT_MIN, LINK_MAX, LONG_MAX, LONG_MIN, MAX_CANON, MAX_INPUT, MB_LEN_MAX, NAME_MAX, NGROUPS_MAX, OPEN_MAX, PATH_MAX, PIPE_BUF, SCHAR_MAX, SCHAR_MIN, SHRT_MAX, SHRT_MIN, SSIZE_MAX, STREAM_MAX, TZNAME_MAX, UCHAR_MAX, UINT_MAX, ULONG_MAX USHRT_MAX
Locale	LC_ALL, LC_COLLATE, LC_CTYPE, LC_MONETARY, LC_NUMERIC, LC_TIME
Math	HUGE_VAL
Pathname	_PC_CHOWN_RESTRICTED, _PC_LINK_MAX, _PC_MAX_CANON, _PC_MAX_INPUT, _PC_NAME_MAX, _PC_NO_TRUNC, _PC_PATH_MAX, _PC_PIPE_BUF, _PC_VDISABLE
POSIX	_POSIX_ARG_MAX, _POSIX_CHILD_MAX, _POSIX_CHOWN_RESTRICTED, _POSIX_JOB_CONTROL, _POSIX_LINK_MAX, _POSIX_MAX_CANON, _POSIX_MAX_INPUT, _POSIX_NAME_MAX, _POSIX_NGROUPS_MAX, _POSIX_NO_TRUNC, _POSIX_OPEN_MAX, _POSIX_PATH_MAX, _POSIX_PIPE_BUF, _POSIX_SAVED_IDS, _POSIX_SSIZE_MAX, _POSIX_STREAM_MAX, _POSIX_TZNAME_MAX, _POSIX_VDISABLE, _POSIX_VERSION
Signal	SA-NOCLDSTOP, SIGABRT, SIGALRM, SIGCHLD, SIGCONT, SIGFPE, SIGHUP, SIGILL, SIGINT, SIGKILL, SIGPIPE, SIGQUIT, SIGSEGV, SIGSTOP, SIGTERM, SIGTSTP, SIGTTIN, SIGTTOU, SIGUSR1, SIGUSR2, SIG_BLOCK, SIG_DFL, SIG_ERR, SIG_IGN, SIG_SETMASK, SIG_UNBLOCK
Stat	S_IRGRP, S_IROTH, S_RUSR, S_IRWXG, S_IRWXO, S_IRWXU, S_ISGID, S_ISUID, S_IWGRP, S_IWOTH, S_IWUSR, S_IXGRP, S_IXOTH, S_IXUSR
Stat Macros	S_ISBLK, S_ISCHR, S_ISDIR, S_ISFIFO, S_ISREG
Stdio	BUFSIZ, EOF, FILENAME_MAX, L_ctermid, L_cuserid, L_tmpname, TMP_MAX
Stdlib	EXIT_FAILURE, EXIT_SUCCESS, MB_CUR_MAX, RAND_MAX
System Configuration	_SC_ARG_MAX, _SC_CHILD_MAX, _SC_CLK_TCK, _SC_JOB_CONTROL, _SC_NGROUPS_MAX, _SC_OPEN_AMX, _SC_SAVED_IDS, _SC_STREAM_MAX, _SC_TZNAME_MAX, _SC_VERSION
Time	CLK_TCK, CLOCKS_PER_SEC
Unistd	R_OK, SEEK_CUR, SEEK_END, SEEK_SET, STDIN_FILENO, STDOUT_FILENO, STDERR_FILENO, W_OK, X_OK
Wait	WNOHANG, WUNTRACED
Wait Macros	WIFEXITED, WEXITSTATUS, WIFSIGNALED, WTERMSIG, WIFSTOPEED, WSTOPSIG

The following table lists the tags you can use when importing sets of POSIX functions.

Tag	Symbols
:assert_h	assert, NDEBUG
:ctype_h	isalnum, isalpha, iscntrl, isdigit, isgraph, islower, isprint, ispuncy, isspace, isupper, isxdigit, tolower, toupper
:errno_h	E2BIG, EACCES, EAGAIN, EBADF, EBUSY, ECHILD, EDEADLK, EDOM, EEXIST, EFAULT, EFBIG, EINTR, EINVAL, EIO, EISDIR, EMFILE, EMLINK, ENAMETOOLONG, ENFILE, ENODEV, ENOENT, ENOEXEC, ENOLCK, ENOMEM, ENOSPC, ENOSYS, ENOTDIR, ENOTEMPTY, ENOTTY, ENXIO, EPERM, EPIPE, ERANGE, EROFS, ESPIPE, ESRCH, EXDEV, errno
:fcntl_h	FD_CLOEXEC, F_DUPFD, F_GETFD, F_GETFL, F_GETLK, F_RDLCK, F_SETFD, F_SETFL, F_SETLK, F_SETLKW, F_UNLCK, F_WRLCK, O_ACCMODE, O_APPEND, O_CREAT, O_EXCL, O_NOCTTY, O_NONBLOCK, O_RDONLY, O_RDWR, O_TRUNC, O_WRONLY, creat, SEEK_CUR, SEEK_END, SEEK_SET, S_IRGRP, S_IROTH, S_IRUSR, S_IRWXG, S_IRWXO, S_IRWXU, S_ISBLK, S_ISCHR, S_ISDIR, S_ISFIFO, S_ISGID, S_ISREG, S_ISUID, S_IWGRP, S_IWOTH, S_IWUSR
:float_h	DBL_DIG, DBL_EPSILON, DBL_MANT_DIG, DBL_MAX, DBL_MAX_10_EXP, DBL_MAX_EXP, DBL_MIN, DBL_MIN_10_EXP, DBL_MIN_EXP, FLT_DIG, FLT_EPSILON, FLT_MANT_DIG, FLT_MAX, FLT_MAX_10_EXP, FLT_MAX_EXP, FLT_MIN, FLT_MIN_10_EXP, FLT_MIN_EXP, FLT_RADIX, FLT_ROUNDS, LDBL_DIG, LDBL_EPSILON, LDBL_MANT_DIG, LDBL_MAX, LDBL_MAX_10_EXP, LDBL_MAX_EXP, LDBL_MIN, LDBL_MIN_10_EXP, LDBL_MIN_EXP
:limits_h	ARG_MAX, CHAR_BIT, CHAR_MAX, CHAR_MIN, CHILD_MAX, INT_MAX, INT_MIN, LINK_MAX, LONG_MAX, LONG_MIN, MAX_CANON, MAX_INPUT, MB_LEN_MAX, NAME_MAX, NGROUPS_MAX, OPEN_MAX, PATH_MAX, PIPE_BUF, SCHAR_MAX, SCHAR_MIN, SHRT_MAX, SHRT_MIN, SSIZE_MAX, STREAM_MAX, TZNAME_MAX, UCHAR_MAX, UINT_MAX, ULONG_MAX, USHRT_MAX, _POSIX_ARG_MAX, _POSIX_CHILD_MAX, _POSIX_LINK_MAX, _POSIX_MAX_CANON, _POSIX_MAX_INPUT, _POSIX_NAME_MAX, _POSIX_NGROUPS_MAX, _POSIX_OPEN_MAX, _POSIX_PATH_MAX, _POSIX_PIPE_BUF, _POSIX_SSIZE_MAX, _POSIX_STREADM_MAX, _POSIX_TZNAME_MAX
:locale_h	LC_ALL, LC_COLLATE, LC_CTYPE, LC_MONETARY, LC_NUMERIC, LC_TIME, NULL, localeconv, setlocale
:math_h	HUGE_VAL, acos, asin, atan, ceil, cosh, fabs, floor, fmod, frexp, ldexp, log10, modf, pow, sinh, tan, tanh
:setjmp_h	longjmp, setjmp, siglongjmp, sigsetjmp
:signal_h	SA_NOCLDSTOP, SIGABRT, SIGALRM, SIGCHLD, SIGCONT, SIGFPE, SIGHUP, SIGILL, SIGINT, SIGKILL, SIGPIPE, SIGQUIT, SIGSEGV, SIGSTOP, SIGTERM, SIGTSTP, SIGTTIN, SIGTTOU, SIGUSR1, SIGUSR2, SIG_BLOCK, SIG_DFL, SIG_ERR, SIG_IGN, SIG_SETMASK, SIG_UNBLOCK, raise, sigaction, signal, sigpending, sigprocmask, sigsuspend

Tag	Symbols
:stddef_h	NULL, offsetof
:stdio_h	BUFSIZ, EOF, FILENAME_MAX, L_ctermid, L_cuserid, L_tmpname, NULL, SEEK_CUR, SEEK_END, SEEK_SET, STREAM_MAX, TMP_MAX, stderr, stdin, stdout, clearerr, fclose, fdopen, feof, ferror, fflush, fgetc, fgetpos, fgets, fopen, fprintf, fputc, fputs, fread, freopen, fscanf, fseek, fsetpos, ftell, fwrite, getchar, gets, perror, putc, putchar, puts, remove, rewind, scanf, setbuf, setvbuf, sscanf, tmpfile, tmpnam, ungetc, vfprintf, vprintf, vsprintf
:stdlib_h	EXIT_FAILURE, EXIT_SUCCESS, MB_CUR_MAX, NULL, RAND_MAX, abort, atexit, atof, atoi, atol, bsearch, calloc, div, free, getenv, labs, ldiv, malloc, mblen, mbstowcs, mbtowc, qsort, realloc, strtod, strtol, stroul, wcstombs, wctomb
:string_h	NULL, memchr, memcmp, memcpy, memmove, memset, strcat, strchr, strcmp, strcoll, strcpy, strcspn, strerror, strlen, strncat, strncmp, strncpy, strpbrk, strrchr, strspn, strstr, strtok, strxfrm
:sys_stat_h	S_IRGRP, S_IROTH, S_IRUSR, S_IRWXG, S_IRWXO, S_IRWXU, S_ISBLK, S_ISCHR, S_ISDIR, S_ISFIFO, S_ISGID, S_ISREG, S_ISUID, S_IWGRP, S_IWOTH, S_IWUSR, S_IXGRP, S_IXOTH, S_IXUSR, fstat, mkfifo
:sys_utsname_h	uname
:sys_wait_h	WEXITSTATUS, WIFEXITED, WIFSIGNALED, WIFSTOPPED, WNOHANG, WSTOPSIG, WTERMSIG, WUNTRACED
:termios_h	B0, B110, B1200, B134, B150, B1800, B19200, B200, B2400, B300, B38400, B4800, B50, B600, B75, B9600, BRKINT, CLOCAL, CREAD, CS5, CS6, CS7, CS8, CSIZE, CSTOPB, ECHO, ECHOE, ECHOK, ECHONL, HUPCL, ICANON, ICRNL, IEXTEN, IGNBRK, IGNCR, IGNPAR, INLCR, INPCK, ISIG, ISTRIP, IXOFF, IXON, NCCS, NOFLSH, OPOST, PARENB, PARMRK, PARODD, TCIFLUSH, TCIOFF, TCIOFLUSH, TCION, TCOFLUSH, TCOOFF, TCOON, TCSADRAIN, TCSAFLUSH, TCSANOW, TOSTOP, VEOF, VEOL, VERASE, VINTR, VKILL, VMIN, VQUIT, VSTART, VSTOP, VSUSP, VTIME, cfgetispeed, cfgetospeed, cfsetispeed, cfsetospeed, tcdrain, tcflow, tcflush, tcgetattr, tcsendbreak, tcsetattr
:time_h	CLK_TCK, CLOCKS_PER_SEC, NULL, asctime, clock, ctime, difftime, mktime, strftime, tzset, tzname
:unistd_h	F_OK, NULL, R_OK, SEEK_CUR, SEEK_END, SEEK_SET, STRERR_FILENO, STDIN_FILENO, STDOUT_FILENO, W_OK, X_OK, _PC_CHOWN_RESTRICTED, _PC_LINK_MAX, _PC_MAX_CANON, _PC_MAX_INPUT, _PC_NAME_MAX, _PC_NO_TRUNC, _PC_PATH_MAX, _PC_PIPE_BUF, _PC_VDISABLE, _POSIX_CHOWN_RESTRICTED, _POSIX_JOB_CONTROL, _POSIX_NO_TRUNC, _POSIX_SAVED_IDS, _POSIX_VDISABLE, _POSIX_VERSION, _SC_ARG_MAX, _SC_CHILD_MAX, _SC_CLK_TCK, _SC_JOB_CONTROL, _SC_NGROUPS_MAX, _SC_OPEN_MAX, _SC_SAVED_IDS, _SC_STREAM_MAX, _SC_TZNAME_MAX, _SC_VERSION, _exit, access, ctermid, cuserid, dup2, dup, execl, execle, execlp, execv, execve, execvp, fpathconf, getcwd, getegid, geteuid, getgid, getgroups, getpid, getuid, isatty, lseek, pathconf, pause, setgid, setpgid, setsid, setuid, sysconf, tcgetpgrp, tcsetpgrp, ttyname

Safe

Functions deny, deny_only, mask, new, permit, permit_only, rdo, reval, root, share, share_from, trap, untrap, varglob

Syntax

```
use Safe;
```

```
$net = new Safe;
```

```
$net->deny(oplist);
```

```
$net->deny_only(oplist);
```

```
$net->mask(mask);
```

```
$net->permit(oplist);
```

```
$net->permit_only(oplist);
```

```
$net->rdo(file);
```

```
$net->reval(string);
```

```
$net->root;
```

```
$net->share(varlist);
```

```
$net->share_from(package, arrayref);
```

```
$net->trap(oplist);
```

```
$net->untrap(oplist);
```

```
$net->varglob(var);
```

Usage The *Safe* module lets you create a safety net or compartment where you can safely evaluate Perl code. This safety net has its own namespace, and variables outside this namespace cannot be accessed. Code outside the net can share variables into the net. The only default variables shared with the net are $_, @_, %_, and _.

Each safety net created has an opmask associated with it. Whenever you compile Perl code, either through eval or do 'file' within a net, it will be subject to the net's opmask. If it tries to access a masked operator, then it will fail. By default the opmask is the :default optag. See the Opcode module to find out what opcodes this optag includes.

The new method creates a new safety net. You can pass an optional namespace to be used for the net. If you don't specify one, it will default to Safe::Root0 and be incremented with each new net. You cannot pass a mask to the new method as with earlier versions of Safe.

The deny method takes a list of opcodes (which can be an optag) and doesn't allow those opcodes to be used within the current net. Any other operators may still be allowed. The deny_only method causes only the listed operators to be denied; all others will be allowed. The trap method is the same as the deny method.

The mask method returns the current mask of the net if no argument is passed. If a *mask* is passed to it, then that mask will be set as the operator mask for the net. In this case, it is similar to the deny_only method.

The permit method takes a list of opcodes and allows them to be used within the net in addition to any other opcodes that are already allowed. The permit_only method only allows those operators to be used; all others will be denied. The untrap method is the same as the permit method.

The rdo evaluates the contents of the file passed to it inside the safety net. The contents of the file are subject to the same constraints as a string passed to the reval method. The code can only see in the net's namespace, which will appear as the main:: package within the code. Any disallowed code that tries to be compiled will cause a compile-time error. If this happens, the code will not be executed and $@ is set to the error message.

If you allow the entereval operator within your safety net, you open up possible security holes. The code being evaluated could call its own eval method to hide using operators that are denied. When the code tries to execute, it will still fail, but it lets the code see what is allowed, which may be potentially harmful.

The root method returns the name of the package that is the root of the net's namespace. This does not allow you to change the namespace as with earlier versions of Safe.

The share method allows you to share variables into the net. The variables must be passed with their identifier (i.e., '$var'). These variables are assumed to be in the package calling this method. The share_from method is similar to share except it takes a package name and an array reference of the names of the variables to be shared, that is:

```
$net->share_from('myPackage', [ '$myvar', '@myarr' ]);
```

The varglob method returns a reference to the symbol table entry of the variable passed to it in the net's package. This allows you to access the qualified name of the variable without having to know the name of the net's package.

Examples The following example creates a safety net and then tries to compile code that won't be allowed. The code to allow the reval method to work is commented out. The code simply tries to run a command on the system:

```
use Safe;

$net = new Safe;
# $net->permit(:subprocess);
$net->reval(system('who'));
```

See Also Opcode

SDBM_File

MODULE

Syntax
```
use SDBM_File;
tie %var, "SDBM_File", filename, mode, permissions;
$var{key} = value;
untie %var;
```

Usage
The *SDBM_File* module allows you to access a simple database. You use the tie function to tie an associative array to the database. When you access or modify a key of the associative array, it reads from or writes to the database file. The SDBM_File module isn't the best database manager to use, but it's available on any system that supports Perl. If you want to guarantee portability, then you should use this module.

Examples
The following example shows how to create a simple database file and read from and write to it:

```
use SDBM_File;
tie %data, "SDBM_File", "phone", O_CREAT|O_RDWR, 0644;
$data{'Terry} = "555-1234";
$data{'Nancy'} = "555-4321";
$data{'Fred'} = "555-5858";
while ( ( $name, $number ) = each %data ) {
   print "$name = $number\n";
}
untie %data;
```

See Also
Modules: AnyDBM_File
Functions:tie

Shell

MODULE

Functions
cat, cp, echo, ps

Syntax
```
use Shell;

$filetext = cat("filename.txt");

cp("file1", "file2");

$var = echo("one", "two");

sub ps;

$var = ps;
```

Usage   The *Shell* module allows you access to a few shell commands directly from Perl. This saves you from having to use a system call or from having to use the backtick to run the program.

The cat method will return the contents of the list of files passed to it. The cp method will copy one file to another. The echo command will return the list of arguments passed to it as a string joined by spaces and ending with a new line. The ps command will give a process list of the processes running on your machine.

Examples   The following script makes use of the Shell functions:

```
use Shell;
$contents = cat("myfile.txt");
print $contents;
cp("myfile.txt", "newfile.txt");
$var = echo("one", "two");
print $var; # displays "one two\n";
sub ps;
print ps;
```

sigtrap
PRAGMA

Syntax   `use sigtrap;`

`use sigtrap @arr;`

Usage   The *sigtrap* pragma enables default signal handlers for the list of signals you pass to it. If you don't pass an argument, the following signals will be handled automatically: ABRT, BUS, EMT, FPE, ILL, PIPE, QUIT, SEGV, SYS, TERM, and TRAP.

The default signal handler it uses will print a stack dump of the Perl program and then send itself a SIGABRT.

After you import the signal handlers, you can override any of them by setting the appropriate handler in the %SIG array.

Examples   Run the following program and then send it one of the signals listed in the Usage section to see this pragma's affect. The QUIT signal has been overridden to be ignored instead of handled by the sigtrap pragma:

```
use sigtrap;
$SIG(QUIT} = "noquit";

$var = <STDIN>;
sub noquit {
   print "Ignoring SIGQUIT\n";
}
```

See Also   The special variable %SIG

Socket

Functions INADDR_ANY, INADDR_LOOPBACK, INADDR_NONE, inet_aton, inet_ntoa, pack_sockaddr_in, pack_sockaddr_un, sockaddr_in, sockaddr_un, unpack_sockaddr_in, unapck_sockaddr_un

Syntax
```
use Socket;

$ip = INADDR_ANY;

$ip = INADDR_LOOPBACK;

$ip = INADDR_NONE;

$ip = inet_aton $hostname;

$hostname = inet_ntoa $ip;

$sockAddr_in = pack_sockaddr_in $port, $ip;

$sockAddr_un = pack_sockaddr_un $path;

($port, $ip) = sockaddr_in $sockAddr_in;

$sockAddr_in = sockaddr_in $port, $ip;

$path = sockaddr_un $sockAddr_un;

$sockAddr_un = sockaddr_un $path;

($port, $ip) = unpack_sockaddr_in $sockAddr_in;

$path = unpack_sockaddr_un $sockAddr_un;
```

Usage The *Socket* module is a translation of the C socket.h include file. It adds the common constants like AF_INET, PF_INET, and SOCK_STREAM to your Perl script so you can use them in your socket calls. The functions included in this module are there to aid in working with the structures associated with socket calls.

The inet_aton method takes a hostname or IP address string as an argument ("**Error! Bookmark not defined.**" or '199.72.13.1') and turns it into a packed 4-byte string. If the hostname can't be resolved, it returns an undefined value. The inet_ntoa method does the opposite of this function. It takes a packed 4-byte structure and returns a string representing the IP address.

The INADDR_ANY method returns a packed string IP address for the host on which the script is running. If a machine has more than one IP address, this method will allow you to affect all of them. It is generally the same as inet_aton('0.0.0.0'). The INADDR_LOOPBACK method returns a packed string representing the loopback address of the host running the script. It is generally the same as inet_aton('localhost'). The INADDR_NONE method returns a packed string representing an invalid IP address. It is generally the same as inet_aton('255.255.255.255').

The functions sockaddr_in, pack_sockaddr_in, and unpack_sockaddr_in are used to convert between an IP address/port pair and a socket address (SOCKADDR_IN structure). The pack_sockaddr_in method takes a port and IP address (the packed string) and returns a socket address. The unpack_sockaddr_in method takes a socket address and returns an array of the port and IP address. The sockaddr_in method works the same as these two functions, depending on its context. If it's returning an array, it will accept a socket address and return the port and IP address like unpack_sockaddr_in. If it's returning a scalar, it will accept a port and IP address and return a socket address.

The functions sockaddr_un, pack_sockaddr_un, and unpack_sockaddr_un work similarly to the sockaddr_in functions except they work on SOCKADDR_UN structures. They convert between a path and the SOCKADDR_UN structure.

Examples The first example creates a server listening on port 2468. See the Perl functions for more information on the socket functions used. Once you connect to this server, it prints a message and then shuts down:

```
Use Socket;
socket(SERVER, PF_INET, SOCK_STREAM, getprotobyname('tcp'));
bind(SERVER, sockaddr_in(3456, INADDR_ANY));
listen(SERVER, SOMAXCONN);
accept(CLIENT, SERVER);
print CLIENT "Welcome!\n";
close CLIENT;
```

The second example creates a client that will connect to the server in the first example and display any output it receives:

```
Use Socket;
$serverIP = inet_aton('your.hostname.com');
$serverAddr = sockaddr_in(3456, $serverIP);
socket(CLIENT, PF_INET, SOCK_STREAM, getprotobyname('tcp'));
connect(CLIENT, $serverAddr);
while ( <CLIENT> ) {
print;
}
```

See Also IO::Socket

strict

Syntax   use strict;

use strict *option*;

no strict;

no strict *option*;

Usage   The *strict* pragma restricts certain unsafe practices. There are three possible options you can pass when you use the strict pragma: refs, subs, and vars. If you don't specify a list to use, then all of them will be used.

The refs option causes a run-time error to occur if you use symbolic references that wouldn't occur normally.

The subs option causes a compile-time error to occur if you use a bareword identifier that isn't a subroutine unless it is within curly braces or to the left of a '=>' symbol.

The vars option causes a compile-time error to occur if you access a variable that isn't fully qualified or made local via *my*. (You can also use the vars pragma to allow certain variables.) Using local doesn't remove the restriction for that variable, however.

Examples   The following script shows where errors will occur using the strict pragma. The lines that would error are commented out:

```
use strict 'refs';
$var = "one";
$ref = \$var;
print $$ref, "\n";    # no error
$ref = "var";
#print $$ref, "\n";    # would cause a runtime error
no strict 'refs';
print $$ref, "\n";    # ok now
use strict 'subs';
#$SIG{INT} = ignore; # would cause a compile time error
$SIG{INT} = "ignore";# no error
no strict 'subs';
$SIG{INT} = ignore;    # ok now
use strict 'vars'
my $var = 1;           # ok
$main::var2 = 2;       # ok
#$var3 = 3;                 # would cause a compile time error
no strict 'vars';
$var3 = 3;             # ok now
```

See Also   vars

subs

Syntax   `use subs @arr;`

Usage   The *subs* pragma predeclares all the subroutines passed to it so that they can subsequently be called without using parentheses.

Examples   The following script predeclares its subroutines using the subs pragma and then calls them without using parentheses. The two subroutines print out the arguments passed to them, one to STDOUT and the other to STDERR:

```
Use subs "simpleOut", "simpleErr";
simpleOut "Here's", "some", "text.";
srand(time ^ $$);
$! = int(rand(10));
simpleErr "Random error:", $!;

sub simpleOut {
   print STDOUT join ( " ", @_), "\n";
}
sub simpleErr {
   print STDERR join ( " ", @_), "\n";
}
```

See Also   Functions: sub

Symbol

Functions   gensym, qualify, ungensym

Syntax   `use Symbol;`

`$symbol = gensym;`

`$var = qualify(var, [package]);`

`ungensym $symbol;`

Usage   The *Symbol* module is used to create anonymous globs and to determine the fully qualified names of variables. The gensym method creates an anonymous glob and returns a reference to it. That reference can then be used as a handle. The ungensym is only provided for backward compatibility and doesn't actually do anything.

The qualify method takes a variable name and an optional package name. If you leave out the package name, it will default to the current package. If you use a global variable name, it will also return with the 'main' package regardless of what you put for the second argument. The qualify method only modifies strings; if you pass a reference as the first argument, it simply returns it assuming it is already qualified.

Examples The first example uses an anonymous glob as a directory handle:

```
use Symbol;
$myDir = gensym;
opendir ($myDir, ".");
@files = readdir($myDir);
print "@files\n";
closedir ($myDir);
```

The second example shows what qualify returns in the various instances:

```
use Symbol;
$tmp = qualify("var");  # returns main::var
package myPackage;
$tmp = qualify("var");  # returns myPackage::var

$tmp = qualify("var", "aPkg");  # aPkg::var
$tmp = qualify("aPkg::var", "bPkg"); # aPkg::var
$tmp = qualify("ENV", "aPkg"); # main::ENV
$tmp = qualify(\$var);    # returns the reference to $var
$tmp = qualify(\$var, "aPkg") # same as previous
```

vars

Syntax use vars @arr;

Usage The *vars* pragma predeclares all the variables passed to it so that they can be used without generating any typo warnings when you're using the strict pragma.

Examples The following example uses the vars pragma to keep errors from happening when accessing variables while using the strict pragma. Normally, using variables this way would cause errors (see the strict pragma entry for more information):

```
Use strict 'vars';
Use vars '$one', '@two';

$one = "testing";
@two = ( '1', '2', '3' );
print "$one @two\n";
```

See Also strict

Optional Modules

This chapter covers a few of the optional modules that you can add to Perl. All these modules and many, many more can be found at any CPAN mirror. You can find a CPAN mirror by visiting http://www.perl.com/perl/CPAN. If you don't place a / after the URL then you will be given a choice of mirror sites. For a direct path, you can visit http://www.perl.com/perl/CPAN/CPAN.html.

From the CPAN mirror, you can find the module you're looking to download. Once you download it, there will be instructions for adding it to your Perl installation.

CGI

Functions append, delete, delete_all, header, import_names, keywords, new, param, query_string, redirect, save, self_url, url

Syntax
```
use CGI;

$query = new CGI ([datahash|FILE_VARIABLE|string]);

@keywords = $query->keywords;

@keys = $query->param;

value(s) = $query->param(key);

$query->param(key, valuelist);

$query->append(key, valuelist);

$query->import_names(namespace);

$query->delete(key);

$query->delete_all;

$query->save(FILE_VARIABLE);

$full_url = $query->self_url;

$url = $query->url;

$query_string = $query->query_string;

$header = $query->header;

$value = $query->header(heading);

$query->header(%hash);

$query->redirect(URL);
```

Usage The CGI module allows you to more easily create CGI scripts with Perl. This entry doesn't cover all the methods of the CGI module because there are so many, but it includes the most important ones for reading in data from an HTML form submitted to your Perl script. Most of the methods that are left out are methods that will return HTML tags with the parameters you pass them.

The new method will create a new query object either from a file handle, from an associative array, or from a string of key value pairs. For most of your scripts you will create the query object from STDIN. The most accepted way to do this is to pass a reference to the STDIN glob:

```
$query = new CGI(\*STDIN);
```

When you create a query object with a string, it must be in a format like:

```
key1=value1&key2=value2
```

The query object represents the HTML form elements that are passed to it (if you used STDIN). These are simply key/value pairs. Sometimes there may be multiple values with the same key.

If the form submitted to your script had the ISINDEX attribute, then you can retrieve the keywords typed into the form via the keywords method. It simply returns an array of the keywords.

The param method is the main interface for accessing the fields in the query object. With no arguments, it returns the keys of the key/value pairs of the query object. If you pass it a key, it returns the value for that key, or if it has multiple values and is requested in an array context, it will return all the values. You can also use the param method to set key/value pairs in the query object by passing the first argument as the key and the rest as the list of values to assign to it. The append method will add the given values to the list of values already associated with a given key.

The import_names method imports all the keys in the query object into the namespace passed to this method. You can then access the scalars and arrays as part of that namespace. For example, if you pass 'myForm' as the namespace you can access the key1 value by $myForm::key1.

The delete method deletes all the values associated with the given key. The delete_all method deletes all the key/value pairs in the query object.

The save method saves all the key/value pairs into the file represented by the file handle passed to this method. The file consists of the 'key=value' pairs, each on one line.

The self_url method returns a URL that can be used to recreate the current query object. It can be used to create HTML links that keep the current state of the query object. The url method simply returns the URL of the script without the QUERY_STRING. The query_string method simply returns the QUERY_STRING associated with the query_object.

The header method can be used to manipulate the header that you send back to the client requesting your page. You can use this to manipulate any of the header variables. When called without any arguments, it returns the content type of the header. When called with a header variable, it returns the value of that header. When called with an associative array, it adds those name/value pairs to the header. The redirect method causes the client to be redirected to the URL you pass to it.

Example   The following CGI script can be used to handle the HTML form from the following HTML file.

```
<html>
<head>
<title>Simple Form</title>
</head>
<body>
<form method=POST action="/cgi-bin/myScript.pl">
Type some data: <input name=data><br>
Select an option: <select name=options multiple size=5>
```

```
<option value=1>One
<option value=2>Two
<option value=3>Three
<option value=4>Four
<option value=5>Five
<option value=6>Six
</select>
<input type=submit value="Submit Form">
</body>
</html>
```

Now the CGI script to handle this form:

```
$query = new CGI (\*STDIN);
print "The data you typed was: ", $query->param('data'), "\n";
@options = $query->param('options');
print "You selected these options: @options\n";
$query->import_names('myForm');
print "The data again was: ", $myForm::data, "\n";
```

DB_File

MODULE

PERL 5

Functions   del, fd, get, get_dup, length, pop, push, put, seq, shift, sync, unshift

Syntax   use DB_File;

$ref = tie *var*, "DB_File"[, *filename*, FLAGS, *mode*, TYPE];

$ref->del(*key*[, FLAGS]);

$fd = $ref->fd;

$ref->get(*key*, *valuevar*[, FLAGS]);

$ref->put(*key*, *value*[, FLAGS]);

$ref->seq(*keyvar*, *valuevar*[, FLAGS]);

$ref->sync([FLAGS]);

$*var*{*key*} = value;

delete $*var*{*key*};

```
undef $var[0];

untie var;

# DB_BTREE functions

$num = $ref->get_dup(key);

@values = $ref->get_dup(key);

%counts = $ref->get_dup(key, 1);

# DB_RECNO functions

$len = $ref->length;

$element = $ref->pop;

$ref->push(@newdata);

$element = $ref->shift;

$ref->unshift(@newdata);
```

Usage   The DB_File module is a Perl interface to the Berkeley DB. You will need to
have Berkeley DB installed on your machine before installing the DB_File
module. The Perl interface allows you access to the three database types that
Berkeley DB supplies: hashes (DB_HASH), binary trees (DB_BTREE), and
record numbers (DB_RECNO). The type of database used is set by the TYPE
argument that you pass to the tie method.

   The DB_HASH and DB_BTREE types both tie to an associative array
while DB_RECNO ties to a regular array. If you don't select a database type,
the DB_HASH will be used. If you don't select a filename where the database will be kept, it will be stored in memory. If you wish to use a binary tree
or record number database, you can pass undef as the filename to get an in-
memory database. The FLAGS option determines how the database is
opened (see the Berkeley DB documentation for more information on the
flags). The *mode* is how the permissions on the file are set if it is created.

   You can add, delete, and retrieve elements from the database by accessing
the array that is tied to the database. You can also use the return value from
the tie function as a reference to the database so you can call the Berkeley DB
functions instead of these.

   All the methods return a 0 if they are successful and a –1 if they fail. The
$! variable will be set with the error code.

   The get method gets the value associated with *key* and sets the variable
passed as the second argument to it. The put method stores the value
passed to it associated with key. The seq function takes two variables and
will cycle through all the entries in the database setting these two variables.
The sync method writes any data in memory to the database. It has no use
with in-memory databases. The fd method returns the file descriptor
associated with the database file.

If you're using a binary tree database, you have the ability to duplicate keys for different data. You do this by setting the $DB_BTREE->{'flags'} variable to R_DUP. You can then set multiple values to the same key. You can't, however, retrieve them using get or the associative array; you must use the get_dup method. If it's called in scalar context, it will return the number of entries that share that key. If it's called in an array context and the second argument is false, it will return a list of all the values that match that key. If it's called in an array context and the second argument is true, it will return an associative array with the keys being the values that match the database key and the values being the number of times that value appears with that key.

If you're using a record number database, there are some additional methods to add and remove elements from the database. The pop method returns the last element in the array and removes it, and the shift method returns the first element of the array and removes it. The push and unshift methods add the given value to the end and beginning of the array respectively. You can find out how many elements are in the array by using the length method.

Example   The following example creates an in-memory hash database using DB_File. It uses the methods instead of the associative array for the data access.

```
use DB_File;
$db = tie %unused, "DB_File";
# add some data from a file of names and email addresses
# the format of the file is:
# email firstname lastname
while ( <> ) {
    ($email, $name) = split(' ', $_, 2);
    $db->put($email, $name);
}

$db->get("nobody@nowhere.com", $who);
print "$who\n";

print "The entire database is:\n";
while ( $status = $db->seq($email, $name, R_FIRST); $status == 0;
    $status = $db->seq($email, $name, R_NEXT) ) {
    print "$name <$email>\n";
}
```

See Also   Modules: Any_DBMFile

File::Copy

Functions   copy, cp, syscopy

Syntax
```
use File::Copy;
copy(startfile, endfile[, buffer]);
use File::Copy 'cp';
cp(startfile, endfile[, buffer]);
use File::Copy 'syscopy';
```

Usage   The File::Copy module allows you to copy files within your Perl script. The copy function takes two arguments: the source file and the destination file. These arguments can be filenames, file handles, or references to file handles (like those when using the FileHandle module). The optional third argument determines how much of the first file to hold in memory until it gets written to the second file.

      The cp function is exactly the same as the copy function, but you must explicitly import it if you wish to use it.

      The syscopy function takes the same arguments but uses the copy routine based on the system the script is run on. This will keep any system-specific file information when the file is copied.

Example   The following example copies the file passed to it from one directory to another.

```
use File::Copy;
copy("$old/$ARGV[0]", "$new/$ARGV[0]");
```

See Also   Modules: File::Tools
Functions: rename

File::Recurse

Functions   recurse

Variables   FOLLOW_SYMLINKS, MAX_DEPTH

Syntax
```
use File::Recurse;
recurse(CODE, directory[, extra]);
$File::Recurse::FOLLOW_SYMLINKS = 0;
$File::Recurse::MAX_DEPTH = 100;
```

Usage   The File::Recurse module allows you to run a code fragment or subroutine on all the files and directories beneath the directory you pass it. The first argument can either be a statement block or a reference to a subroutine. The code won't be called on the directory passed as the second argument.

      The third optional argument isn't used by the recurse function, but will be passed to your subroutine as a second argument in case you have a need for it.

      The MAX_DEPTH variable determines how many directories deep to traverse. The default is 100. The FOLLOW_SYMLINKS variable can either be 1 or 0. If it's 0 then the recurse function won't read any directories that are symlinks. If it's 1, it will traverse symlinks like any other directory.

      If you have your subroutine return –1 and the current file is a directory, then the recurse function won't enter that directory and will skip to the next element. If your subroutine returns –2 the recurse function will stop.

Example   The following script recurses all directories beneath the current directory and prints all filenames that end in ".pl." It ignores any directories that have "old" in the name.

```
use File::Recurse;
sub isPL {
   local ($file) = shift;
   return -1 if ( -d $file and $file =~ m/old/i );
   print $file, "\n" if ( $file =~ m/\.pl$/i );
}
recurse( \&isPL, "." );
```

See Also   Modules: File::Tools

File::Tools
MODULE

PERL 5

Syntax   `use File::Tools;`

Usage   The File::Tools module simply imports functions from other File modules.
This currently consists of the File::Copy and File::Recurse modules but more
will be added later.

See Also   Modules: File::Copy, File::Recurse

Getopt::Std
MODULE

PERL 5

Functions   getopt, getopts

Syntax   `use Getopt::Std;`

`getopt(options);`

`getopts(options);`

Usage   The Getopt::Std module contains functions for reading in command line
options with your scripts. The *options* list is a string of characters that are
accepted as options. With the getopt function, all the options take an argument which will be assigned to $opt_*letter*. The getopts function allows you
to set whether the option takes an argument or not. If the character is
followed by a colon, it takes an argument and assigns it to $opt_*letter*; if there
is no colon $opt_*letter* is set to true if the option was used and false if other-
wise. Any options passed to a script using getopt that aren't in the string
passed to getopt will be set to 1 if they appear. The getopts function only
allows options that are in the *options* string.

   Any option that takes an argument must be the last option if you combine
options. For example, if a doesn't take an argument and b does, then the
following would be fine:

```
myscript.pl -ab arg
myscript.pl -a -b arg
myscript.pl -abarg
myscript.pl -a -barg
```

   The following invocation of your script would set $opt_b to 'a' and $opt_a
wouldn't be set at all.

```
myscript.pl -ba
```

Example
The following example uses the getopt function and then prints the options given to it.

```
use Getopt::Std;
getopt('b');
if ( $opt_a ) {
    print "You used the -a option.\n";
}
if ( $opt_b ) {
    print "You passed '$opt_b' as the -b option.\n";
}
```

This example uses the getopts function to provide an alternate method of the above script. This script will give the same output as before except that if the user tries an option other than –a or –b he or she will see 'Unknown option: *x*.'

```
use Getopt::Std;
getopts('ab:');
...
```

See Also
Modules: File::Tools
Functions: rename

IO::Select

MODULE

PERL 5

Functions
add, bits, can_read, can_write, count, exists, handles, has_error, new, remove, select

Syntax
```
use IO::Select;
```
```
$selectObj = new IO::Select [FILE_VARIABLE];
```
```
$selectObj->add(FILE_VARIABLE);
```
```
$selectObj->bits;
```

```
@handles = $selectObj->can_read([timeout]);

@handles = $selectObj->can_write([timeout]);

$num = $selectObj->count;

$handle = $selectObj->exists(FILE_VARIABLE);

@handles = $selectObj->handles;

@handles = $selectObj->has_error;

$selectObj->remove(FILE_VARIABLE);

($readref, $writeref, $errorref) = IO::Select::select( $selectObj,
    $selectObj, $selectObj[, timeout]);
```

Usage   The IO::Select module is an object interface to the select system call. It lets
you keep a list of file handles and determines which of them are ready for
reading or writing or which have errors. All the file handles passed to these
methods must be references to file handle globs.

The new method creates a new instance of the IO::Select object and can
optionally take a list of file handles. This is the same as creating a new object
and then calling the add method with the list of handles. The add method
adds the list of file handles to the set of handles that will be checked by the
object. The remove method removes the list of handles from the set of active
handles to be checked. The exists method determines if the handle is in the
set of handles and returns it if it is there or undef if it's not.

The count method returns the number of handles that will be checked by
the select object. The handles method returns an array of handles that are
stored in the object.

The can_read method will return an array of handles that are ready to be
read from. The timeout determines how long the method will wait for a file
handle to be ready to read from. The can_write method will return an array
of handles that are ready to be written to. The has_error method returns a list
of handles that have an error condition on them (such as eof).

The bits method returns a string that can be passed to the core select call.
The select method returns an array of three array references: the first being a
list of handles ready to be read from, the second being a list of handles ready
to be written to, and the third being a list of handles with an error condition.
The three arguments to select can either be undefined or an IO::Select object.

Example   The following example takes a few file handles and displays which can be
written to and read from.

```
use IO::Select;
$selObj = new IO::Select;
$selObj->add(\*STDIN);
open ( ALIAS, "</etc/mail/aliases" );
$selObj->add(\*ALIAS);
open ( NEW, ">/tmp/newfile" );
$selObj->add(\*NEW);

@read = $selObj->can_read(5);
@write = $selObj->can_write(5);

# display the reference info for each handle
print "Key:  STDIN -> ", \*STDIN, "  ALIAS -> ", \*ALIAS, "  NEW -> ",
   \*NEW, "\n";
print "Read: @read\n";      # prints the handles that can
                            # be read from
print "Write: @write\n";    # prints the handles that can
                            # be written to.
```

See Also   Bundled Modules: IO

Appendices

III

Appendix A
About the Companion CD-ROM

The CD-ROM included with your copy of *The Perl 5 Programmer's Reference* contains the Perl compiler source code for various platforms, sample scripts for processing Internet data, valuable software, and a hypertext version of the book.

To View the CD-ROM

To find out more about the CD-ROM and its contents, please open the "README.HTM" file in your favorite browser. You will see a small menu offering links to software descriptions and to the contents of the book.

Software

JavaFTP — JavaFTP is one of the first graphical FTP clients written with Java. To use JavaFTP, you need to have a 1.0.x version of the Java Virtual Machine. (Note: this program will not work with version 1.1.x) You can download Sun's JDK 1.0.2 at http://www.javasoft.com or you can use Microsoft's virtual machine. To launch this application please enter the following command line:

- Using Sun's JDK:

  ```
  java JavaFTP
  ```

- Using Microsoft's Java Virtual Machine:

  ```
  jview JavaFTP
  ```

To find out more about this FTP client, visit http://www.princeton.edu/~dragones/JavaFTP.

Note: A copy of the GNU Public License is included on this CD. In compliance with the terms of the GNU Public License, Ventana Communications Group hereby disclaims all copyright interest in the program Perl Win 32.

Perl 5.004_01 — This CD-ROM contains version 5.004_01 of Perl. Perl is an interpreted language optimized for scanning arbitrary text files, extracting information from those text files, and printing reports based on that information. For more information about Perl, visit www.perl.com/perl on the WWW.

Perl for ISAPI Intel — The Perl for ISAPI Intel/x86 binary allows the Microsoft IIS Web server to execute Perl programs directly, without having to use the CGI method of Web programming. This eliminates a lot of the overhead of CGI and speeds up your Perl-based Web programs. For more information, visit ActiveWare's home page at http://www.activeware.com.

Perl for Win 32 — ActiveWareTool Corp.'s Perl for Win32 Intel/x86 binary is a port of most of the functionality in Perl, with extra Win32 API calls that allow you to take advantage of native Windows functionality. Perl for Win32 runs on Windows 95 and Windows NT 3.5 and later. The Perl for Win32 package contains perl.exe, perlx00.dll, supporting documents, and extensions that allow you to call Win32 functionality. For more information, visit ActiveWare's home page at http://www.activeware.com.

Perl Script — The PerlScript Intel/x86 binary allows the user to utilize Perl variables and programming constructs (if, while, etc.) that are embedded directly into HTML pages. For more information, visit ActiveWare's homepage at http://www.activeware.com.

TextPad — TextPad is designed to provide the power and functionality to satisfy the most demanding text editing requirements. It is Windows-hosted, and comes in 16- and 32-bit editions. Huge files can be edited by either; just choose the edition that works best with your PC. The 32-bit edition can edit files up to the limits of virtual memory, and it will work with Windows 95, NT, and 3.1 with Win32 extensions.

Note: The 16-bit version has been included for OS/2 users. You should install this application in a Win-OS2 session. You can also save files in PC, Mac, and Unix formats. Visit http://www.textpad.com for more information.

Technical Support

Technical support is available for installation-related problems only. The technical support office is open from 8:00 A.M. to 6:00 P.M. EST Monday through Friday and can be reached via the following methods:

Phone: (919) 544-9404 extension 81

Faxback Answer System: (919) 544-9404 extension 85

E-mail: help@vmedia.com

FAX: (919) 544-9472

World Wide Web: **http://www.vmedia.com/support**

America Online: keyword *Ventana*

Limits of Liability & Disclaimer of Warranty

The authors and publisher of this book have used their best efforts in preparing the CD-ROM and the programs contained in it. These efforts include the development, research, and testing of the theories and programs to determine their effectiveness. The authors and publisher make no warranty of any kind expressed or implied, with regard to these programs or the documentation contained in this book.

The authors and publisher shall not be liable in the event of incidental or consequential damages in connection with, or arising out of, the furnishing, performance, or use of the programs, associated instructions, and/or claims of productivity gains.

Some of the software on this CD-ROM is shareware; there may be additional charges (owed to the software authors/makers) incurred for their registration and continued use. See individual programs' README or VREADME.TXT files for more information.

Appendix B
Perl Special Variables

There are five types of special variables listed in this section:

- **Global** variables are accessible anywhere in your program.
- **Format** variables are used when you use the format and write functions. They generally exist globally but have a special use.
- **Regular expression** variables are created when you use any of Perl's pattern matching capabilities.
- **File handle** variables are mostly variables that refer to special file handles, but some modify how file handles are used.
- **Subroutine** variables are only valid while in a subroutine.

$!

Usage   The $! variable holds the value of the most recent system error that occurred in your program. If it's accessed in a numeric context, it will return the value of errno on the system. If it's accessed in a string context, it will print the error message corresponding to the error number. You can assign a value to $! to see an error number. If you try to access this variable before a system error has occurred, you will get unexpected results.

Examples   The following code fragment tries to open a file, and if it fails, it dies and prints the error that occurred:

```
Open(FILE, "<$myfile") or die "Can't open $myfile: $!";
```

See Also $@
Bundled modules: English

$"

Usage   The value of the $" variable will be printed between elements of an array that is interpolated between a double-quoted string. The default value is a space.

Examples   The following code shows the difference between the default value of $" and a value you assign to it:

```
@test = ( 'one', 'two' );
print "@test\n";  # prints "one two\n"

$" = ", ";
```

See Also $,
Bundled modules: English

$#

Usage   The $# variable should no longer be used in new programs. It is only
supplied in Perl 5 to be compatible with old scripts. It was meant to emulate
awk's OFMT variable and is used as a format for printing numbers. The
default value for the OFMT variable in awk is %.6g, while the $# variable
default is %.14g. It is better to use printf to format your numeric values
instead of this variable.

See Also   Bundled modules: English

$$

Usage   The $$ holds the process ID of the Perl script that is currently running.

Examples   The following code fragment outputs the process ID of the running script:

```
print "The process ID is $$\n";
```

See Also   Bundled modules: English

$%

Usage   The $% variable represents the current page number when you're using the
write function. It is most often used in the "top of page" format to display
how many pages have been output.

Example   The following example uses the $% variable to print the current page
number at the top of every page printed. This script reads in a comma-
delimited file and prints it in a more readable format. The lines of the file are
in the format:

```
one, two, three
```

The script follows:

```
format STDOUT_TOP =
@>>>>>>>>>>>>>>>>>>>>>>>>>>>>>>>>>>>>>>>>>>>>>>>>>>>>
"Page $%"
--------------------------------------------------
.

format STDOUT =
@>>>>>>>>>> @||||||||||| @<<<<<<<<<<<<<
$var1, $var2, $var4
.

open ( UGLY, "<ugly.txt" );
while ( <UGLY> ) {
  ( $var1, $var2, $var3 ) = split ( ',', $_ );
  write;
}
```

With the line above, this script would output:

```
                                                 Page 1
--------------------------------------------------
            one        two        three
```

See Also $-, $=
Bundled modules: English, FileHandle
Functions: format, write

$&

Usage   The $& variable holds the value of the last successful pattern match. This is a read-only variable.

Examples   The following code fragment performs a pattern match and displays what was matched:

```
$temp = "1234567890";
$temp =~ /.\d{3,4}/;
print = "$&\n";  # will print 12345
```

See Also $digit, $', $'
Bundled modules: English
Functions: m//, s///

$'

REGULAR EXPRESSION

PERL 4   PERL 5

Usage   The $' variable holds the value of the string following the last successful pattern match. This is a read-only variable.

Examples   The following code fragment performs a pattern match and displays what is after the match which in this case will be 67890:

```
$temp = "1234567890";
$temp =~ /.\d{3,4}/;
print = "$'\n";   # will print 67890
```

See Also $*digit*, $&, $'
Bundled modules: English

$(

GLOBAL

PERL 4   PERL 5

Usage   The $(variable holds the value of the real group ID that is running the current process. If the system you're on supports multiple simultaneous groups, then this will return a space-delimited list of all the groups.

Examples   The following code fragment prints the real group ID of the running script:

```
print = "$(\n";
```

See Also $)
Bundled modules: English
Functions: getgrid

$)

GLOBAL

PERL 4   PERL 5

Usage   The $) variable holds the value of the effective group ID that is running the current process. If the system you're on supports multiple simultaneous groups, then this will return a space-delimited list of all the groups. The effective group ID may be different from the real group ID if you're running a setgid script.

Examples   The following code fragment prints the effective group ID of the running script:

```
print = "$)\n";
```

See Also $(
Bundled modules: English
Functions: getgrid

$*

REGULAR EXPRESSION

PERL 4

Usage   The $* variable should no longer be used in Perl 5 programs. It only remains to be compatible with older Perl scripts. You should use the /m extension instead of setting this variable.

    If this variable is set to 1, then regular expressions will assume that there may be more than one line in the string being searched. If it's set to 0, then it will assume a single line. Setting this variable only changes the way the regular expression interprets the ^ and $ characters in the expression. If it's set to 0, then $ will match after the first new line, not necessarily after the end of the string.

See Also   Bundled modules: English

$+

REGULAR EXPRESSION

PERL 4   PERL 5

Usage   The $+ variable holds the value of the last parenthetical pattern match. This is most often used when the number of the match may be different.

Example   This example shows how you can pull out the data you want even if you don't know the number of the parenthetical match you've made. In this example, you want to find the number following "Message: " or "Data: ", but you don't want to have to do any extra parsing to find whether it found "Message" or "Data":

```
$temp = "Message: 123";
$temp =~ /Message: (\d+)|Data: (\d+)/;
# $+ == $1
print "$+\n" # prints 123

$temp2 = "Data: 456";
```

```
$temp2 =~ /Message: (\d+)|Data: (\d+)/;
# $+ == $2
print "$+\n" # prints 456
```

See Also *$digit*
Bundled modules: English

$,

GLOBAL

PERL 4 PERL 5

Usage   The $, variable is what is displayed between fields passed to the print
function. This variable defaults to being nothing. It simply replaces the
commas in the print statement with the value of this variable.

Examples The following code fragment shows the effects of changing $,:

```
print "123", "456", "789", "0", "\n"
# prints 1234567890
$, = "-";
print "123", "456", "789", "0", "\n"
# prints 123-456-789-0-
```

See Also Bundled modules: English
Functions: print

$-

FORMAT

PERL 4 PERL 5

Usage   The $- variable holds the value of the number of lines left to be printed
before the end of the current output page. When this variable equals 0 and
you call a write, then the "top of page" format is printed.

Examples This example uses the $- variable to determine when a whole page has been
printed and then prints a footer for the page. I'll shorten the page length so
it'll be easier to see:

```
format STDOUT_TOP =
@>>>>>>>>>>>>>>>>>>>>>>>>>>>>>>>>>>>>>>>>>>>>>
"Page $%"
-------------------------------------------------
.
```

```
format STDOUT =
@>>>>>>>>> @||||||||||| @<<<<<<<<<<<<<
$var1, $var2, $var4
.


$= = 5;
open ( UGLY, "<ugly.txt" );
while ( <UGLY> ) {
   ( $var1, $var2, $var3 ) = split ( ',', $_ );
  write;
  if ( $- == 0 ) {
     printf "--------------------------------------------- %4d\n", $%;
   }
}
if ( $- != 0 ) {
printf "--------------------------------------------- %4d\n", $%;
}
```

Assuming ugly.txt was a file with the following data:

```
one,two,three
four,five,six
seven,eight,nine
ten,eleven,twelve
thirteen,fourteen,fifteen
```

running the program would produce the following output:

```
                                                Page 1
---------------------------------------------
        one      two     three
       four     five     six
      seven     eight    nine
---------------------------------------------  1
                                                Page 2
---------------------------------------------
        ten      eleven   twelve
   thirteen   fourteen    fifteen
---------------------------------------------  2
```

See Also $=
Bundled modules: English, FileHandle
Functions: format, write

$.

GLOBAL

PERL 4   PERL 5

Usage   The $. variable holds the input line number of the last filehandle that was read. When you close the filehandle, $. is reset. See the example for a way to use this variable effectively when reading files using the <> operator.

Examples The following script prints the lines of the files passed to it with their line numbers:

```
while ( <> ) {
    printf "%4d: %s", $., $_;
    # resets $. if there are multiple files
    # passed to the script.
    close ARGV if eof;
}
```

See Also   Bundled modules: English

$/

GLOBAL

PERL 4   PERL 5

Usage   The $/ variable is the input record separator. When you read in a file using the <> operator, it determines how much of the file to read in. This defaults to a newline character so that you read one line of the file at a time. This variable can be set to multiple characters as well.

If you wish to read in the file a paragraph at a time based on a blank line between paragraphs, you can set this variable to "". If you set it to "\n\n", it will only match two newlines beside each other and may cause problems if there are three newlines. Setting it to blank will cause the file to be read in sections divided by one or more blank lines. If you "undef" $/, it will read in the entire file.

Examples The following script reads in a line of data from standard input, then changes the input record separator to a '.' on a line by itself, and then reads in data until that period:

```
print "Type in a single line of data: ";
chop ( $temp = <STDIN> );
print "You typed: ", $temp, "\n";
```

```
$/ = "\n.\n";
print "Type in multiple lines of data. ";
print "End by typing a '.' on a line by itself.\n";
$temp2 = <STDIN>
$temp2 =~ s/\n.\n$//m;
print "You typed:\n", $temp2, "\n";
```

See Also $\
Bundled modules: English

$0
GLOBAL

PERL 4   PERL 5

Usage   The $0 variable holds the name of the file containing the currently running Perl script. You can modify this variable and it will change how the 'ps' (process list) program shows the name of your program.

See Also   Bundled modules: English

$digit
REGULAR EXPRESSION

PERL 4   PERL 5

Usage   The $digit variables are a set of variables that are created when you use parentheses in your regular expression. The first set of parentheses matched is $1, the second $2, and so on. The number is based on the order of the opening paren, so nested parentheses are numbered with the enclosing set being the first number, that is:

```
( ( ( ) ( ( ) ) ) ( ) )
1 2 3   4 5       6
```

Examples   The following code fragment will parse out the area code, exchange, and suffix of a phone number in a standard format:

```
$text = "Phone #: 1 (888) 555-1212";
$text =~ /\((((\d{3})\)\s*(\d{3})-(\d{4})))/;
#              12    2   3      3 4      41
$fullnumber = $1;
$areacode = $2;
$exchange = $3;
$suffix = $4;
```

See Also $&

$:

Usage   The $: holds the set of characters on which a string may be broken to display in a continuation field. The default value is " \n-" so that it may break on white space, newlines, or dashes.

Examples   The following example uses a continuation field in the format and only allows it to be split on a pipe character, |. If the string can't be split, it will wrap at the max length provided by the format:

```
format STDOUT =
@>>>>> ^<<<<<<<<<<<<<<<<<<<<<<<<<<
$id,    $info
        ^<<<<<<<<<<<<<<<<<<<<<<<<<<
        $info
        ^<<<<<<<<<<<<<<<<<<<<<<<<<<
        $info
.

$: = "|";
$id = 1;
$info = "This is the first line|This is the second line|This is the
   third line";
write;
```

This script will produce the following output:

```
1 This is the first line|
  This is the second line|
  This is the third line
```

See Also   Bundled modules: English, FileHandle
Functions: format, write

$;

Usage   The $; variable was useful for emulating multiple-dimension arrays in Perl 4. With Perl 5, you can create multiple-dimension arrays using references, which is the preferable method.

When you access an associative array as:

```
$array{0,0} = "new data";
```

it is the same as:

```
$array{join($;, 0, 0)} = "new data";
```

The default value is "\034", which is an unprintable character. If your array keys include binary data then you might need to change this character, but there also might not be any safe character for this value.

See Also   Bundled modules: English

$<

GLOBAL

PERL 4   PERL 5

Usage   The $< variable holds the value of the real user ID that is running the current process.

Examples   The following code fragment prints the real user ID of the running script:

```
print = "$<\n";
```

See Also $>
            Bundled modules: English
            Functions: getpwuid

$=

FORMAT

PERL 4   PERL 5

Usage   The $= variable holds the number of lines per page when you're using the write function. Once you've written the specified number of lines, the "top of page" format is displayed and the next page begins. The default page length is 60, but you can set it to your desired page length.

Examples   The following script reads a file of any type and then writes it back in pages of five lines each. Note that the page header is counted in the lines per page:

```
Format STDOUT_TOP =
@<<<<<<<<<<<<<<<<<<<<
"Page $%"
--------------------
```

```
.
format STDOUT =
<<<<<<<<<<<<<<<<<<<
$_
.

$= = 5;
while ( <> ) {
  write;
}
```

See Also $-
Bundled modules: English, FileHandle
Functions: format, write

$>

GLOBAL

PERL 4   PERL 5

Usage The $> variable holds the value of the effective user ID that is running the current process. The effective user ID may be different from the real user ID if you're running a setuid script.

Examples The following code fragment prints the effective user ID of the running script:

```
print = "$<\n";
```

See Also $<
Bundled modules: English
Functions: getpwuid

$?

GLOBAL

PERL 4   PERL 5

Usage The $? variable holds the status returned from the last child process that ended either through closing a pipe, ending a system call, or running a command using ". This is a status word returned from the wait system call. You should bitshift right by 8 to find out the exit code of the child ($? >> 8). You can also do $? & 255 to find out from what signal the process died and whether there was a core dump. If the subprocess ended normally, this variable should be 0.

Examples   The following code fragment makes an invalid system call and then displays the values of $?:

```
system('nocommand');
print "Status: ", $?, "\n";
print "Exit code: ", $? >> 8, "\n";
print "signal: ", $? & 255, "\n";
```

See Also   Bundled modules: English

$@

GLOBAL

PERL 4   PERL 5

Usage   The $@ holds a Perl syntax error message from the last eval call you made. This variable is null if the eval was parsed correctly. Any errors that occur as a result of the eval will happen normally.

Examples   The following code fragment shows how to check your syntax of eval using $@. The eval statement will cause an error because it will interpolate $a and effectively try to evaluate " = 2". This code won't cause an error in your program, and when you try to access $a in the second line, it won't be 2 like you expected:

```
eval "$a = 2" or die $@;
print "$a\n";
```

See Also   Bundled modules: English

$ARGV

GLOBAL

PERL 4   PERL 5

Usage   The $ARGV variable holds the name of the current file that's being parsed by <ARGV>. Note that <> is the same as <ARGV>.

Examples   The following script prints out the files passed to the script followed by text giving the name of each file and the number of lines in the file:

```
while ( <> ) {
  print;
  if (eof) {
```

```
        print "--End of file $ARGV ($. Lines)\n\n";
        close (ARGV );
    }
}
```

See Also   ARGV
           Bundled modules: English

$[

Usage   The $[variable contains the value of the index of the first element in an array.
           This defaults to 0. If you want your array's index to start at 1, then set this
           variable to 1.

Examples   The following code fragment causes any subsequent arrays to be 1-based
           instead of 0-based arrays:

```
$[ = 1;
@days = ( "Sunday", "Monday", "Tuesday", "Wednesday", "Thursday",
    "Friday", "Saturday");
print "$days[1]\n"; # prints Sunday
```

See Also   Bundled modules: English

$\

Usage   The $\ variable is the output record separator. It is what is printed at the end
           of each print statement. It defaults to nothing. So you don't have to type it
           each time, you can set this to "\n" if you want a newline at the end of each
           print statement.

Examples   The following code fragment changes the output record separator to "\n\t"
           so that all lines except the first are indented when they're printed:

```
$\ = "\n\t";
print "This is line one.";
print "This is line two.";
print "This is line three.";
```

See Also   Bundled modules: English

$]

Usage   The $] holds the current version number of Perl so your scripts can check to make sure the required version of Perl is available.

Examples   The following code fragment makes sure the Perl interpreter is at least version 5 before continuing:

```
Die "Old version of Perl, you must have Perl 5.002 or higher.\n" if $]
    < 5.002;
```

See Also   Bundled modules: English

$^

Usage   Setting the $^ variable changes what the write function uses for its "top of page" format for the currently selected output handle. By default, it uses the name of the handle followed by _TOP. You can set this variable if you change the output handle often but want to use the same "top of page" format.

Examples   The following code fragment uses a standard "top of page" format. At the top of the page, it will print the page number followed by a line of dashes. If you decide to change the current file handle, you can simply set the $^ variable instead of creating a "_TOP" format for each of them:

```
format my_top =
@>>>>>>>>>>>>>>>>>>>>>>>>>>>>>>>>>>>
"Page $%"
------------------------------------
.

format MYFILE =
@<<<<<<<<<
$temp
.
```

```
select (MYFILE);
$^ = "my_top";
foreach $temp ( 0..3 ) {
   write;
}
```

See Also $~
Bundled modules: English
Functions: format, write

$^A

FORMAT

PERL 5

Usage   The $^A variable holds the current value of the write accumulator for formatted lines. When you call write, it calls formline, which sets its result to $^A, which is then printed and cleared. You won't be able to access $^A unless you call formline yourself.

Examples   The following subroutine mimics the behavior of write:

```
$one = "test1";
$two = "test2";
&mywrite;

sub mywrite {
   formline ("@>>>>> @<<<<<", $one, $two);
   print $^A, "\n";
}
```

See Also   Bundled modules: English
Functions: formline and write

$^D

GLOBAL

PERL 4   PERL 5

Usage   The $^D variable holds the value of the current debugging flags; the value is generally set by the –D switch.

See Also   Bundled modules: English

$^E

GLOBAL

PERL 5

Usage The $^E variable holds more information about the last system error than $!. If there is no more specific data, it is the same as $!. In most cases it will be the same.

See Also $!
Bundled modules: English

$^F

GLOBAL

PERL 4   PERL 5

Usage The $^F variable holds the value of the maximum number for a system file descriptor, which is usually 2. System file descriptors are special because they are passed to processes that are 'exec'ed to, while other file descriptors are not. System file descriptors are also preserved if an open fails. Normally the file descriptor would be closed before the new open was tried.

See Also Bundled modules: English

$^H

GLOBAL

PERL 5

Usage The $^H variable holds the current set of syntax checks that are enabled when you use the strict pragma.

See Also Bundled modules (pragma): strict

$^I

GLOBAL

PERL 4   PERL 5

Usage The $^I variable holds the current value of the in-place edit flag. This flag is set by using the –i switch when invoking the Perl interpreter. You can disable in-place editing by 'undef'ing this variable.

See Also Bundled modules: English

$^L

FORMAT

PERL 5

Usage The $^L variable holds the value that format outputs when it does a formfeed. The default value is \f.

See Also Bundled modules: English, FileHandle
Functions: format, write+

$^O

GLOBAL

PERL 5

Usage The $^O variable holds the name of the operating system that the Perl interpreter you're using was compiled on.

Examples The following code fragment prints the operating system of the Perl interpreter:

```
print = "$^O\n";
```

See Also Bundled modules: English

$^P

GLOBAL

PERL 4   PERL 5

Usage The $^P variable is a flag that the debugger clears so that it doesn't debug itself. You can disable debugging by clearing the value of this variable.

See Also Bundled modules: English

$^T

GLOBAL

PERL 4   PERL 5

Usage The $^T variable holds the time when the script began running. This time is stored as seconds since the epoch. You can parse this data using the localtime function and the ctime.pl library. This value is used when you use the –A, -C, or –M file tests.

Examples   The following code fragment prints the time the script began running:

```
sleep 5;
($sec, $min, $hour) = localtime($^T);
print "This script began at $hour:$min:$sec\n";
($sec, $min, $hour) = localtime(time);
print "It is now $hour:$min:$sec\n";
```

See Also   Bundled modules: English
Functions: localtime

$^W

Usage   The $^W variable holds the current value of the warning switch, which is set by using the –w switch.

Example   The following code fragment prints a warning if you don't have warnings enabled on your script:

```
if (!$^W) {
    print STDERR "You don't have warnings enabled!\n";
}
```

See Also   Bundled modules: English

$^X

Usage   The $^X variable holds the name of the Perl executable that is being used to interpret the current script. Unless you've changed it, this will most often be perl.

See Also   Bundled modules: English

$_

Usage   The $_ variable is the default variable that is used with many Perl functions. The $_ variable is set in the following cases:

- When you use:

```
while (<FILE>) { … }
```

which is equivalent to:

```
while ( defined($_ = <FILE>) ) { … }
```

- When you use:

```
foreach ( @arr ) { … }
```

which is equivalent to:

```
foreach $_ ( @arr ) { … }
```

- When you use the grep and map functions, $_ is set to the current iteration in the array used.

The following cases assume using $_ if no variable is passed to them:

- The unary functions including int and ord.
- All file tests except –t, which uses STDIN by default.
- The list functions like print and unlink.
- The pattern matching operations m//, s///, and tr/// when used without =~.

Examples   The following script prints out the contents of the file passed to the script:

```
while ( <> ) {  # $_ is set
   print;        # defaults to print $_
}
```

See Also   Bundled modules: English

$'

Usage   The $' variable holds the value of the string preceding the last successful pattern match. This is a read-only variable.

Examples   The following code fragment performs a pattern match and displays what was before the match which in this case should be 12345:

```
$temp = "1234567890";
$temp =~ /.\d{3,4}$/;
print = "$'\n";  # will print 12345
```

See Also   *$digit*, *$&*, *$'*
Bundled modules: English

$|

Usage   If $| is set to anything other than 0, then a flush will occur after every print or write statement on the currently selected output channel. The default is 0. It is most often useful when you're writing data to a pipe or simply when you want to see output as it's happening.

See Also   Bundled modules: English

$~

Usage   Setting the $~ variable changes what the write function uses for its format for the currently selected output handle. By default, it uses the name of the handle. You can set this variable if you change the output handle often but want to use the same format.

Examples   The following code fragment uses a standard format. If you decide to change the current file handle, you can simply set the $^ variable instead of creating a format for each of them:

```
format my_format =
@<<<<<<<<<
```

```
$temp
   .

select (MYFILE);
$~ = "my_format";
foreach $temp ( 0..3 ) {
  write;
}
```

See Also $^
Bundled modules: English
Functions: format, write

%ENV

GLOBAL

PERL 4   PERL 5

Usage   The %ENV associative array holds all of the environment variables of the
current process. These values can be used to read or change the environment
variables. If you wish to remove one of these variables, you should use the
delete function. If you change or remove any of the variables, then any child
process will use this modified environment.

Examples   The following script checks for a certain directory in the PATH environment
variable and then adds it if it's not there:

```
if ( $ENV{'PATH'} !~ m#^/usr/new/bin:# and $ENV{'PATH'} !~ m#:/usr/new/
  bin$# and $ENV{'PATH'} !~ m#:/usr/new/bin:# ) {
  $ENV{'PATH'} .= ":/usr/new/bin";
}
```

See Also   Bundled modules: Env

%INC

GLOBAL

PERL 4   PERL 5

Usage   The %INC associative array holds each file that has been included in the
current script by using do or require. The key is the name of the file that was
included, and the value is the path to that file. This is used by the require
function to determine if a file has already been included so that it isn't
included twice.

See Also   @INC

%SIG

Usage   You can use the %SIG associative array to set up handlers for various signals
           your script may receive. If you decide to remove a handler, you can set the
           associated signal to 'DEFAULT'. If you simply want to ignore certain signals,
           you can set it to 'IGNORE'.
               The routine specified by $SIG{__WARN__} is called when a warning is
           about to be printed. The warning message is passed to this routine so you
           can handle the warnings your own way instead of printing the warning to
           STDERR. You can do the same thing for fatal exceptions by setting
           $SIG{__DIE__}. Within these subroutines, warn and die, respectively, work
           as they originally would so as not to cause an endless loop.

Examples   The following script will catch a HUP signal and die. If you run this script
           and then send the process a HUP signal, it will print the message and die:

```perl
$SIG{HUP} = 'nohup';
$tmp = <STDIN>;
sub nohup {
   die "Caught a SIGHUP\n";
}
```

@ARGV

Usage   The @ARGV variable holds all the arguments passed to the script. Note that
           the first argument is $ARGV[0], not $ARGV[1] with the script name being
           $ARGV[0]. If you wish to access the script name, use $0.

Examples   The following script spits back the arguments passed to it separated by
           newlines:

```perl
print join ( "\n", @ARGV ), "\n";
```

See Also   @_

@F

Usage   This @F variable is the array that an input line is auto-split into when you use the –a switch. If –a is not used, then this is not a special variable.

Examples   The following script will print the first word of each line in the file passed to it:

```
#!/usr/local/bin/perl -na
print $F[0], "\n";
```

See Also   Command-line switches: -a

@INC

Usage   The @INC variable includes a list of directories in which your script will look when you use the do, require, or use functions. It defaults to the value of the –I switch followed by the default locations. You can modify it for any custom libraries to load.

Examples   The following code fragment modifies the @INC variable and requires a custom library file:

```
push ( @INC, "/usr/local/lib/custom" );
require "custom.pl";
...
```

See Also   Functions: do, require, use

@_

Usage   The @_ variable is created local to a subroutine when you invoke the subroutine. It holds the arguments passed to the subroutine in a way that is similar to @ARGV does when the program is running.

Examples   The following subroutine spits back the arguments passed to a subroutine
separated by newlines:

```
sub showArgs {
    print join ( "\n", @_ ), "\n";
}
```

See Also   @ARGV

ARGV

Usage   ARGV is a special file handle that is opened when you pass a file or list of
files to a Perl script. When it reaches the end of the first file, it automatically
opens on the second file. This is the default file handle when you use the <>
operator, so <ARGV> is the same as <>/.

Examples   The following script reads in from a list of files and counts the total number
of lines in all the files:

```
while ( <ARGV> ) { }
print "$. Lines.\n";
```

DATA

Usage   DATA is a special file handle that is opened on any text in the file containing
the script after the __END__ token. It can also refer to any text following the
__DATA__ token in a required file as long as you read it in the same package
that the token was found in.

Examples   The following script will print out the lines following the __END__ token:

```
while ( <DATA> ) {
    print;
}
__END__
Testing
One
Two
Three
```

STDERR

Syntax   `print STDERR "Bad things happening.\n"`

Usage   STDERR is a special file handle that is opened when your script begins. You
          can write any error message by printing to this file handle. The die and warn
          functions print to this file handle.

STDIN

Usage   STDIN is a special file handle that refers to the standard input. When you try
          to read from this file handle, the script will wait for the user input before
          continuing.

Example   The following script asks for a user's name and then prints it back to the
          user. I use the chop function to remove the newline character since that will
          be read in as well when the user presses Enter:

```
print "What is your name? ";
chop ($name = <STDIN>);
print "Hello, $name, welcome to my program.\n";
```

STDOUT

Syntax   `print STDOUT "Standard message.\n"`

Usage   STDOUT is the default output file handle, which refers to the standard output.
          When you use print without a file handle, it will print to this file handle.

—

Usage   This is a special file handle that is used to cache information from the last file
          test operator or the last lstat or stat function calls.

See Also Functions: lstat, stat

Appendix C
Reference Tables & Lists

As you know, not all of Perl's glory lies in its commands and modules. There are many built-in operators and functionality options that allow a programmer to expand the potential of their scripts.

This appendix references some of Perl's most useful options and operators. The following pages define these operators and options and are laid out for easy reference and usability.

Perl Options

The following is a short description and list of the options that you can pass to Perl when executing a script. These options are either implemented in the command line or in the first line of your script where you specify the Perl compiler location.

Syntax	Description
--	Terminates all following options. It will translate them as files to be read in for processing. This is a good option to include in the #! Line in your script if you want no options to be implemented on your script.
-0 num	Allows you to specify an end-of-line marker for your input data file. This option accepts num as the octal representation for the ASCII location you wish to specify. By default, a newline character is sought, but this option allows you to specify another location to end your processing.

➡

Syntax	Description
-a	Used with the -n or -p option; splits each input line read into a list of individual words. The list is then stored in the @F special variable for processing within your script.
-c	Verifies the syntax of your script without running it.
-Dnum	Allows you to set the Perl interpreter's debugging flags. See your system's Perl man pages for a list of values to pass to this option.
-d	Tells Perl to run your script in the debugger mode.
-e command	Executes command as if it were contained in a script. It can be as long as your system will allow you to type on one line. Be sure to enclose the command in quotation marks.
-F original	Used in conjunction with the -a option. It specifies a pattern, defined by original, on which to perform the split.
-h	Acts as your help resource. It will print a summary of the command-line options.
-I directory	Used in conjunction with the -P option to specify a directory to search for additional include files to be used by the C preprocessor.
-i fileExtension	Tells Perl that the files you wish to execute your script on should be done so in place. It will take the passed file, create a backup with the same name with fileExtension added to it, and open the original file for editing. This allows you to back up the files you wish to edit before you do so.
-l num	Works in the same manner as the -0 option, but the octal number you pass specifies an end location on an output file rather than an input file.
-M module	Executes 'use module' before executing your script.
-M -module	Executes 'no module' before executing your script.
-m module	Executes 'use module' before executing your script.
-m -module	Executes 'no module' before executing your script.
-n	Allows you to specify multiple files to pass to your script instead of running your program multiple times on these multiple files. You can use the -n option to pass all the files at once.
-P	Allows you to use the C preprocessor to search your script for preprocessor statements.
-p	Works in the same manner as the -n option, but it prints each line of the input files passed to it.
-S	Tells the Perl compiler to search your PATH for the script you wish to execute.
-s	Allows you to pass options to your script for more control of the script's execution. If the -s option is contained on the command line, your entry may look like this: perl -s testfile.pl -w.
-T	Turns on "taint" checking for scripts running setuid on UNIX systems.
-U	Allows you to perform unsafe operations in your script, such as those that can be performed by the superuser on UNIX systems.
-u	Tells Perl to do a core dump after the execution of your script. If you have the undump program, this core dump can be turned into an executable for quicker implementation.
-V	Prints your Perl configuration characteristics.

Syntax	Description
-v	Returns the version of Perl you are using.
-w	Puts the compiler in "warn" mode. It will let you know of instances where your script might compile and work but may cause you problems in the long run.
-x	Allows you to execute a script that is embedded in the middle of a file. Perl will search the file for your #! line and then execute the rest of the script as normal. If there is data after the script as well, then you must specify a __END__ to let Perl know not to continue processing.

Literals

The following is a list of literals (nonstandard characters) and other Perl conventions. This reference will be helpful for both parsing files for nonalphanumeric characters and for the layout of various Perl information.

Syntax	Type	Description
__DATA__	Token	Designates that the following information is not part of the script.
__END__	Token	Signifies the end of the script.
__FILE__	Token	Signifies the filename of your program.
__LINE__	Token	Signifies the current line of your program.
\a	String	Alert (bell) character.
\b	String	Backspace character.
\cC	String	*Ctrl+C* character.
\E	Escape	Ends implementation of \L , \Q, and \U character.
\e	String	*Esc.* character.
\f	String	Form-feed character.
\L	Escape	All characters lowercase.
\l	Escape	Next character lowercase.
\n	String	Newline character.
\Q	Escape	Place a backslash before nonalphanumeric characters.
\r	String	Carriage return.
\t	String	Tab character.
\U	Escape	All characters uppercase.
\u	Escape	Next character uppercase.
\x7f	String	DEL in octal.
num	Numeric	Designates that the value of num is an integer.
num.num	Numeric	Designates the value of num is a float.
0xalphanumeric	Numeric	Hexadecimal number where alphanumeric is a hexadecimal number.

Syntax	Type	Description
Onum	Numeric	Octal number where num is an octal number.
num.numEpower	Numeric	Allows you to specify an integer or float to a power of 10.
q//	Quote	Encloses the information in ´´ characters.
qq//	Quote	Encloses the information in "" characters.
qw//	Quote	Encloses the information in() characters.
qx//	Quote	Encloses the information in ´´ characters.

Pattern Matching

You will find most all parsing you perform will not be simple one-character or word searches. There may be many restrictions on finding a correct occurrence or special instances on how it may repeat. Perl has several built-in conventions to help your parsing needs. These conventions can narrow your search, like requesting only four numerical digits in a row, and fine-tune your searching location, like beginning at the end of a string. The following table lists Perl's conventions with a short description of what they do.

Pattern Matching Conventions	
Convention	**Description**
.	Matches any character but a newline character.
^	Matches pattern at the beginning of a string.
$	Matches pattern at the end of a string.
$1	Holds the value of the first "(string)" for later reference. Any following searches for other (string) will be held in $2, $3, etc.
*	Matches your string 0 or more times.
+	Matches your string at least 1 time.
?	Matches your string 0 or 1 time.
string1|string2	Matches string1 or string2. Note that you are not limited to only one occurrence of | in an expression.
(string)	Stores the value of string for later references. See the entry for $1 for the storing variable.
(?#string)	Contains a comment in which string is ignored.
(?string)	Matches if the search will match string next.
(?=string)	Matches if the search will match string next, but it will not include string in $&.
(?!string)	Matches if the search will not match string next.
{a}	Your string must be matched exactly *a* times.
{a,}	Your string must be matched at least *a* times.
{a, b}	Matches at least *a* times, but no more than *b*.

Convention	Description
\A	Matches at the beginning of the string you passed.
\B	Matches a word boundary. If placed before your search string, it will find the instances that do not begin with your string. If at the end, it will find those instances that do not end with your string. This option is the reverse of the \b option.
\b	Matches at word boundaries. If placed before your search string, it will find instances that begin with your string. If placed after your search string, it will find instances ending with your string.
\D	Matches nondigit characters.
\d	Matches a numeric digit from 0 to 9.
\S	Matches anything that is not white space. This is the same as [^ \f\n\r\t].
\s	Matches any white space. This is the same as [\f\n\r\t].
\W	Matches a nonword character that is not a-z, A-Z, 0-9, or an underscore (_).
\W	Matches a word character that is a-z, A-Z, 0-9, or an underscore (_).
\Z	Matches at the end of the string you passed.

You will also run across entries that are not your normal alphanumeric characters (A - Z, a-z, 0 - 9). These characters could represent anything from a carriage return to a tab, and their presence can not be ignored when parsing files that contain them. Common representations have been set up to allow you to find entries that are not alphanumeric. The following table lists these representations along with a brief description of what entry each representation will match.

Character Representations	
Representation	**Matches**
\metacharacter	Escapes *metacharacter* so you can search for it as well. This will allow you to search for characters that Perl uses in its syntax, such as \. See the entry for *quotemeta* in the Perl Commands section for more information on metacharacters.
\octal	Represents the ASCII character via its *octal* value.
\0	Represents *NULL*.
\a	Represents an alert character.
\cChar	Represents the ASCII control character specified by *Char*.
\e	Represents ESC character.
\f	Represents form-feed character.
\n	Represents newline character.
\r	Represents carriage return character.
\t	Represents tab character.
\xhex	Represents the ASCII character via its *hex* value.

One of the major advantages to Perl is its built-in options that can be passed to its various parsing operators. These options allow programmers to modify the default search characteristics of the operators to better suit their needs. If, for instance, you wish to parse a string for a certain run of characters, but you are not sure of the case to be passed, you could use the *i* option to your *m* or *s* search to make the search case insensitive. These small functionality features allows a programmer to be truly efficient in his or her coding.

The following table lists the options that can be passed to the various searching operators. Each entry is accompanied by the type of search it can be used with as well as a brief description of what it does.

Parsing Options		
Option	Search Used With	Description
c	tr, y	Replaces all non*original* characters with *replacement*. See the second example of y for this type of implementation.
d	tr, y	Deletes all *original* instances found. After the deletion, the blank space is removed. See the second example of *tr* for this type of implementation.
e	s	Tells Perl to evaluate the right side as an expression.
g	m, s	Finds all occurrences in the string passed.
i	m, s	Performs a case-insensitive search.
m	m, s	Tells Perl to treat the string being parsed as multiple lines.
o	m, s	Tells Perl to compile the pattern only once.
s	m, s	Tells Perl to treat the string being parsed as a single line.
s	tr, y	Replaces any sequential *original* occurrences with only one *replacement*. For instance, if you replaced all the *o*'s in "look" with *i*, then the resultant string would be "lik."
x	m, s	Tells Perl to use its extended regular expressions. See the table in "Perl Options" earlier in this appendix for a list of extended regular expressions.

Formatting

When creating output for your various Perl implementations, you will find it helpful to know that Perl has a few built-in formatting options to cover your basic formatting needs. These options can help you organize your output and make your report more readable. For more information on implementing these options, see the entries for *format* and *printf* in the Perl Commands section of this book. The following table lists the formatting options you can specify in your scripts.

Option	Description
@	Field initializer that signifies the start of a single-line field. When the end of a line is reached, a field initialized with @ will be truncated.
^	Field initializer that signifies the start of a multiple-line field. This is different from the @ field initializer in that it is allowed to wrap to multiple lines.
<	Left-justify the text in the field.
>	Right-justify the text in the field.
|	Center the text in the field.

To help you understand the implementation of these options, I have included a single example to implement each option. The first field formats a left-justified name up to 14 characters and the second field centers an age of up to 3 characters. The third field right-justifies the person's sex up to six characters, with the final entry initializing a left-justified field that has the option of wrapping to multiple lines:

```
format MYFORMAT =
@<<<<<<<<<<<<<<  @||     @>>>>>  ^<<<<<<<<<<<<<<<<<<<<<<<<<<<<<<
$name,              $age,$sex,   $occupation
.
```

Operators

The following table lists operators in order of their precedence. The *level* column specifies the level of precedence each operator has. This is used to distinguish between operators on separate lines but with the same precedence.

Expression Operators			
Level	Operator	Assoc'ty	Description / Version
1	(	Left	Terms and leftward list operators / P4, P5
2	->	Left	De-reference operator / P5
3	++	Non	Auto-increment / P4, P5
3	--	Non	Auto-decrement / P4, P5
4	**	Right	Exponential / P4, P5
5	+ (unary)	Right	Only used to separate a function from a parenthesis list that is not part of the function's arguments / P5
5	- (unary)	Right	Arithmetic negation if performed on a numeric value; otherwise, a string concatenated with value of the argument is returned / P4, P5
5	! (unary)	Right	Negation / P4, P5
5	~ (unary)	Right	Bitwise complement / P4, P5

Level	Operator	Assoc'ty	Description / Version
5	\ (unary)	Right	Reference / P5
6	=~	Left	Pattern matching / P4, P5
6	!~	Left	Negated pattern matching / P4, P5
7	*	Left	Multiplication / P4, P5
7	/	Left	Division / P4, P5
7	%	Left	Modulo division / P4, P5
7	x	Left	Returns the left operand repeated by the number of times specified by the right operand / P4, P5
8	+	Left	Addition / P4, P5
8	-	Left	Subtraction / P4, P5
8	.	Left	Concatenation / P4, P5
9	<<	Left	Bitwise shift left / P4, P5
9	>>	Left	Bitwise shift right / P4, P5
10	Named unary operators	Non	These include the following Perl functions: alarm, caller, chdir, chroot, cos, defined, delete, do, eval, exists, exit, exp, gethostbyname, getnetbyname, getgrp, getprotobyname, glob, gmtime, goto, hex, int, lc, lcfirst, length, local, localtime, log, lstat, my, oct, ord, quotemeta, rand, readlink, ref, require, reset, return, rmdir, scalar, sin, sleep, sqrt, srand, stat, uc, ucfirst, umask, undef / P4, P5
11	<	Non	Numeric less than / P4, P5
11	lt	Non	String less than / P4, P5
11	<=	Non	Numeric less than or equal to / P4, P5
11	le	Non	String less than or equal to / P4, P5
11	>	Non	Numeric greater than / P4, P5
11	gt	Non	String greater than / P4, P5
11	>=	Non	Numeric greater than or equal to / P4, P5
11	ge	Non	String greater than or equal to / P4, P5
12	==	Non	Numeric equality / P4, P5
12	eq	Non	String equality / P4, P5
12	!=	Non	Numeric inequality / P4, P5
12	ne	Non	String inequality / P4, P5
12	<=>	Non	Numeric comparison / P4, P5
12	cmp	Non	String comparison / P4, P5
13	&	Left	Bitwise AND / P4, P5
14	|	Left	Bitwise OR / P4, P5
14	^	Left	Bitwise XOR (exclusive OR) / P4, P5
15	&&	Left	Logical AND / P4, P5
16	||	Left	Logical OR / P4, P5
17	..	Non	Range in scalar context. Enumeration in array context. / P4, P5

Level	Operator	Assoc'ty	Description / Version
18	?:	Right	Conditional (if..then..else) operator / P4, P5
19	=	Right	Assignment / P4, P5
19	+=	Right	Addition and assignment / P4, P5
19	-=	Right	Subtraction and assignment / P4, P5
19	*=	Right	Multiplication and assignment / P4, P5
19	/=	Right	Division and assignment / P4, P5
19	%=	Right	Modulo division and assignment / P4, P5
19	**=	Right	Exponential and assignment / P4, P5
19	&&=	Right	Logical AND and assignment / P4, P5
19	&=	Right	Bitwise AND and assignment / P4, P5
19	||=	Right	Logical OR and assignment / P4, P5
19	|=	Right	Bitwise OR and assignment / P4, P5
19	^=	Right	Bitwise XOR (exclusive OR) and assignment / P4, P5
19	>>=	Right	Bitwise shift right and assignment / P4, P5
19	<<=	Right	Bitwise shift left and assignment / P4, P5
19	.=	Right	Concatenation and assignment / P4, P5
19	x=	Right	Left operand repeated by the number of times specified by the right operand and assignment / P4, P5
20	,	Left	Comma operator and list element separator / P4, P5
20	=>	Left	Mimics the comma operator / P5
21	)	Non	Rightward list operators / P4, P5
22	not	Right	Low-precedence negation / P5
23	and	Left	Low-precedence AND / P5
24	or	Left	Low-precedence OR / P5
24	xor	Left	Low-precedence XOR (exclusive OR) / P5

In addition to the various expression operators, Perl has built in file test operators. These operators simply test the properties and attributes of the expression passed. The following is a list and description of various file test operators:

File Test Operators	
Operator	**Description**
-A	Determines how long its has been since expression was accessed.
-B	Determines if the expression passed is a binary file.
-b	Determines if the expression passed is a block device.
-C	Determines how long its has been since expression's inode was accessed.
-c	Determines if the expression passed is a character device.
-d	Determines if the expression passed is a directory.
-e	Determines if the expression passed exists.

Operator	Description
-f	Determines if the expression passed is a non-text file.
-g	Determines if the expression passed has its setgid bit set.
-l	Determines if the expression passed is a symbolic link.
-M	Determines how long it has been since expression was modified.
-o	Determines if the expression passed is owned by the user executing the script.
-p	Determines if the expression passed is a named pipe command.
-r	Determines if the expression passed is readable.
-S	Determines if the expression passed is a socket.
-s	Determines if the expression passed contains information.
-T	Determines if the expression passed is a text file.
-t	Determines if the expression passed represents a terminal.
-u	Determines if the expression passed has its setuid bit set.
-w	Determines if the expression passed can be written to.
-x	Determines if the expression passed is an executable.
-z	Determines if the expression passed is an empty file.

Loop Control

The following table contains a list of the loop control commands that can be used in Perl. Not all of these commands fully qualify as loop control commands, but these can be used in the body of a loop for better control. Only a brief syntax has been given, so please see each individual entry in the Perl Commands section of this book for a more defined explanation of their usage.

Type	Syntax
for	for(EXPRESSION; CONDITION; CONTROL){CODE}
	for(EXPRESSION1, EXPRESSION2; CONDITION1, CONDITION2; CONTROL1, CONTROL2){CODE}
	for(;;){CODE}
foreach	foreach $variable(@list){CODE}
goto	goto SECTION
if	if (CONDITION){CODE}
	CODE if(CONDITION)
if..else	if (CONDITION){CODE}else{CODE}
last	last SECTION
next	next(SECTION)
redo	redo(SECTION)
unless	unless(*CONDITION*){*CODE*}
until	until(*CONDITION*){*CODE*}
until..continue	until(*CONDITION*){*CODE*}continue{*CODE*}
while	while(*CONDITION*){*CODE*}
while..continue	while(*CONDITION*){*CODE*}continue{*CODE*}

Debugger Commands

The following table contains a list of the commands that you can execute on the Perl debugger along with a short description of each. You can enter the Perl debugger by using the –D switch to Perl.

Syntax	Description
<CR>	Repeats last *n* or *s* option.
< *command*	Tells the debugger to execute *command* after going through the script but before another debugger command is entered.
> *command*	Tells the debugger to execute *command* before continuing through the script.
! *num*	Repeats command indexed by *num*. See the entry for *H* to display the command index number.
! -*num*	Repeats command back *num* entries. See the entry for *H* to display the command index number.
! *original*	Redoes the last command that began with *original*.
-	Lists previous several lines.
= *alias*	Defines a command alias for those commands you may be using multiple times.
^D	Exit.
/*original*/	Searches for *original*.
?*original*?	Searches for *original* starting at end.
A	Deletes all actions.
a *num command*	Tells the debugger to execute *command* at line *num*.
b *num*	Sets a breakpoint at *num*.
b *num CONDITION*	Sets a breakpoint at *num* based on *CONDITION*.
b *subroutine CONDITION*	Sets a breakpoint at *subroutine* based on *CONDITION*.
c	Tells the script to execute until a breakpoint is reached.
c *num*	Tells the script to execute until line *num* is reached.
command	Executes *command* as a Perl statement.
D	Deletes all breakpoints.
d *num*	Deletes the breakpoint at *num*.
f *filename*	Switches to viewing *filename*.
H	Lists the preceding debugger commands you have entered. This is much like the **history** command on UNIX machines.
H -*num*	Lists the preceding *num* debugger commands you have entered. This is much like the **history** command on UNIX machines.
h *COMMAND*	Prints a help message on the debugger *COMMAND* passed.
L	Lists the actions and breakpoints.
l	Lists next several lines.
l *minimum + num*	Lists *num* lines starting at *minimum*.

Syntax	Description
l *minimum - maximum*	Lists lines from *minimum* to *maximum*.
l *num*	Lists line *num*.
l *subroutine*	Lists several lines from *subroutine*.
n	Executes a single line of code as well as displaying the next line to be executed, but will not enter subroutines as the *s* command will.
p *EXPRESSION*	Prints the value of *EXPRESSION* passed.
q	Exits the debugger.
r	Tells the debugger to go ahead and finish executing the complete subroutine if you are in a subroutine and you are executing a line at a time.
R	Restarts the debugger.
S	Lists all the subroutines, each on a new line.
S *original*	Lists the subroutines matching *original*, each on a new line.
S *!original*	Lists the subroutines not matching *original*, each on a new line.
s	Executes a single line of code as well as displaying the next line to be executed.
T	Displays all subroutines that have been called.
t	Turns on trace mode.
t[*EXPRESSION*]	Traces through the execution of *EXPRESSION*.
V *package variable*	Displays the variable and value in the passed *package*.
w num	List several lines around num.
X *variable*	Displays the *variable* passed and its value.
x *EXPRESSION*	Evaluates and prints a formatted result of the *EXPRESSION* passed. The evaluation is done in list context.

ASCII Character Set

The following table contains a list of the ASCII characters and their decimal representation. Do note that not all systems support this character set and a call to the *chr* function may not return the correct character. For a safe implementation, try to stick with the basic alphanumeric characters (a-z, A-Z, and 0-9).

Note: these characters may vary on different operating systems.

Dec. Value	ASCII Char.	Dec. Value	ASCII Char.	Dec. Value	ASCII Char.
0		40	(	79	O
1	☺	41	)	80	P
2	☻	42	*	81	Q
3	♥	43	+	82	R
4	♦	44	,	83	S
5	♣	45	-	84	T
6	♠	46	.	85	U
7	•	47	/	86	V
8	bksp	48	0	87	W
9	tab	49	1	88	X
10	⊞	50	2	89	Y
11	♂	51	3	90	Z
12	♀	52	4	91	[
13	return	53	5	92	\
14	♫	54	6	93	]
15	*	55	7	94	^
16	▶	56	8	95	_
17	◀	57	9	96	‘
18	◊	58	:	97	a
19	!!	59	;	98	b
20	¶	60	<	99	c
21	§	61	=	100	d
22	–	62	>	101	e
23	◊	63	?	102	f
24	↑	64	@	103	g
25	↓	65	A	104	h
26	→	66	B	105	i
27	←	67	C	106	j
28	∟	68	D	107	k
29	↔	69	E	108	l
30	▲	70	F	109	m
31	▼	71	G	110	n
32	space	72	H	111	o
33	!	73	I	112	p
34	"	74	J	113	q
35	#	75	K	114	r
36	$	76	L	115	s
37	%	77	M	116	t
38	&	78	N	117	u
39	'				

Dec. Value	ASCII Char.	Dec. Value	ASCII Char.	Dec. Value	ASCII Char.
118	v	157	¥	196	─
119	w	158	₧	197	┼
120	x	159	ƒ	198	╞
121	y	160	á	199	╟
122	z	161	í	200	╚
123	{	162	ó	201	╔
124	|	163	ú	202	╩
125	}	164	ñ	203	╦
126	~	165	Ñ	204	╠
127	⌂	166	ª	205	═
128	Ç	167	º	206	╬
129	ü	168	¿	207	╧
130	é	169	⌐	208	╨
131	â	170	¬	209	╤
132	ä	171	½	210	╥
133	à	172	¼	211	╙
134	å	173	¡	212	╘
135	ç	174	«	213	╒
136	ê	175	»	214	╓
137	ë	176	░	215	╫
138	è	177	▒	216	╪
139	ï	178	▓	217	┘
140	î	179	│	218	┌
141	ì	180	┤	219	█
142	Ä	181	╡	220	▄
143	Å	182	╢	221	▌
144	É	183	╖	222	▐
145	æ	184	╕	223	▀
146	Æ	185	╣	224	α
147	ô	186	║	225	ß
148	ö	187	╗	226	Γ
149	ò	188	╝	227	π
150	û	189	╜	228	Σ
151	ù	190	╛	229	∂
152	ÿ	191	┐	230	μ
153	Ö	192	└	231	ì
154	Ü	193	┴	232	Φ
155	¢	194	┬	233	Θ
156	£	195	├	234	Ω

Dec. Value	ASCII Char.
235	δ
236	∞
237	$\emptyset$
238	$\in$
239	$\cap$
240	$\equiv$
241	$\pm$
242	$\geq$
243	$\leq$
244	$\lceil$
245	$\rfloor$
246	$\div$
247	$\approx$
248	$\circ$
249	$\circ$
250	$\cdot$
251	$\sqrt{}$
252	^{n}
253	^{2}
254	■
255	

Appendix D
Error Messages

This appendix includes all the error messages you should see in Perl. Some of the messages have pieces that will be replaced by Perl when they occur to give you more information. These places are indicated by a string in all caps.

There are six main types of Perl errors, which are listed in the following table in order of severity.

Error Type	Notes
Warning	A warning message that you will only see if you're using the -w switch of Perl. These warnings can be trapped by assigning a sub-routine reference to $SIG{__WARN__}.
Deprecation	This error is indicating that you're using a construct of Perl that has been deprecated and should no longer be used. These messages are only seen if you use the -w switch.
Severe warning	This indicates a more extreme warning. These warnings can be trapped by assigning a subroutine reference to $SIG{__WARN__}.
Fatal	These errors are fatal and will cause your script to stop executing. They can be trapped with an eval statement.
Very fatal	These errors are very fatal and will cause your script to stop executing with no hope of trapping them.
External	These error messages come from a source other than Perl.

There is one other error type: Panic. These errors come from an internal problem in Perl or your system. It would be very rare that you would actually see one of these messages.

The error messages are sorted alphabetically with error messages that start with odd characters coming first. If the odd character is simply a quote around an alpha character, then it is sorted by the first alpha character. The messages beginning with a string that will be replaced by Perl are listed first.

OP (...) interpreted as function   WARNING

Occurrence   You will see this warning when you use a list operator with parentheses and additional processing after the ending paren.

Example   The following code will generate the error. In this case, it will try to multiple the return value of print(3) by two, which is most likely not what you were after:

```
print (3) * 2;
```

```
print (...) interpreted as function
```

FUNC argument is not a HASH element   FATAL

Occurrence   If you try to pass anything other than a hash element to a function expecting one, you will generate an error. Currently this only happens with the exists and delete operators. The delete operator can accept a hash element or a hash slice (i.e., @var{'one', 'two', 'three'}).

Example   The following code will generate the error:

```
if (exists($var)) { ... }
```

```
exists operator argument is not a HASH element
```

See Also   delete, exists

FILE did not return a true value   FATAL

Occurrence   When you import a file using the use or require functions, the file must
return a true value to indicate that it compiled and initialized correctly.
Generally these files end with a 1;, but they can end with any value that
evaluates as true.

Example   The following code will generate the error. Assume there's a file named
"myLib.pl" in the library search path (@INC) that doesn't return with a true
value:

```
require "myLib.pl";
```

```
myLib.pl did not return a true value
```

See Also   require, use

VAL found where operator expected   SEVERE WARNING

Occurrence   You will see this error when Perl sees a term where it was expecting an
operator. This generally occurs when you leave out an operator or a semicolon.

Example   The following code will generate the error:

```
print "howdy\n"
$var = "partner";
```

```
Scalar found where operator expected
```

FILE had compilation errors   FATAL

Occurrence   You will see this as the last error message if errors occur when you compile a
script using the –c option to Perl.

Example   If you invoke Perl from the command line on your script and errors occur,
you will generate this error:

```
perl -c myScript.pl
myScript.pl had compilation errors
```

FILE has too many errors

FATAL

Occurrence   You will see this error when the Perl parser has encountered too many errors (usually 10) in your script.

VAL matches null string many times

WARNING

Occurrence   You will see this error when your regular expression pattern would cause an infinite loop if the regexp engine didn't specifically check for it.

SYM never introduced

SEVERE WARNING

Occurrence   You will get this warning when the symbol listed was declared but went out of scope before it could be used.

FILE syntax OK

FATAL

Occurrence   You will see this as the last error message if your script compiled correctly when you compiled a script using the –c option to Perl .

Example   If you invoke Perl from the command line on your script it compiled successfully, you will see the following:

```
perl -c myScript.pl

myScript.pl syntax OK
```

FUNC: Command not found

EXTERNAL

FUNC: Expression syntax

EXTERNAL

FUNC: Undefined variable

EXTERNAL

FUNC: not found

Occurrence   You will see one of these four error messages if you run your script through csh instead of Perl. This may be because of the #! line in your script or the way your shell interprets scripts. You can correct it by fixing the #! line or by running your script through the Perl interpreter manually.

-P not allowed for setuid/setgid script

Occurrence   This error will occur if you use the –P option (which causes the C preprocessor to preprocess your script) on a setuid/setgid script; it will break a security condition and fail.

-T and –B not implemented on filehandles

Occurrence   You will get this error message if Perl can't peek at the stdio buffer of filehandles because it doesn't know about your type of stdio. To get around this, you can simply use the filename instead of the filehandle.

/REGEXP/: ?+* follows nothing in regexp

Occurrence   You will see this message if you have a ?, +, or * in a regular expression without anything preceding it. If you want to match the specific character, you need to escape it with a backslash.

Example   The following code will generate the error:

```
print if /+2/;
```

```
/+2/: ?+* follows nothing in regexp
```

@ outside of string

Occurrence   You will see this error message if you had a pack template that specified an absolute position that was outside the string being unpacked.

See Also   pack

% may only be used in unpack
FATAL

Occurrence You can't use % in the format string in the pack function to supply a checksum. This is only usable in the unpack function.

Example The following code will generate the error:

```
$packed = pack ('%L', 1);
```

See Also unpack

\1 better written as $1
WARNING

Occurrence You will see this warning if you have *digit* in the replacement portion of a s/// regular expression. It will still work, but it's better to use $1 since it does the exact same thing and doesn't run into problems after the first nine occurrences.

'I' and '<' may not both be specified on command line
FATAL

'I' and '>' may not both be specified on command line
FATAL

Occurrence These errors are specific to the VMS operating system. You will see one of these two errors if you try to use both a pipe and redirection on the command line at the same time. With <, Perl would be confused about which should be STDIN since both should be. With >, Perl is confused about where to send its STDOUT output.

accept() on closed fd
WARNING

Occurrence   You will get this warning if you try to call the accept function on a filehandle
that has been closed. This might be because the socket function failed and
you didn't check to make sure it succeeded.

Example   The following code will generate this error:

```
socket(SOCKET, PF_INET, SOCK_STREAM, $proto);
# assume this failed
accept(CLIENT, SOCKET);
```

Allocation too large:
VERY FATAL

Occurrence   You will generate this error message on an MS-DOS machine if you try to
allocate more than 64K.

Allocation too large
FATAL

Occurrence   You will get this error if you try to allocate more than 2^31+x (where x is a
very small amount) bytes for holding data in your script.

Arg too short for msgsnd

Occurrence   You will see this error message if you try to pass an MSG to msgsnd that is
shorter than sizeof(long). This is because the message must be a packed
value that begins with a long specifying the message type.

Example   The following code will generate the error:

```
msgsnd($id, 1, $flags);
```

Ambiguous use of EXPR resolved as EXPR   WARNING

Occurrence   An expression in your script may have been interpreted differently than what you expected. This can generally be resolved by adding a missing quote, operator, parentheses, or declaration.

Args must match #! line   FATAL

Occurrence   If you have a setuid script, the arguments you invoke Perl with must match the arguments on the #! line of the script. If your system only allows one argument on the #! line, you can match this by combining switches (i.e., making –p –i be –pi).

Argument "STR" isn't numeric OP   WARNING

Occurrence   You will get this warning if you try to pass a string to an operator that was expecting a numeric value. You will possibly see in the warning which operator received the string.

Example   The following code will generate the error:

```
print "test" * 2;
```

```
Argument "test" isn't numeric in multiply
```

Array @VAR missing the @ in argument # of FUNC()   DEPRECATED

Occurrence   In very old versions of Perl, you were allowed to pass arrays to some functions without the @. This behavior has been deprecated.

Assignment to both a list and a scalar FATAL

Occurrence You will see this error message if you try to assign to a conditional operator and the second and third arguments aren't both scalars or both lists. This is because Perl won't know which context to supply to the right side of the assignment.

Example The following code will generate the error:

```
$check ? $var : @var = (1,2);
```

Attempt to free temp prematurely WARNING

Occurrence Mortalized values should be freed by the free_tmps internal routine. If something else is freeing the SV before free_tmps, this warning will be generated because when free_tmps does try to free it, it will be freeing an unreferenced scalar.

Attempt to free unreferenced scalar WARNING

Occurrence You will see this warning if Perl tried to decrement the reference count of a scalar to 0 only to find it was already at 0 and should already be freed.

Bad arg length for FUNC, is # should be # FATAL

Occurrence You will get this error if you passed a buffer that wasn't the correct size to msgctl, semctl, or shmctl.

See Also msgctl, semctl, shmctl

Bad filehandle: HANDLE FATAL

Occurrence You will see this message if you try to use a symbol in a function expecting a filehandle if the symbol doesn't refer to a filehandle.

Bad free() ignored

SEVERE WARNING

Occurrence   You will see this warning if an internal routine called free on a variable that had never been malloc'd.

Bad name after PACKAGE::

FATAL

Occurrence   You will see this error if you try to name a symbol using a fully qualified variable name but didn't pass the whole symbol. This most often happens if you try to interpolate a variable outside quotes.

Example   The following code would generate this error:

```
$var = "packageVariable";
$symbol = myPackage::$var;

Bad name after myPackage::
```

Badly placed ()'s

EXTERNAL

Occurrence   You will see this message if you run your script through csh instead of Perl. This may be because of the #! line in your script or the way your shell interprets scripts. You can correct it by fixing the #! line or by running your script through the Perl interpreter manually.

BEGIN failed—compilation aborted

FATAL

Occurrence   You will see this error if an untrapped exception occurred while the BEGIN subroutine was being executed.

bind() on closed fd

WARNING

Occurrence   You will get this warning if you try to call the bind function on a filehandle that has been closed. This might be because the socket function failed and you didn't check to make sure it succeeded.

Example   The following code will generate this error:

```
socket(SOCKET, PF_INET, SOCK_STREAM, $proto);
# assume this failed
bind(SOCKET, $iaddr);
```

Bizarre copy of VAL in VAR

PERL

Occurrence   You will see this error if Perl found a copy of an internal value that shouldn't have the ability to be copied.

Callback called exit

FATAL

Occurrence   You will see this error if a subroutine was invoked from an external package through the perl_call_sv function and called exit.

Can't "X" outside a block

FATAL

Occurrence   In this error, X may be one of last, next, or redo. You will get this error if you try to use one of these statements when you're not in a loop block. This means that the block in an if/then statement isn't considered a loop block. You could add an extra set of curly braces to add a single loop block.

Example   The following code will generate this error:

```
print "howdy\n";
last;
```

```
Can't "last" outside a block
```

Can't bless non-reference value

FATAL

Occurrence You will get this error if you try to bless a variable that isn't a reference. Perl does this to enforce encapsulation of objects.

Example The following code will generate this error:

```
package myPackage;

sub new {
    my $class = shift;
    my $var = shift;
    bless $var, $class;
}
```

Can't call method "METHOD" in empty package "PACKAGE"

FATAL

Occurrence You will get this error if you try to invoke a method on a package that is acting as a class but doesn't have anything defined in it, including methods.

Can't call method "METHOD" on unblessed reference

FATAL

Occurrence You will get this error message if you try to call a method on something that isn't an object reference. A reference can't be an object reference if it hasn't been blessed.

Example The following code will generate this error:

```
package myPackage;
sub new { return {} }
# sub new { bless {} } wouldn't make this error
$obj = new myPackage;
$obj->myMethod

Can't call method "myMethod" on unblessed reference
```

Can't call method "METHOD" without a package or object reference
FATAL

Occurrence   You will get this error message if you try to call a method on something that isn't an object reference or a package name. You will generally get this if the object reference you're passing is null.

Example   The following code will generate this error:

```
$obj->myMethod
```

```
Can't call method "myMethod" without a package or object reference
```

Can't chdir to DIR
FATAL

Occurrence   You will get this message if you invoke Perl with the –x option but the directory you specified can't be chdir'd to. This most likely occurs if the directory doesn't exist or you don't have permission to change to it.

Example   The following code will generate this error:

```
perl -x/abc myScript.pl
```

```
Can't chdir to /abc
```

Can't coerce VAR to X in OP
FATAL

Occurrence   You will get this error message if you try to force an SV to stop being what it is. The possible values for X in this message are integer, number, or string.

Example   The following code will generate this error:

```
*var .= "one";
```

```
Can't coerce GLOB to string in concat
```

Can't declare TYPE in my
FATAL

Occurrence   You will get this error if you try to declare anything other than an array, associative array, or scalar with the my function.

Example   The following code will generate this error:

```
my \$var;

Can't declare scalar ref constructor in my
```

Can't do inplace edit on FILE: REASON
SEVERE WARNING

Occurrence   You will get this if Perl can't create a new file while doing an in-place edit (using the –i option of Perl).

Can't do inplace edit without backup
FATAL

Occurrence   You will get this error if you're trying to do an in-place edit without specifying a backup file to use on systems that don't allow reading from a deleted but still open file. You can specify a backup by listing it after the –i, that is –i.old.

Can't do inplace edit: FILE > 14 characters
SEVERE WARNING

Occurrence   You will get this warning if the backup file you're creating for an in-place edit has a longer filename than is allowed by the system you're working on.

Can't do inplace edit: FILE is not a regular file
SEVERE WARNING

Occurrence   You will get this error if you try to do an in-place edit on a file that isn't a regular file. This file could be in the /dev directory or may be a FIFO. The file will be skipped.

Can't do setuid

FATAL

Occurrence You will get this error message if Perl tried to exec to suidperl so that it could do setuid emulation but failed for some reason. You can look for a corresponding Perl binary that is preceded by an s (i.e., perl5.003 -> sperl5.003) in the directory where your Perl binary is. If the file is there, make sure it is executable. If it's not there, ask your systems administrator why it's not.

Can't do waitpid with flags

FATAL

Occurrence You will get this error message if you try to pass flags to a waitpid call and your system doesn't have waitpid or wait4. You'll need to pass 0 as your flags in this case.

See Also waitpid

Can't do {n,m} with n > m

FATAL

Occurrence You will get this error if you try to set the minimum value greater than the maximum value in a regular expression match. If for some reason you wish to match 0 times, use {0}.

Example The following code will generate this error:

```
$var = "1111111";
$var =~ s/1{5,4}/2/;
```

Can't emulate –SWITCH on #! line

FATAL

Occurrence You will get this error if you try to pass a switch on the #! line of a Perl script when it doesn't make sense at that point. Using –x is one instance where it doesn't make sense.

Example The following code will generate this error:

```
#!/usr/local/bin/perl -x/tmp

Can't emulate -x on #! line
```

Can't exec "PROGRAM": MESSAGE

Occurrence   You will get this warning if you have a system, exec, or piped open call that
              couldn't execute the program you passed it. The reason it couldn't execute
              will be given in the error message.

Example   The following code will generate this error:

```
system("noprog");
```

```
Can't exec "noprog": No such file or directory
```

See Also   exec, open, system

Can't exec PROGRAM

Occurrence   You will get this error if Perl tries to execute a specific program based on the
              #! line in your script. If you don't want that program to be run, then make
              sure Perl is in the #! line.

Example   The following code will generate this error:

```
#!/usr/no/program
```

...

    Then if you pass this script to Perl by:

```
perl myprog.pl
```

```
Can't exec /usr/no/program
```

Can't execute PROGRAM

Occurrence   You will get this error when you run Perl with the –S switch but Perl can't
              find the program you listed or it can't execute it.

Example   The following command-line invocation may generate this error:

```
perl -S myProg.pl
```

```
Can't execute myProg.pl
```

Can't find label LABEL

Occurrence   You will get this error if you have a goto statement without a valid label. This may be because of a typo or because the label doesn't exist in the file.

Example   The following script will generate this error:

```
goto MyLabel; # typo, should be myLabel
print "not printed\n";
myLabel:
print "printed\n";

Can't find label MyLabel
```

Can't find string terminator EXPECTED anywhere before EOF

Occurrence   You will get this message if Perl can't find the expected string terminator before the end of your script.

Example   The following code will generate this error:

```
print <<"END";
Line One
Line Two

Can't find string terminator END anywhere before EOF
```

Can't fork

Occurrence   You will get this error if a fatal error occurred while your script tried to fork.

See Also   fork

Can't get filespec—stale stat buffer?

SEVERE WARNING

Occurrence This warning is specific to the VMS operating system. You may get this message due to the fact that VMS access checking is different from UNIX access checking, which Perl assumes. You shouldn't see this warning as an error to running a Perl command; it will only appear from internal code.

Can't get pipe mailbox device name

FATAL

Occurrence This error is specific to the VMS operating system. You will get this error if Perl can't retrieve a mailbox name that was created to act as a pipe.

Can't get SYSGEN parameter value for MAXBUF

FATAL

Occurrence This error is specific to the VMS operating system. You will get this error if Perl asked $GETSYI how big the mailbox buffers should be and didn't get a response.

Can't goto subroutine outside a subroutine

FATAL

Occurrence You will get this error if you try to pass a subroutine to the goto command and you're not inside a subroutine.

Example The following code will generate this error:

```
goto &mySub;
sub mySub {
   print "One\n";
}
```

See Also   goto

Can't localize a reference   FATAL

Occurrence   You will get this error if you try to pass a reference to the local command. This causes an error because the compiler can't tell whether the reference will point to something with a symbol table entry, which is required to be local.

Example   The following code will generate this error:

```
local $$ref;
```

See Also   local

Can't localize lexical variable VAR   FATAL

Occurrence   You will get this error if you try to pass a variable to the local command that you've already declared as a lexical variable using the my command. If you want to localize a variable with the same name in a package, use the fully qualified name.

Example   The following code will generate this error:

```
my $var;
local $var;

Can't localize lexical variable $var
```

See Also   local, my

Can't locate FILE in @INC   FATAL

Occurrence   You will get this error if you import a file using do, require, or use and the file can't be found in the directories listed in the @INC array. You may need to add the directory to the @INC array or make sure you don't have a typo in the filename.

Example   The following code may generate this error:

```
use NoFile;

Can't locate NoFile.pm in @INC
```

See Also   do, require, use

Can't locate object method "METHOD" via package "PACKAGE"

FATAL

Occurrence   You will get this error if you invoke a method on a package where the package or any of its base classes don't define the method.

Example   The following code will generate this error:

```
package myPackage;
sub new { bless {} }
package main;
$obj = new myPackage;
$obj->myMethod;

Can't locate object method "myMethod" via package "myPackage"
```

Can't locate package PACKAGE for @PACKAGE::ISA

WARNING

Occurrence   You will get this warning if there is a package listed in the @ISA array of your package and it can't be found.

Example   The following code will generate this error:

```
package myPackage;
@ISA = {"noPackage"};
sub new { bless {} }
package main;
$obj = new myPackage;

Can't locate package noPackage for @myPackage::ISA
```

Can't mktemp()

FATAL

Occurrence   You will get this error message when using the –e switch and the mktemp function failed. This could be because the /tmp filesystem is full or corrupt.

Can't modify TYPE in OP   FATAL

Occurrence   You will get this error if you try to assign a value to the type given or try to change it.

Example   The following code will generate this error:

```
1++;
```

```
Can't modify constant item in postincrement
```

Can't modify non-existent substring   FATAL

Occurrence   You will see this error if the internal function that handles assigning a value to a substr was passed a NULL.

Can't msgrcv to read-only variable   FATAL

Occurrence   You will get this error if the buffer you pass to the msgrcv function isn't assignable.

See Also   msgrcv

Can't open FILE: REASON   SEVERE WARNING

Occurrence   You will get this message if you are using in-place edit and can't open the file for the reason given. This is most often because you don't have permission to read the file.

Example   The following command-line invocation may generate this error:

```
perl -pi -e 's/ 1 / one /g;' myFile.txt
```

```
Can't open myFile.txt: Permission denied
```

Can't open bidirectional pipe

WARNING

Occurrence   You will get this warning if you try to open a bidirectional pipe using the open function. You could use the IPC::Open2 module to open a bi-directional pipe or you could write the pipe's output to a filehandle and read it in through another.

Example   The following code will generate this error:

```
open ( ECHO, "|echo|" );
```

Can't open error file FILE as stderr
Can't open input file FILE as stdin
Can't open output file FILE as stdout
Can't open output pipe (name: PIPE)

FATAL

Occurrence   These four errors are specific to the VMS operating system. Perl handles command-line redirections itself, and in these cases, the file (or pipe) given after 2>, 2>>, <, >, >> or | couldn't be opened.

Can't open Perl script "FILE": REASON

FATAL

Occurrence   You will see this error if the Perl script you're trying to run can't be opened. The reason for the error will be appended to the error message.

Can't rename FILE to FILE: REASON, skipping file

SEVERE WARNING

Occurrence   You will see this error if you're using the –i switch and couldn't rename the file for the reason specified. This most likely happens when you don't have write permission for the directory the file is in.

Example   The following command-line invocation will generate this error:

```
perl -pi -e 's/ 1 / one /g;' myFile.txt
```

```
Can't rename myFile.txt to myFile.txt: Permission denied, skipping file
```

Can't reopen input pipe (name: PIPE) in binary mode

FATAL

Occurrence This error is specific to VMS. This error will occur if Perl thinks stdin is a pipe and tries to reopen stdin to accept binary data.

Can't reswap uid and euid

FATAL

Occurrence You will see this error if the setreuid function failed in the setuid emulator of suidperl.

Can't return outside a subroutine

FATAL

Occurrence You will see this error if you have a return statement that isn't in a subroutine block.

Example The following code will generate this error:

```
return $var;
```

Can't stat script "FILE"

FATAL

Occurrence If you do see this error, it is because Perl can't fstat the script even though it's already been opened.

Can't swap uid and euid

FATAL

Occurrence You will see this error if the setreuid function failed in the setuid emulator of suidperl.

Can't take log of #   FATAL

Occurrence   You will see this error if you try to take the log of a negative number.

Example   The following code will generate this error:

```
print log -1;

Can't take log of -1
```

Can't take sqrt of #   FATAL

Occurrence   You will see this error if you try to take the square root of a negative number.
              You can use the Complex module if you want to take square roots of nega-
              tive numbers.

Example   The following code will generate this error:

```
print sqrt -1;

Can't take sqrt of -1
```

Can't undef active subroutine   FATAL

Occurrence   You will see this error if you try to undef the currently running subroutine.

Example   The following code will generate this error:

```
&mySub;
sub mySub {
  print "@_\n";
  undef &mySub;
}
```

Can't unshift   FATAL

Occurrence   You will see this error if you try to unshift an array that isn't real. The main
              Perl stack is such an array.

See Also   unshift

Can't use "my VAR" in sort comparison

FATAL

Occurrence   You will see this error if you've declared either $a or $b as a lexical variable and then use them in a sort routine. You can avoid this by using the fully qualified name for the variable in question.

Example   The following code will generate this error:

```
my $a;
@arr = ( 1, 10, 100, 2, 20, 200 );
@sorted = sort bynumber @arr;
print "@sorted\n";
sub bynumber { $a <=> $b; }

Can't use "my $a" in sort comparison
```

Can't use VAR for loop variable

FATAL

Occurrence   You will see this error if you try to use anything other than a scalar variable as the loop variable in a foreach loop.

See Also   foreach

Can't use TYPE ref as TYPE ref

FATAL

Occurrence   You will see this error if you mix up your reference types. The ref function will tell you what type of reference you have.

See Also   ref

Can't use \1 to mean $1 in expression

WARNING

Occurrence   You may get this warning if you try to use \1 outside of a regular expression. This construct is only valid inside a regular expression. You should use $1 outside the regexp.

See Also   foreach

Can't use string ("STR") as TYPE ref while "strict refs" in use

FATAL

Occurrence You will see this error if you're using strict refs and you try to use a symbolic reference. You can only use hard references while strict refs is in effect.

Example The following code will generate this error:

```
use string "refs";
$var = 1;
print $$var, "\n";

Can't use string ("1") as a SCALAR ref while "strict refs" in use
```

Can't use an undefined value as TYPE reference

FATAL

Occurrence You will see this error if you try to create a reference without a defined value.

Can't use global VAR in "my"

FATAL

Occurrence You will see this error if you try to make a global special variable a lexical variable.

Example The following code will generate this error:

```
my $$;

Can't use global $$ in "my"
```

Can't use subscript on TYPE

FATAL

Occurrence   You will see this error if the compiler interpreted a bracketed expression as a subscript but couldn't determine that the left side of the bracket was an array.

Example   The following code will generate this error:

```
print var[1];
```

```
Can't use subscript on constant item
```

Can't write to temp file for –e: REASON

FATAL

Occurrence   The temp file for the –e switch couldn't be written to for the given reason. This most likely occurs if the /tmp filesystem is full or is corrupt.

Can't x= to readonly value

FATAL

Occurrence   You will see this error if you try to use the repeat operator on a read-only variable (since you can't modify that variable).

Example   The following code will generate this error:

```
$var = "12345";
$var =~ m/\d/;
$& x= 5;
print "$&\n";
```

Cannot open temporary file

FATAL

Occurrence   The temp file for the –e switch couldn't be created for the given reason. This most likely occurs if the /tmp filesystem is full or is corrupt.

chmod: mode argument is missing initial 0   WARNING

Occurrence   The mode argument of the chmod function expects an octal value. All octal values begin with 0 in Perl. (You could use decimal numbers, but the numbers wouldn't be readable by other users of your program.)

Example   The following code will generate this error:

```
chmod 644, "myFile.txt"
```

Close on upopened file <FILE>   WARNING

Occurrence   You will see this warning if you close a filehandle that wasn't opened.

Example   The following code will generate this error:

```
use Symbol;
$fh = gensym;
close ( $fh );

Close on upopened file <GEN0>
```

connect() on closed fd   WARNING

Occurrence   You will get this warning if you try to call the connect function on a filehandle that has been closed. This might be because the socket function failed and you didn't check to make sure it succeeded.

Example   The following code will generate this error:

```
socket(SOCKET, PF_INET, SOCK_STREAM, $proto);
# assume this failed
connect(CLIENT, $iaddr);
```

Deep recursion on subroutine "SUB" WARNING

Occurrence   You will get this warning if a subroutine calls itself 100 times more than it has returned. This is assumed to be an infinite recursion.

Example   The following code will generate this message:

```
print &recurse(1), "\n";
sub recurse {
  $num = shift;
  if ( $num < 150 ) {
  return $num + &recurse($num+1);
  } else {
    return $num+1;
  }
}
```

```
Deep recursion on subroutine "recurse"
```

Did you mean &SUB instead? WARNING

Occurrence   You will get this warning if you refer to an imported subroutine as a scalar instead of a subroutine (i.e., $SUB instead of &SUB).

(Did you mean $ or @ instead of %?) WARNING

Occurrence   You will get this warning if you try to access an associative array element (or list of elements) with % instead of $ or @.

Example   The following code will generate this error:

```
%list = ( 'one', 1, 'two', 2 );
print %list{'one'}, "\n";
```

Died
FATAL

Occurrence   You will get this message if you call die with the empty string or with no arguments and $@ was undefined.

Example   The following code will generate this error:

```
die "";
```

(Do you need to predeclare SUB?)
SEVERE WARNING

Occurrence   You will get this warning if you refer to a subroutine or module that hasn't been declared yet. You can declare an empty subroutine or package to make a forward declaration for the subroutine or package.

Example   The following code will generate this error:

```
$var = doNothing "one";
sub doNothing {
    return shift;
}

String found where operator expected
    (Do you need to predeclare doNothing?)
```

Duplicate free() ignored
SEVERE WARNING

Occurrence   You will get this warning if an internal function called free on something that was already free.

elseif should be elsif
SEVERE WARNING

Occurrence   You will get this error if you try to use elseif instead of elsif; elseif isn't a valid keyword in Perl so the compiler will think you are passing the block following elseif to an undeclared method.

Example   The following code will generate this error:

```
if (1) {
    print "Ok\n";
} elseif {
    print "Not Ok\n";
}
```

END failed—cleanup aborted   FATAL

Occurrence   You will get this error if an untrapped exception occurs in the END subroutine of your script.

Error converting file specification SPEC   FATAL

Occurrence   This error is specific to VMS. You will see this error if you pass an invalid file specification to Perl or its internal conversion routines can't handle the current case.

Execution of FILE aborted due to compilation errors.   FATAL

Occurrence   This is the last error message you will see when a fatal error occurs in your program.

Exiting X via FUNC   WARNING

Occurrence   You will see this warning if you exit an eval, pseudo-block, subroutine, or substitution abnormally. This could be because of a goto or loop control statement (or a return in the case of a substitution).

fcntl is not implemented

Occurrence   You will see this error if you try to use any of the file control functions and your system doesn't implement fcntl.

Filehandle HANDLE never opened

Occurrence   You will see this warning if you try to read from or write to a filehandle that hasn't been opened.

Example   The following code will generate this error:

```
print FILE "Message\n";
```

```
Filehandle main::File never opened
```

Filehandle HANDLE opened only for input

Occurrence   You will get this warning if you try to write to a read-only filehandle.

Example   The following code will generate this error:

```
open ( FILE, "<myFile.txt" );
print FILE "Message\n";
close ( FILE );
```

```
Filehandle main::FILE opened only for input
```

See Also   open

Final $ should be \$ or $name

Occurrence   You will get this error if you have a $ at the end of a string. If you meant it to be a variable, you need to add the variable name. If you meant it to be a dollar sign, you need to escape it with a backslash.

Example   The following code will generate this error:

```
socket(SOCKET, PF_INET, SOCK_STREAM, $proto);
# assume this failed
connect(CLIENT, $iaddr);
```

Format HANDLE redefined

WARNING

Occurrence   You will get this message if you redefine a format for a filehandle.

Example   The following code will generate this error:

```
format STDOUT =
@<<<<<<<<<<<<<<
$var
.

format STDOUT =
@>>>>>>>>>>>>>
$var

.


Format STDOUT redefined
```

Format not terminated

FATAL

Occurrence   You will see this error if you forgot to end a format with a period on a line by itself.

Example   The following code will generate this error:

```
format STDOUT =
@>>>>>>>>>>>>>
$var

$var = "one";
write;
```

Found = in conditional, should be ==
WARNING

Occurrence You will get this warning if you have an assignment operator in a conditional statement where the equality operator should be.

Example The following code will generate this error:

```
$var = $ARGV[0];
if ( $var = 1 ) { print "Is one\n"; }
else { print "Isn't one\n"; }
```

gdbm store returned #, errno #, key "KEY"
SEVERE WARNING

Occurrence You will only see this warning if you're using the GDBM_File module. It occurs if you try to store a key to the database and it fails for the given reason.

gethostent not implemented
FATAL

Occurrence You will get this error if you make a call to gethostent and gethostent isn't implemented on your system.

getpeername() on closed fd &
getsockname() on closed fd
WARNINGS

Occurrence You will get one of these errors if you try to get the socket name or peer socket name on a socket that has been closed.

Example The following code will generate this error:

```
socket(SOCKET, PF_INET, SOCK_STREAM, $proto);
# assume this failed
$name = getsockname(SOCKET);
```

getpwnam returned invalid UIC # for user "USER"
SEVERE WARNING

Occurrence   This error is specific to VMS. You will get this error if the sys$getuai function returned an invalid UIC.

[gs]etsockopt() on closed fd
WARNING

Occurrence   You will get this error if you try to get or set a socket option on a socket that has been closed.

Glob not terminated
FATAL

Occurrence   You will get this error if you have a left angle bracket (<) where Perl was expecting a term; it assumes there should be a > but there isn't one.

Global symbol "VAR" requires explicit package name
FATAL

Occurrence   You will see this error if you're using the strict vars pragma and you've used a variable that you didn't declare as a lexical variable (with my) or you didn't fully qualify it with its package name.

Example   The following code will generate this error:

```
use strict 'vars';
$var = "one";

Global symbol "var" requires explicit package name
```

goto must have a label   FATAL

Occurrence	You will get this error if you use the goto statement but don't give it a label to go to.
Example	The following code will generate this error:

```
goto;
```

See Also	goto

Had to create SYM unexpectedly   SEVERE WARNING

Occurrence	You will get this warning if a routine tried to access a symbol from the symbol table and the symbol didn't exist when it should have. The routine created the symbol to prevent a core dump.

Hash %VAR missing the % in argument # of
FUNC()   DEPRECATED

Occurrence	You will get this error if you try to pass a hash variable to a function without using the % like you could do with older versions of Perl.

Identifier "PACKAGE::SYM" used only once:
possible typo   WARNING

Occurrence	You will get this warning message if you only use a variable once in your program. If you only need the variable once, you can get rid of this warning by using the strict vars pragma.

Ill-formed logical name |NAME| in prime_env_iter

WARNING

Occurrence   This error is specific to VMS. You will see it if the logical name found while iterating over the environment variables with %ENV wasn't allowed based on the syntactic rules governing logical names. This entry will be skipped.

Illegal division by zero

FATAL

Occurrence   You will get this error if you try to divide by 0 (zero). This is generally caused by not checking input to make sure it's not 0.

Example   The following code will generate this error:

```
# assume the script was passed 0 for the 1st argument
$var = $ARGV[0];
print 10/$var, "\n";
```

Illegal modulus zero

FATAL

Occurrence   You will get this error if you try to find the remainder of a number when you divide it by 0 using the modulus operator. See the preceding error message.

Example   The following code will generate this error:

```
# assume the script was passed 0 for the 1st argument
$var = $ARGV[0];
print 10 % $var, "\n";
```

Illegal octal digit

FATAL

Occurrence   You will get this error if you tried to use an 8 or 9 in an octal number. .

Example   The following code will generate this error:

```
$var = 09;
```

Illegal octal digit ignored
WARNING

Occurrence   You will get this error if you tried to use an 8 or 9 in an octal number. The invalid digits will be ignored, and the octal will be the value before the 8 or 9 occurred.

Example   The following code will generate this error:

```
$var = 08;
```

Insecure dependency in %s
FATAL

Occurrence   You will get this error if you did something unsafe in your script that the tainting mechanism didn't like. Tainting is turned on when you use the –T switch or if you have a setuid/setgid script. All user input is considered untrustworthy, so you will get this error if you allow user input in a dangerous situation.

Example   The following code will generate this error:

```
$ENV{'PATH'} = "/usr/bin";  # to prevent other errors
system(@ARGV);

Insecure dependency in system while running with -T switch
```

Insecure directory in DIR
FATAL

Occurrence   You will get this error if you use an exec, open a pipe, or use a system call in a setuid/setgid script and the PATH environment variable has a directory that is world writable.

Insecure $ENV{PATH}
FATAL

Occurrence   You will get this error if you're script is taint checking (either because of –T or it is setuid/setgid) and the PATH environment variable came from data supplied by the user. Your script must set this variable with a trusted value.

Internal inconsistency in tracking vforks

SEVERE WARNING

Occurrence
This error is specific to VMS. You will get this warning if Perl has lost count of the number of times your script has called fork and exec. If this happens, the next time you call exec it execs the current process instead of a subprocess even if a subprocess should be exec'd instead.

invalid [] range in regexp

FATAL

Occurrence
You will get this error if you have an invalid range in a regular expression. This may be because the minimum value is greater than the maximum value.

Example
The following code will generate this error:

```
$var =~ /[k-a]/;
```

```
/[k-a]/: invalid [] range in regexp
```

ioctl is not implemented

FATAL

Occurrence
You will get this error if ioctl is not implemented on your system.

Label not found for "X LABEL"

FATAL

Occurrence
You will get this warning if you try to use last, next, or redo to end, continue, or restart a loop but you're not inside a loop with the given label. The X will be replaced with the function you used.

Example
The following code will generate this error:

```
MYLOOP:
while ( 1 ) {
    last LOOP if 1;
}
```

```
Label not found for "last LOOP"
```

Line # not breakable
SEVERE WARNING

Occurrence   You can only get this warning if you're using the Perl debugginer (perl –d). This occurs if you try to set a break point on a line where Perl cannot stop the execution of the script.

listen() on closed fd
WARNING

Occurrence   You will get this warning if you try to call the listen function on a filehandle that has been closed. This might be because the socket function failed and you didn't check to make sure it succeeded.

Example   The following code will generate this error:

```
socket(SOCKET, PF_INET, SOCK_STREAM, $proto);
# assume this failed
listen(SOCKET, SOMAXCONN);
```

Literal @STR now requires backslash
FATAL

Occurrence   You will get this error if you use an @ in a string and the text that follows it isn't a variable. If you want to use a literal '@', you must use a backslash before it.

Example   The following code will generate this error:

```
$email = "someone@somewhere.com";

Literal @somewhere now requires backslash
```

Method for operation OP not found in package PACKAGE during blessing
FATAL

Occurrence   You will get this error if you try to overload an operator in a package but the entry isn't a valid subroutine in the package.

Might be a runaway multi-line STR string starting on line # SEVERE WARNING

Occurrence   This warning generally follows another error and tries to explain why the previous error occurred. The parse is guessing that you forgot to end a string or pattern in a previous line because it ended on the line causing the error.

Example   The following code will generate this error:

```
$var = "Howdy dude\n';
print "$var\n";
```

```
Scalar found wher eoperator expected at FILE line 4 near print "$var"
    (Might be a runaway multi-line "" string starting on line 3)
```

Misplaced _ in number WARNING

Occurrence   You will see this warning if an underline in a decimal constant wasn't on a three-digit boundary.

Missing $ on loop variable FATAL

Occurrence   You will get this error if you leave off the $ in a loop variable. All scalars must always begin with $ in Perl.

Example   The following code will generate this error:

```
foreach var ( @arr ) { … }
```

Missing comma after first argument to FUNC function

FATAL

Occurrence   You will get this error if you pass a filehandle to a function as an argument and don't follow the filehandle with a comma. Some functions allow (or require) this behavior, but not in the current case.

Example   The following code will generate this error:

```
open FILE "<myFile.txt";
while ( <FILE> ) { … }
close FILE;

Missing comma after first argument to open function
```

(Missing operator before SYM?)

SEVERE WARNING

Occurrence   You will get this warning when Perl tries to help you figure out why a "VAL found where operator expected" error occurs.

Example   The following code will generate this error:

```
$var = 'one';
print "\$var is " $var;

Scalar found where operator expected …
    (Missing operator before $var?)
```

Missing right bracket

FATAL

Occurrence   You will get this error if you have more opening curly braces than closing curly braces in your script.

Example   The following code will generate this error:

```
if ( 1 ) {
    # a whole lot of code with no ending }
```

Missing semicolon on previous line? SEVERE WARNING

Occurrence   You will see this warning when Perl is trying to help you figure out why a "VAL found where operator expected" error occurred. This doesn't necessarily mean you should place a semicolon at the end of the previous line.

Modification of a read-only value attempted FATAL

Occurrence   You will get this error if you try to change the value of a constant.

Example   The following code will generate this error:

```
$var = "12345";
$var =~ m/123/;
$& = "12";
```

Modification of non-creatable array value attempted, subscript # FATAL

Occurrence   You will get this error if you try to create an array value with an invalid subscript. This is most often because it is negative.

Example   The following code will generate this error:

```
$arr[-1] = 'negative';
```

```
Modification of non-creatable array value attempted, subscript -1
```

Modification of non-creatable hash value attempted, subscript "KEY" FATAL

Occurrence   You will get this error if you try to create a hash value with an invalid subscript.

Module name must be a constant
FATAL

Occurrence   You will get this error if you pass anything other than a bare module name to the use function as the first argument.

msgFUNC not implemented
FATAL

Occurrence   You will get this error if you try to use one of the System V IPC messaging calls and it's not available on your system.

Multidimensional syntax SYNTAX not supported
WARNING

Occurrence   You will get this warning if you try to declare a multidimensional array any way other than $arr[0][0].

Example   The following code will generate this error:

```
$arr[0,0] = 'first';
```

```
Multidimensional syntax $arr[0,0] not supported
```

"my" variable VAR can't be in a package
FATAL

Occurrence   You will see this error when you try to declare a variable with the my function qualified with a package name. Since these variables are lexical, they aren't a party of a specific package.

Example   The following code will generate the error:

```
my $myPackage::var = "one";
```

```
"my" variable $myPackage::var can't be in a package
```

See Also   my

Negative length
FATAL

Occurrence   You will see this error if you try to pass a buffer with a length of less than 0 to a read, write, send, or recv function.

nested *?+ in regexp
FATAL

Occurrence   You will get this error if you have two regular expression quantifiers beside each other (i.e., **, +*).

No #! line
FATAL

Occurrence   You will get this error if you don't have a #! line in your setuid script. The setuid emulator requires this line even if your system doesn't support it.

No FUNC allowed while running setuid
FATAL

Occurrence   You will get this error if you try to call any of the functions that are too insecure to be run in a setuid/setgid script.

No -e allowed in setuid scripts
FATAL

Occurrence   You will get this error if the user tries to define a setuid script with the –e switch.

No comma allowed after TYPE
FATAL

Occurrence   You will get this error if you put a comma after a filehandle or indirect object that isn't supposed to have a comma after it for the function. This keeps it from being passed to the function as an argument.

Example   The following code will generate this error:

```
print STDERR, "Error message\n";
```

```
No comma allowed after filehandle
```

No command into which to pipe on command line
FATAL

Occurrence	This error is specific to the VMS operating system. This error will occur if you have a pipe at the end of your command line and Perl doesn't know where to pipe the output.

No DB::DB routine defined
FATAL

Occurrence	You will get this error if you're using Perl with the –d switch and the perl5db.pl file didn't define a routine to run at the beginning of each statement. Normally, other errors would occur before you get to this point.

No DBsub routine defined
FATAL

Occurrence	You will get this error if you're using Perl with the –d switch and the perl5db.pl file didn't define a DB::sub routine to run at the beginning of each subroutine.

No error file after 2> or 2>> on command line
FATAL

No input file after < on command line
FATAL

No output file after > on command line
FATAL

No output file after > or >> on command line
FATAL

Occurrence	These errors are specific to the VMS operating system. You will get one of these errors if you use one of the command-line redirection operators without a filename following it.

"no" not allowed in expression

FATAL

Occurrence | Since the no command is only used to remove imported symbols from an external source, it has no meaning in an expression. You will generate this error if you try to use no in an expression.

Example | The following code will generate the error:

```
$var = no Socket;
```

See Also | no

No Perl script found in input

FATAL

Occurrence | You will get this error if you invoke Perl with the –x switch but no #! line with Perl was found in the file.

No setre[gu]id available

FATAL

Occurrence | You will get this error if Configure couldn't find setreuid or setregid on your system.

No space allowed after -I

FATAL

Occurrence | You will get this error if you put a space after the –I switch. The argument must follow the –I with no space.

No such signal: SIGSIGNAL

WARNING

Occurrence | You will get this warning if you define a signal handler for a signal that isn't valid on your machine.

Example | The following code will generate this error:

```
$SIG{NONE} = \&mySub;
sub mySub { exit; }

No such signal: SIGNONE
```

Not a X reference

FATAL

Occurrence
You will get this error if Perl was trying to evaluate a reference but discovered it wasn't the reference type it was expecting. The possible values for X are CODE, format, GLOB, HASH, SCALAR, subroutine, ARRAY.

Not a perl script

FATAL

Occurrence
You will get this error if you're running a setuid script that doesn't have a valid #! line in it. The setuid emulate requires this even if your machine doesn't support it.

Not a subroutine reference in %OVERLOAD

FATAL

Occurrence
You will get this error if you specify a reference to something that isn't a valid subroutine.

Not enough arguments for FUNC

FATAL

Occurrence
You will get this error if you don't pass the correct number of arguments to a function.

Example
The following code will generate this error:

```
socket();
```

```
Not enough arguments for socket
```

Not enough format arguments

Occurrence   You will get this warning if you don't have enough arguments to match the pictures you defined in a format.

Example   The following code will generate this error:

```
format STDOUT =
@<<<<< @||||| @>>>>>
$var,  $var2

$var = "one";
$var2 = "two";
write;
```

Null filename used

Occurrence   You will get this error if you try to require a null filename.

Null picture in formline

Occurrence   You will get this error if the first argument to formline wasn't a valid picture specification.

Odd number of elements in hash list

Occurrence   You will get this warning if you try to assign an odd number of elements to a hash table. You can't do this since they are assigned as key/value pairs.

Offset outside string

Occurrence   You will get error if you try to call read, write, send, or recv with an offset that is outside the buffer.

oops: oopsAV

SEVERE WARNING

oops: oopsHV

SEVERE WARNING

Occurrence   These internal warnings mean that you haven't used the correct grammar.

Operation 'OP': no method found, FUNC

FATAL

Occurrence   You will get this error if you're trying to access an overloaded operation and there was no method defined for it.

See Also   Module: overload

Operator or semicolon missing before SYM

SEVERE WARNING

Occurrence   You will get this warning if you use a variable or subroutine call where an operator was expected.

Out of memory!

(VERY) FATAL

Occurrence   You will get this error if malloc couldn't allocate any more memory.

Out of memory during request for VAL

FATAL

Occurrence   You will get this error if the malloc couldn't allocate any more memory.

Out of memory for yacc stack

FATAL

Occurrence   You will get this error if the yacc parser tried to grow its stack using realloc but the call failed.

page overflow

WARNING

Occurrence   You will get this warning if a call to write produces more output lines than will fit on a single page.

Parens missing around "FUNC" list

WARNING

Occurrence   You will get this warning if Perl thinks you left out some parens where they're necessary.

Example   The following code will generate this warning:

```
local $var1, $var2 = @ARGV;

Parens missing around "local" list
```

Perl VER required—this is only version VER, stopped

FATAL

Occurrence   You will get this error if you try to load a module that requires a newer version of Perl than you have.

Permission denied

FATAL

Occurrence   You will get this error if the setuid emulator decides you're trying to do something you shouldn't.

pid # not a child

WARNING

Occurrence   This warning is specific to the VMS operating system. You will get this warning if you make a call to waitpid to wait for a process but that process isn't a child of the current process. VMS will happily wait for that process to end, but you may have meant to wait for a child process.

POSIX getpgrp can't take an argument FATAL

Occurrence   You will get this error when you make a call to getpgrp with a PID as an argument and you're using a POSIX getpgrp. This getpgrp can't take an argument (or it must be 0).

Possible memory corruption: VAL overflowed 3rd argument FATAL

Occurrence   You will get this error if ioctl or fcntl returned more to the buffer than Perl was expecting. Perl assumes that the memory is corrupt if this happens.

Precedence problem: open FILE should be open(FILE) SEVERE WARNING

Occurrence   You will generally get this warning when trying to run an old Perl script with a newer version of Perl. Due to a change in Perl's grammar, 'open MYFILE || die;' is not assumed to mean 'open(MYFILE || die);'. You can fix this by using or instead of || or by placing parentheses around the filehandle.

print[f] on closed filehandle HANDLE WARNING

Occurrence   You will see this warning if you try to use print (or printf) on a filehandle that has been closed.

Example   The following code will generate this error:

```
open ( FILE, ">newfile.txt" );
...
close ( FILE );
print FILE "new data\n";

print on closed filehandle main::FILE
```

Probable precedence problem on OP WARNING

Occurrence You will get this warning if there is a bare word where Perl is expecting a conditional. You can generally fix this by putting in parentheses to make sure the precedence will be how you want it.

Example The following code will generate this error:

```
open FILE || die;
```

```
Probable precedence problem on logical or
```

Prototype mismatch: (PROTO) vs (PROTO) SEVERE WARNING

Occurrence You will see this warning if you define a subroutine's prototype differently than how you predeclared it earlier in the script.

Example The following code will generate this error:

```
sub mySub($$);
mySub 1, 2;
sub mySub($$$) {
   print "@_\n";
}
```

```
Prototype mismatch: ($$) vs ($$$)
```

Read on closed filehandle <HANDLE> WARNING

Occurrence You will see this warning if you try to read from a filehandle that has been closed.

Example The following code will generate this warning:

```
open ( FILE, ">newfile.txt" );
...
close ( FILE );
$var = <FILE>
```

```
Read on closed filehandle <FILE>
```

Reallocation too large: # FATAL

Occurrence   You will get this error on an MS-DOS system if you try to allocate more than 64K.

Recompile Perl with –DDEBUGGING to use –D switch FATAL

Occurrence   You will get this error if you try to use the -D switch without compiling the ability into Perl. You'll need to recompile your executable with this option.

Recursive inheritance detected FATAL

Occurrence   You will get this error if more than 100 levels of inheritance are used in your program.

Reference miscount in sv_replace() WARNING

Occurrence   You will see this warning if the internal sv_replace function was passed an SV with a reference count that wasn't 1.

regexp too big FATAL

Occurrence   You will get this error if you try to compile a large regular expression (more than 32,767 bytes). You can usually break up your expression into multiple regexps instead.

Reversed OP= operator

Occurrence You will get this warning if you have one of the assignment operators written backwards. The equal sign must always be last.

Example The following code will generate this warning:

```
$var = 1;
$var =+ 1;
print "$var\n";

Reversed += operator
```

Runaway format

Occurrence You will see this error if you have ~~ in your format definition and it created 200 lines at once with the 199th and 200th line looking exactly alike. This is most likely because you didn't use a ^ instead of an @ or you neglected to shift or pop your array.

Scalar value @ARR[SUB] better written as $ARR[SUB]

Occurrence You will get this warning if you refer to a single element of an array in array context. It is usually preferable to refer to it in a scalar context so that it will always behave as a scalar.

Example The following code will generate this warning:

```
@arr = ( 'one', 'two', 'three' );
print "@arr[1]\n";

Scalar value @arr[1] better written as $arr[1]
```

Scalar value @ARR{'KEY'} better written as $ARR{'KEY'}

Occurrence   You will get this warning if you refer to a single element of an associative
array in array context. It is usually preferable to refer to it in a scalar context
so that it will always behave as a scalar.

Example   The following code will generate this warning:

```
%arr = ( 'one' => 1, 'two' => 2, 'three' => 3 );
print "@arr{'three'}\n";

Scalar value @arr{'three'} better written as $arr{'three'}
```

Script is not setuid/setgid in suidperl

Occurrence   You will get this error if you are running a script with suidperl but the
setuid/setgid bit isn't set on the file. It's rather odd for this to happen.

Search pattern not terminated

Occurrence   You will get this error if you leave off the end delimiter when using m//.
This could be from a typo or you may be using a bracket for your delimiter,
which would count nesting levels.

Example   The following code will generate this warning. If you made the search
pattern m{{\d}}, it wouldn't error and $& would be {3}:

```
$var = "12{3}45";
$var =~ m{{\d};
print $&, "\n";
```

seek() on unopened file WARNING

Occurrence You will see this warning if you try to seek on a filehandle that is not open.

Example The following code will generate this warning:

```
open ( FILE, ">newfile.txt" );
...
close ( FILE );
seek(FILE, 10, 0);
```

select not implemented FATAL

Occurrence You will see this error if you try to use the select function and it isn't supported on your system.

semFUNC not implemented FATAL

Occurrence You will get this error if you try to use one of the System V IPC semaphore calls and it's not available on your system.

semi-panic: attempt to dup freed string SEVERE WARNING

Occurrence You will get this warning if the newSVsv function was passed a scalar to duplicate that had already been marked as free.

Semicolon seems to be missing WARNING

Occurrence You may get this warning when a syntax error occurs and Perl finds there may be a semicolon or some other operator missing.

Send on closed socket
WARNING

Occurrence   You will get this warning if you try to call the send function on a socket that has been closed. This might be because the socket function failed and you didn't check to make sure it succeeded.

Example   The following code will generate this error:

```
socket(SOCKET, PF_INET, SOCK_STREAM, $proto);
# assume this failed
...
send(SOCKET, $msg, $flags);
```

Sequence (?#... not terminated
FATAL

Occurrence   You will get this error if you're using a regular expression comment and you neglect to terminate it with an ending paren. You are not allowed to nest parens in a comment. You can, however, use the /x option with the regular expression and use normal comments.

Sequence (?STR...) not implemented
FATAL

Occurrence   You will get this error if you try to use an extension to regular expressions that hasn't been implemented yet.

Sequence (?STR...) not recognized
FATAL

Occurrence   You will get this error if you try to use an extension to regular expressions that isn't supported.

Example   The following code will generate this error:

```
$var = "12345";
$var =~ m/1{?nothing)/;

Sequence (?n...) not recognized
```

setXid() not implemented

Occurrence   You will get this error if you try to set one of the special variables that is equivalent to a system call that isn't supported on your system: $) for setegid(), $> for seteuid(), $(for setrgid(), and $< for setruid().

Setuid/gid script is writable by world

Occurrence   You will get this error if you try to run a setuid/setgid script that is world writable. This is because the script may have been tampered with by anyone else using the system and is thus unsafe to run.

shmFUNC not implemented

Occurrence   You will get this error if you try to use one of the System V IPC shared memory calls and it's not available on your system.

shutdown() on closed fd

Occurrence   You will get this warning if you try to shut down a socket that is already closed.

SIGSIGNAL handler "FUNC" not defined

Occurrence   You will get this warning if you've defined a signal handler for SIGNAL in the %SIG array but it can't be found.

sort is now a reserved word

Occurrence   You will probably never see this error, but in really old scripts, someone may have used sort, which long ago wasn't a reserved word.

Sort subroutine didn't return a numeric value   FATAL

Occurrence   You will get this error if you write a sort subroutine that doesn't return a
numeric value. This most often happens if you don't use <=> or cmp
correctly (or at all).

Sort subroutine didn't return a single value   FATAL

Occurrence   You will get this error if your sort routine returns a list that doesn't have
exactly one element.

Stat on unopened file <FILE>   WARNING

Occurrence   You will get this warning if you tried to use the stat function (or one of the
file test operators) on a filehandle that isn't open.

Statement unlikely to be reached   WARNING

Occurrence   You will get this warning if you have a statement after an exec call that isn't
die. You should probably use system instead of exec because exec only
returns if an error occurred.

Subroutine SUB redefined   WARNING

Occurrence   You will get this warning if you redefine a subroutine.

Substitution pattern not terminated   FATAL

Occurrence   You will get this error if Perl can't find the ending delimiter of an s///
expression. If you're using brackets for your delimiters, then be careful when
searching for a bracket in your expression because it will be counted as a
nested level.

Substr outside of string

Occurrence   You will get this warning if you try to get a substring of a string at an offset that is greater than the length of the string.

Example   The following code will generate this warning:

```
$var = "123456";
$subvar = substr($var, 10);
```

suidperl is no longer needed since REASON

Occurrence   You will get this error if the setuid emulator is running but your version of Perl was compiled with the -DSETUID_SCRIPTS_ARE_SECURE_NOW flag.

Syntax error

Occurrence   You will get this error if Perl found a problem with the syntax in your script. There will usually be another error to help you track down where this occurred. You can also turn on extra warning messages with the -w switch to narrow your search further.

Syntax error at line #: 'EXPR' unexpected

Occurrence   You may get this error if you're trying to execute your script with the Bourne shell instead of with Perl. This may be because the #! isn't correct in your script.

System V IPC is not implemented on this machine

Occurrence   You will get this error if you try to use one of the System V IPC functions and they aren't supported on your system. These functions begin with msg, sem, or shm.

Syswrite on closed filehandle

Occurrence   You will see this warning if you try to use syswrite on a filehandle that has been closed.

Example   The following code will generate this error:

```
open ( FILE, ">newfile.txt" );
...
close ( FILE );
syswrite FILE, $data, $len
```

tell() on unopened file

Occurrence   You will see this warning if you try to do a tell on a filehandle that is not open.

Example   The following code will generate this warning:

```
open ( FILE, ">newfile.txt" );
...
close ( FILE );
$pos = tell(FILE);
```

Test on unopened file <FILE>

Occurrence   You will get this warning if you try to use one of the file test operators on a filehandle that isn't open.

That use of $[is unsupported

Occurrence   You will get this error if you try to use $[in a way that isn't allowed by Perl. The only valid way to use it is '$[= #', where # is 0 or a positive integer. (You can also preclude that statement with local.) This is so that one module can't change this value from what another module is expecting.

The FUNC function is unimplemented

Occurrence   You will get this error if the function named wasn't found on your system by Configure.

The crypt() function is unimplemented due to excessive paranoia   FATAL

Occurrence   You will get this error if you try to use the crypt function and it isn't available on your system.

The stat preceding -l _ wasn't an lstat   FATAL

Occurrence   You will get this error if you try to test the current stat buffer to see if it's a symbolic link when the last stat call that wrote to the stat buffer went past the symbolic link to get the real file.

times not implemented   FATAL

Occurrence   You will get this error if your system doesn't support the times system call. This is most likely because you're not running on UNIX.

Too few args to syscall   FATAL

Occurrence   You will get this error if you make a call to syscall without any arguments. You have to pass at least one argument which is the system call to make.

Too late for "-T" option   VERY FATAL

Occurrence   There are two ways to get this error. The first way is if your script is invoked as a command using the #! line but the -T wasn't the first switch. Place it as the first one to fix this. The second way is if your script is invoked as an argument to call Perl from the command line (perl myScript.pl) and the -T was in the #! line but not passed on the command line.

Too many ('s   EXTERNAL

Too many)'s   EXTERNAL

Occurrence You will get this error if you're executing your script using csh instead of Perl. Make sure the #! line is correct or execute the script using Perl from the command line (perl myScript.pl).

Too many args to syscall   FATAL

Occurrence You will get this error if you try to pass more than 14 arguments to the syscall function.

Too many arguments for FUNC   FATAL

Occurrence You will get this error if you passed too many arguments to the given function.

Example The following code will generate this warning:

```
socket(SOCK, AF_INET, SOCK_STREAM, $proto, $extra);
```

```
Too many arguments for socket
```

Trailing \ in regexp   FATAL

Occurrence You will get this error if you end a regular expression with a backslash. You need to either put a backslash before the ending one to escape it or place a character after the backslash.

Translation pattern not terminated   FATAL

Occurrence You will get this error if Perl can't find the middle delimiter of a tr/// construct. (Remember this can also be written as tr[][].)

Example The following code will generate this warning:

```
$var = "12345";
$var =~ tr[123[312];
print "$var\n";
```

Translation replacement not terminated   FATAL

Occurrence You will get this error if Perl can't find the ending delimiter of a tr///
construct.

Example The following code will generate this warning:

```
$var = "12345";
$var =~ tr/123/312;
print "$var\n";
```

truncate not implemented   FATAL

Occurrence You will get this error if your system doesn't have a function to truncate a
file that Configure can find.

Type of arg # to FUNC must be TYPE (not TYPE)   FATAL

Occurrence You will get this error if you've passed the wrong type of argument to the
given function. Arrays must begin with @ and associative arrays with %.

umask: argument is missing initial 0   WARNING

Occurrence The argument of the umask function expects an octal value. All octal values
begin with 0 in Perl. (You could use decimal numbers, but the numbers
wouldn't be readable by other users of your program.)

Example The following code will generate this warning:

```
umask 644;
```

Unable to create sub name "SUB" FATAL

Occurrence   You will get this error if you try to make a subroutine that has an illegal name.

Unbalanced context: # more PUSHes than POPs WARNING

Unbalanced saves: # more saves than restores WARNING

Unbalanced scopes: # more ENTERs than LEAVEs WARNING

Unbalanced tmps: # more allocs than frees WARNING

Occurrence   You will see this warning if your script's exit code found an internal inconsistency in your program. This could be that more execution contexts were
entered than were left, there is an inconsistency in the number of values that
were temporarily localized, more blocks were entered than were left, or more
scalars were allocated than were freed.

Undefined format "FORMAT" called FATAL

Occurrence   You will see this error if the format you're trying to write to can't be found.

Example   The following code will generate this error:

```
$var = 1;
write;
```

```
Undefined format "main::STDOUT" called
```

Undefined sort subroutine "SUB" called   FATAL

Occurrence   You will get this error if the sort subroutine you tried to use couldn't be found.

Example   The following code will generate this error:

```
@arr = ( 3, 2, 1 );
@sorted = sort bySub @arr;
print "@sorted\n";

Undefined sort subroutine "main::bySub" called
```

Undefined subroutine &SUB called   FATAL

Occurrence   You will get this error if the subroutine you tried to use couldn't be found.

Example   The following code will generate this error:

```
print &noSub;

Undefined subroutine &main::noSub called
```

Undefined subroutine called   FATAL

Occurrence   You will get this error if you tried to call an anonymous subroutine that couldn't be found.

Undefined subroutine in sort   FATAL

Occurrence   You will get this error if the sort routine you tried to use hasn't been defined.

Undefined top format "FORMAT" called   FATAL

Occurrence   You will get this error if the top format you're trying to write can't be found.

unexec of PROG into PROG failed!   FATAL

Occurrence   The unexec function on your system failed for some reason.

Unknown BYTEORDER   FATAL

Occurrence   You will get this error if you try to use one of the byte-swapping functions on a machine where Perl doesn't understand your byte order.

unmatched () in regexp   FATAL

Occurrence   You will get this error if you have more opening parentheses in your regular expression than closing parentheses. Unless you escape one of the parentheses with a backslash, they must balance.

Example   The following code will generate this error:

```
$var = "(123)";
$var =~ m/(\d/;
```

Unmatched right bracket   FATAL

Occurrence   You will get this error if there are more closing curly braces in your script than opening curly braces.

Unmatched [] in regexp   FATAL

Occurrence You will get this error if your [] characters don't balance in a regular expression. This is most often caused by having a] as part of the characters you want to match and neglecting to escape it.

Unquoted string "STR" may clash with future reserved word   WARNING

Occurrence You will get this warning if you have a bare word that may one day be a reserved word in Perl. You can get rid of this warning by putting the word in quotes, putting an underscore in it, or making one or more characters capital.

Example The following code will generate this error:

```
$var = frog;

Unquoted string "frog" may clash with future reserved word
```

Unrecognized character \### ignored   SEVERE WARNING

Occurrence You will get this warning if Perl found a character it didn't recognize in its input. The character was ignored.

Unrecognized signal name "SIGNAL"   FATAL

Occurrence You will get this error if you pass a signal to the kill function and the signal isn't recognized.

Unrecognized switch: -SWITCH   FATAL

Occurrence You will get this error if you pass a switch to Perl that doesn't exist.

Unsuccessful FUNC on filename containing newline

WARNING

Occurrence You will get this warning when a file operation fails on a filename and the filename contained a newline character. This most often happens when you forget to chop input from the user.

Example The following code will generate this error:

```
print "Which file? ";
$file = <STDIN>;
if ( -d $file ) { print "It's a directory\n"; }

Unsuccessful stat on filename containing newline
```

Unsupported directory function "FUNC" called

FATAL

Occurrence You will get this error if you tried to call opendir or readdir and they aren't implemented on your system.

Unsupported function FUNC

FATAL

Occurrence You will get this error if you try to use a function that isn't implemented on your system or Configure couldn't find it.

Unsupported socket function "FUNC" called

FATAL

Occurrence You will get this error if you try to use one of the socket functions and the Berkeley socket library isn't available on your machine or Configure couldn't find it.

Unterminated <> operator   FATAL

Occurrence   You will get this error if Perl saw a < where it was expecting a term so it tried to find the matching > but didn't find it. This is generally caused by a typo or by leaving out parentheses where needed when you meant to use < as the less than operator.

"use" not allowed in expression   FATAL

Occurrence   Since the use command is only used to import symbols from an external source, it has no meaning in an expression. You will generate this error if you try to use the use function in an expression.

Example   The following code will generate the error:

```
$var = use Socket;
```

See Also   use

Use of $# is deprecated   DEPRECATED

Occurrence   You will get this error if you try to use the $# special variable. You should use printf or sprintf instead.

Use of $* is deprecated   DEPRECATED

Occurrence   You will get this error if you try to use the $* variable, which used to allow you to do multiline pattern matching. Now you can use the /m option of s/ // (or /s to make sure you only match a single line).

Use of VAL in printf format not supported   FATAL

Occurrence   You will get this error if you try to use a feature of printf that is implemented in C but not in Perl. This is usually because there's a better option in Perl.

Use of FUNC is deprecated
DEPRECATED

Occurrence   You will get this error if you use a function or construct that is no longer recommended to use. This is usually because there is a better way to do it now or because the deprecated way causes bad things to happen.

Use of bar << to mean <<"" is deprecated
DEPRECATED

Occurrence   It is generally better if you supply the "" when you wish to use a blank line as the terminator of the here-document operator.

Use of implicit split to @_ is deprecated
DEPRECATED

Occurrence   You will get this error if you implicitly split a subroutine's argument list. This is bad because splitting a subroutine's argument list takes a lot of work by the compiler; it's better to do it explicitly and assign the results to an array.

Use of uninitialized value
WARNING

Occurrence   You will get this warning if you use an undefined variable as if it has been defined. It will be interpreted as a null string or 0, which may not be what you wanted.

Useless use of VAL in void context
WARNING

Occurrence   You will get this warning if you perform an operation where nothing is done with the return value. This is usually caused by a misunderstanding of Perl precedence.

Example   The following code will generate this error. Putting parentheses around the right side of the assignment would probably be what you want.

```
@var = 'one', 'two';
print "@var\n"; # prints 'one'

Useless use of a constant in void context
```

Variable "VAR" is not exported   FATAL

Occurrence   You will get this error if you're using the strict pragma and you tried to use a variable you thought was exported from a module because another symbol with that name (most likely a subroutine) was exported from that module. This is most often caused by placing the wrong variable identifier before the variable ($ instead of &).

Variable name "PACKAGE::VAR" used only once: possible typo   WARNING

Occurrence   You will get this warning if you have a variable in your program that is used only once. This generally indicates a typo in the variable name. If you really want to use the variable only once, then you can use the 'use vars VAR' pragma to get rid of this warning.

Example   The following code will generate this error:

```
$var = 1;

Variable name "main::var" used only once: possible typo
```

Variable syntax   EXTERNAL

Occurrence   You will see this message if you run your script through csh instead of Perl. This may be because of the #! line in your script or the way your shell interprets scripts. You can correct it by fixing the #! line or by running your script through the Perl interpreter manually.

Warning: something's wrong   WARNING

Occurrence   You will see this warning if you call the warn function with an empty string or with no arguments and the $_ variable is undefined or empty.

Warning: unable to close filehandle HANDLE properly
SEVERE WARNING

Occurrence   You will see this warning if an error occurred when an implicit close was done by a call to open. This generally means that there is no available space left on the disk.

Warning: Use of "FUNC" without parens is ambiguous
SEVERE WARNING

Occurrence   You will get this warning if you have a function in an expression that generally needs parentheses but they can be left out when the function is on the right side of an assignment with nothing following it.

Example   The following code uses sin without an argument because it uses the value of $_ if there's no argument.

```
$_ = 1;
print sin + 20, "\n";
# meant to do sin() + 20, but did
# sin(+20);

Warning: Use of "sin" without parens is ambiguous
```

Write on closed filehandle
WARNING

Occurrence   You will see this warning if you try to write to a filehandle that has been closed.

Example   The following code will generate this warning:

```
format FILE =
@>>>>>>>>>>>
$var
.

open ( FILE, ">newfile.txt" );
...
close ( FILE );
$var = 1;
write FILE;
```

x outside of string
FATAL

Occurrence You will see one of these errors if you were using a pack template that specified a relative position that ends up past the end of the string being unpacked.

Xsub "SUB" called in sort
FATAL

Xsub called in sort
FATAL

Occurrence You will see this error if you try to use an external subroutine as your sort subroutine. This behavior isn't supported yet.

You can't use -l on a filehandle
FATAL

Occurrence You will get this error if you try to use the symbolic link file test on a filehandle. This is because a filehandle is an opened file and any opened file would have read where the symbolic link pointed to and would no longer care about whether it's a symbolic link or not. You should simply use the filename instead.

Example The following code will generate this warning:

```
open ( FILE, ">newfile.txt" );
if ( -l FILE ) {
    print "It's a symbolic link\n";
}
```

YOU HAVEN'T DISABLED SET-ID SCRIPTS IN THE KERNEL YET!

FATAL

Occurrence You will see this error if you try to use a setuid/setgid script and you haven't disabled set-id scripts in your kernel. If you're unable to disable set-id scripts in your kernel, you can use the wrapsuid script that should have come with your Perl distribution in the eg directory to create a setuid C wrapper for your script.

You need to quote "WORD"

WARNING

Occurrence You will get this warning if you've assigned a bare word as a signal handler name. You also have a subroutine with that name defined so Perl will try to call that subroutine when the assignment is done, which is probably not what you want.

Appendix E
Additional Resources

W hen programming in Perl, you may find it necessary to call on additional resources for your scripts. Whether you are having troubles with syntax or you are searching for a module, the Internet could have the information you need. The following list contains sites, newsgroups, and other locations that we often use when programming in Perl.

ActiveWare - Perl for Win32

http://www.activeware.com/

This Web site contains the binaries and source for Perl for Win32, Perl for ISAPI, and PerlScript.

comp.lang.perl

This is a newsgroup that discuss the language on a day-to-day basis. In addition to this main group, you'll find other groups nearby that contain recent Perl announcements (such as comp.lang.perl.announce) and discuss the miscellaneous features of the language (such as comp.lang.perl.misc).

Comprehensive Perl Archive Network (CPAN)

http://www.perl.com/perl/CPAN

CPAN is an archive of Perl modules and is generally a pretty handy resource. Once you go there, you may be passed to a mirror site for faster access. If you're looking for a Perl module, you'll most likely find it here.

Macintosh, Perl, Scripting & WWW Authoring Resources

http://www.best.com/~jtmax/

This Web site contains information on the various aspects of Perl as well as a very resourceful guide to implementing Perl on a Macintosh System (MacPerl).

MacPerl

ftp://www.iis.ee.ethz.ch/pub/neeri/MacPerl/

This FTP site contains the binaries and source for MacPerl.

Perl5 Information, Announcements & Discussion

http://www.metronet.com/perlinfo/perl5.html

The site contains information, announcements, patches, complete source, referencing and dereferencing, functions, object-oriented programming—you name it, this site has it or a link to it.

Perl FAQ Index

http://fohnix.metronet.com/1/perlinfo/faq/

Perl FAQ Index provides in various formats the most frequently asked questions about Perl. It addresses different operating system implementations as well.

PerlRing Homepage

http://www.netaxs.com/~joc/perlring.html

The PerlRing Homepage site was created to help link various Perl pages together. This effort envelops almost any page that you will wish to find—it is a definite bookmark!

The Perl Institute

http://www.perl.org/

The Perl Institute is a nonprofit organization that was established to support the users of Perl and the language's development.

The Perl Journal

http://orwant.www.media.mit.edu/the_perl_journal/

The Perl Journal's site says, "The first and only periodical devoted to Perl"—'nuff said!

The Perl Language Home Page

http://www.perl.com/perl

This is the one. If you want information, documentation, bug reports, source code, listservs, newsgroups, or any other information (even to e-mail the author of Perl, Larry Wall), this is the place to go.

perlWWW

http://www.oac.uci.edu/indiv/ehood/perlWWW

This is a site that indexes Perl programs, libraries, and other World Wide Web/Perl-related material.

Perl Ported Source

ftp://ftp.metronet.com/pub/perl/ports/
This FTP site contains source code for multiple ports of the Perl compiler.

The University of Florida Perl Archive

http://www.cis.ufl.edu/perl/

This Web site contains online documentation for the language.

Yahoo! —Computers & Internet:Programming Languages:Perl

http://www.yahoo.com/Computers_and_Internet/
Programming_Languages/Perl/

This is a Yahoo! index of Perl resources. This location contains links to resources about every subject of Perl.

http://www.vmedia.com

VENTANA

Official Netscape Enterprise Server 3 Book

Richard Cravens
$49.99, 480 pages, part #: 1-56604-664-5

- Detailed examination of web-site security issues and benefits.

- Complete coverage of installation, configuration and maintenance, along with troubleshooting tips.

- Shows how to enrich web sites with multimedia and interactivity.

CD-ROM contains sample HTML editors, HTML references, current Netscape plug-ins.

For Windows NT & UNIX • Intermediate to Advanced

Official Netscape Technologies Developer's Guide

Luke Duncan, Sean Michaels
$39.99, 352 pages, part #: 1-56604-749-8

- Guide to the most critical ONE SDKs and APIs—CORBA/IIOP, IFC, plug-ins and server-side JavaScript.

- Overview of Internet/intranet application development with IFC.

- Example plug-in project to integrate multiple aspects of Netscape ONE.

All Platforms • Intermediate to Advanced

VENTANA

Net Security: Your Digital Doberman

$29.99, 312 pages, illustrated, part #: 1-56604-506-1

Doing business on the Internet can be safe . . . if you know the risks and take appropriate steps. This thorough overview helps you put a virtual Web watchdog on the job—to protect both your company and your customers from hackers, electronic shoplifters and disgruntled employees. Easy-to-follow explanations help you understand complex security technologies, with proven technologies for safe Net transactions. Tips, checklists and action plans cover digital dollars, pilfer-proof "storefronts," protecting privacy and handling breaches.

Intranet Firewalls

$34.99, 360 pages, illustrated, part #: 1-56604-506-1

Protect your network by controlling access—inside and outside your company—to proprietary files. This practical, hands-on guide takes you from intranet and firewall basics through creating and launching your firewall. Professional advice helps you assess your security needs and choose the best system for you. Includes tips for avoiding costly mistakes, firewall technologies, in-depth reviews and uses for popular firewall software, advanced theory of firewall design strategies and implementation, and more.

VENTANA

Principles of Object-Oriented Programming in Java

$39.99, 400 pages, illustrated, part #: 1-56604-530-4

Move from writing programs to designing solutions—with dramatic results! Take a step beyond syntax to discover the true art of software design, with Java as your paintbrush and objects on your palette. This in-depth discussion of how, when and why to use objects enables you to create programs—using Java or any other object-oriented language that not only work smoothly, but are easy to maintain and upgrade. The CD-ROM features the Java SDK, code samples and more.

The Comprehensive Guide to Visual J++

$49.99, 792 pages, illustrated, part #: 1-56604-533-9

Learn to integrate the Java language and ActiveX in one development solution! Master the Visual J++ environment using real-world coding techniques and project examples. Includes executable J++ sample projects plus undocumented tips and tricks. The CD-ROM features all code examples, sample ActiveX COM objects, Java documentation and an ActiveX component library.

VENTANA

Java 1.1 Programmer's Reference

Daniel I. Joshi, Pavel Vorobiev
$49.99, 1000 pages, illustrated, part #: 1-56604-687-4

The ultimate resource for Java professionals! And the perfect supplement to the JDK documentation. Whether you need a day-to-day reference for Java classes, an explanation of new APIs, a guide to common programming techniques, or all three, you've got it—all in an encyclopedic format that's convenient to refer to again and again. Covers new Java 1.1 features, including the AWT, JARs, Java Security API, the JDBC, JavaBeans, and more, with complete descriptions that include syntax, usage and code samples. **CD-ROM:** Complete, hyperlinked version of the book.
For all platforms • Intermediate to Advanced

Migrating From Java 1.0 to Java 1.1

Daniel I. Joshi, Pavel Vorobiev
$39.99, 600 pages, illustrated, part #: 1-56604-686-6

Your expertise with Java 1.0 provides the perfect springboard to rapid mastery of Java 1.1 and the new tools in the JDK 1.1. Viewing what's new from the perspective of what you already know gets you up to speed quickly. And you'll learn not only what's changed, but why—gaining deeper understanding of the evolution of Java and how to exploit its power for your projects. **CD-ROM:** All the sample Java 1.1 programs, plus extended examples.
For Windows NT/95, Macintosh, UNIX, Solaris
Intermediate to Advanced

The Comprehensive Guide to the JDBC SQL API

Daniel I. Joshi, Rodney Runolfson
$49.99, 456 pages, illustrated, part#: 1-56604-637-8

Develop high-powered database solutions for your Internet/intranet site! Covers the basics of Java and SQL, interface design with AWT and instructions for building an Internet-based search engine. **CD-ROM:** OpenLink Serverside JDBC driver, SQL databases and tables from the book, sample code, JDBC API specification and example sites.
For Windows 95/NT • Intermediate to Advanced

VENTANA

The Mac Web Server Book

$49.95, 662 pages, illustrated, part #: 1-56604-341-7

Get the most from your Internet server with this hands-on resource guide and toolset. *The Mac Web Server Book* will help you choose the right server software; set up your server; add graphics, sound and forms; and much more. The CD-ROM includes demo software, scripts, icons and shareware.

The Windows NT Web Server Book

$49.95, 680 pages, illustrated, part #: 1-56604-342-5

A complete toolkit for providing services on the Internet using the Windows NT operating system. This how-to guide includes adding the necessary web server software, comparison of the major Windows NT server packages for the Web, becoming a global product provider and more! The CD-ROM features Alibaba™ Lite (a fully licensed web server), support programs, scripts, forms, utilities and demos.

The UNIX Web Server Book, Second Edition

$49.99, 752 pages, illustrated, part #: 1-56604-480-4

Tools and techniques for building an Internet/intranet site. Everything you need to know to set up your UNIX web site—from basic installation to adding content, multimedia, interactivity and advanced searches. The CD-ROM features Linux, HTTP, CERN Web Server, FTP daemon, conversion software, graphics translators and utilities.

VENTANA

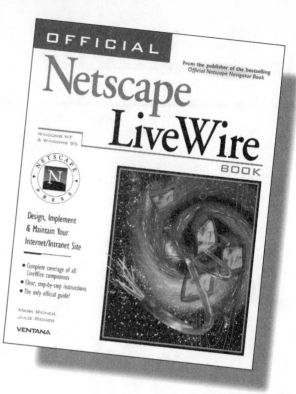

Official Netscape LiveWire Book

$49.95, 700 pages, illustrated, part #: 1-56604-382-4

Master web-site management visually! Now even new webmasters can create and manage intranet and Internet sites. And experienced developers can harness LiveWire's advanced tools for maintaining highly complex web sites and applications. Step-by-step tutorials cover all LiveWire components. Learn to design powerful distributed applications—without extensive programming experience.

Official Netscape LiveWire Pro Book

$49.99, 700 pages, illustrated, part #: 1-56604-624-6

High-end database management and connectivity techniques highlight this examination of LiveWire Pro, featuring sophisticated site development and mangement skills that ease the task for webmasters. Learn to maintain databases, update links, process online orders, generate catalogs and more. The CD-ROM features all the code from the sample applications in the book.

VENTANA

Official Netscape SuiteSpot Book

$49.99, 640 pages, illustrated, part #: 1-56604-502-9

Integrate your intranet with Netscape's power tools!
Here's all you need to set up, configure and manage
an intranet using any or all five Netscape SuiteSpot
servers. With thorough coverage of each server, you'll
learn to choose the SuiteSpot servers that best fit
your needs. Follow step-by-steps to maximize the
myriad advanced features and build an integrated
intranet with SuiteSpot. Or get to know its features
and benefits before you invest.

Official Netscape ONE Book

$49.99, 500 pages, illustrated, part #: 1-56604-632-7

Your ONE-Stop Reference for Internet/intranet
Solutions. Netscape's Open Network Environment
(ONE) provides the tools and technology for
developing versatile applications with cross-
platform functionality. This in-depth guide helps
you harness ONE to create integrated Web
solutions that balance ease of use with economy of
resources—both financial and human. Learn to
master the basic tools, streamline development with
Internet Foundations Classes (IFC) and much
more. The CD-ROM features all the code examples
from the book; complete step-by-step plug-in
example.

VENTANA

Novell IntranetWare: The Comprehensive Guide

Heath Ramsey, Mark R. Bell
$54.99, 1152 pages, illustrated, part #: 1-56604-666-1

The latest Network Operating System (NOS) from Novell
enables you to add all the functionality of Internet technologies to your internal network and open it to global
resources in the bargain. Learn how to start from scratch
with IntranetWare—or make the smooth transition from
an existing Novell LAN or WAN—to build a powerful,
versatile system that's easy to administer. More readable
than typical networking study guides and packed with
real-life examples.

Platform-independent • Intermediate to Advanced

ActiveX Development With Visual Basic 5

Evangelos Petroutsos
$49.99, 600 pages, illustrated, part #: 1-56604-648-3

Developing ActiveX controls is just the beginning! This
advanced guide takes VB programmers into the wider
world of ActiveX, as it applies to the desktop, intranets,
the Internet and more. Also covers VBScript. **CD-ROM:**
Extensive collection of ActiveX controls; shareware,
links and source code for examples.

For Windows 95/NT, Macintosh
Intermediate to Advanced

The Comprehensive Guide to Visual Basic 5

$49.99, 600 pages, illustrated, part #: 1-56604-484-7

From the author of Ventana's bestselling *Visual Guide to Visual Basic for Windows*! Command and syntax descriptions feature real-world examples. Thoroughly covers new features, uses, backward compatibility and much more. The CD-ROM features a complete, searchable text version of the book including all code.

Visual C++ 5 Power Toolkit, Second Edition

$49.99, 800 pages, part #: 1-56604-528-2

Completely updated to cover all new features in the latest version of Visual C++ — including graphics, animation, sound, connectivity and more. Class libraries, tutorials and techniques offer programmers a professional edge. The CD-ROM features fully compiled class libraries, demo programs and complete standards files for all major picture formats.

Excel 97 Power Toolkit

Lisa A. Bucki, James Kinlan, Scott Tucker, Mike Griffin
$49.99, 720 pages, illustrated, part #: 1-56604-657-2

Power users want more than tutorials—now they have
it. Hands-on examples, source files and complete
how-to's for all of Excel's powerful capabilities enable
readers to move to a higher level of productivity and
customization. **CD-ROM:** Templates, examples and
applications from KMT Software.

For Windows 95/NT • Intermediate to Advanced

Microsoft Office 97 Internet Developer's Guide

Kevin Marlowe, Jeff Rowe
$34.99, 1000 pages, illustrated, part #: 1-56604-682-3

Learn how to use the productivity tools included in
Office 97 to build a high-impact, low-cost Web site.
This in-depth guide—packed with of tips on what you
can and can't do with Office 97—focuses on the
techniques that will help you get the job done. Step-
by-step tutorials address each component application
individually, with guidelines for using them together
effectively to create a professional-quality site.
CD-ROM: Fully functional sample Web site—practice
working with the projects in the book!

For Windows 95/NT • Intermediate

VENTANA

The Windows NT 4 Server Book

$49.99, 760 pages, illustrated, part #: 1-56604-495-2

Optimize your Windows NT 4 network with this definitive, easy-to-read reference. Packed with figures, examples, diagrams, and illustrations, it focuses on the unique needs of NT Server users. An indispensable guide covering installation, add-in systems, advanced security, maintenance and more. Plus, extensive appendices—tools, online help sources, glossary of terms.

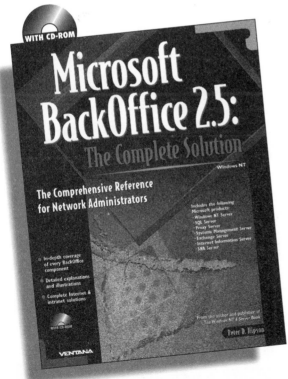

Microsoft BackOffice 2.5: The Complete Solution

$49.99, 864 pages, illustrated, part #: 1-56604-296-8

Link desktops with data via BackOffice's integrated suite of server software. Features tips and tools for devising network solutions and managing multiple systems. Indispensable for IS professionals, network managers and programmers. The CD-ROM features all sample applications, configurations and code in the book; plus sample custom controls and demos.

VENTANA

Web Publishing With Adobe PageMill 2

$34.99, 480 pages, illustrated, part #: 1-56604-458-8

Now, creating and designing professional pages on the Web is a simple, drag-and-drop function. Learn to pump up PageMill with tips, tricks and troubleshooting strategies in this step-by-step tutorial for designing professional pages. The CD-ROM features Netscape plug-ins, original textures, graphical and text-editing tools, sample backgrounds, icons, buttons, bars, GIF and JPEG images, Shockwave animations.

Web Publishing With QuarkImmedia

$39.99, 552 pages, illustrated, part #: 1-56604-525-8

Use multimedia to learn multimedia, building on the power of QuarkXPress. Step-by-step instructions introduce basic features and techniques, moving quickly to delivering dynamic documents for the Web and other electronic media. The CD-ROM features an interactive manual and sample movie gallery with displays showing settings and steps. Both are written in QuarkImmedia.

VENTANA

Interactive Web Publishing With Microsoft Tools

$49.99, 848 pages, illustrated, part #: 1-56604-462-6

Take advantage of Microsoft's broad range of development tools to produce powerful web pages, program with VBScript, create virtual 3D worlds, and incorporate the functionality of Office applications with OLE. The CD-ROM features demos/lite versions of third party software, sample code.

Web Publishing With Microsoft FrontPage 97

$34.99, 500 pages, illustrated, part #: 1-56604-478-2

Web page publishing for everyone! Streamline web-site creation and automate maintenance, all without programming! Covers introductory-to-advanced techniques, with hands-on examples. For Internet and intranet developers. The CD-ROM includes all web-site examples from the book, FrontPage add-ons, shareware, clip art and more.

Web Publishing With ActiveX Controls

$39.99, 688 pages, illustrated, part #: 1-56604-647-5

Activate web pages using Microsoft's powerful new ActiveX technology. From HTML basics to layout, find all you need to make web pages come alive, add multimedia punch to pages and streamline work with ActiveX Controls. The CD-ROM features example files from the book, Working Scripts for using Explorer's built-in controls, 3D Viewer, HTML editor, image map editor and more!

VENTANA

HTML Publishing on the Internet, Second Edition

$39.99, 700 pages, illustrated, part #: 1-56604-625-4

Take advantage of critical updates and technologies that have emerged since this book's bestselling predecessor was published. Learn to create a home page and hyperlinks, and to build graphics, video and sound into documents. Highlighted throughout with examples and templates, and tips on layout and nonlinear organization. Plus, save time and money by downloading components of the new technologies from the Web or from the companion CD-ROM. The CD-ROM also features HTML authoring tools, graphics and multimedia utilities, textures, templates and demos.

The HTML Programmer's Reference

$39.99, 376 pages, illustrated, part #: 1-56604-597-5

The ultimate professional companion! All HTML categories, tags and attributes are listed in one easy-reference sourcebook, complete with code examples. Saves time and money testing—all examples comply with the top browsers! Provides real-world JavaScript and HTML examples. The CD-ROM features a complete hyperlinked HTML version of the book, viewable with most popular browsers.

VENTANA

The Comprehensive Guide to VBScript

$39.99, 864 pages, illustrated, part #: 1-56604-470-7

The only complete reference to VBScript and HTML commands and features. Plain-English explanations; A-to-Z listings; real-world, practical examples for plugging directly into programs; ActiveX tutorial. The CD-ROM features a hypertext version of the book, along with all code examples.

The Microsoft Merchant Server Book

$49.99, 600 pages, illustrated, part #: 1-56604-610-6

Open the door to your online store! Now the long-awaited promise of retail sales is closer to fulfillment. From basic hardware considerations to complex technical and management issues, you'll find everything you need to create your site. Features case studies highlighting Microsoft Banner sites and a step-by-step guide to creating a working retail site. The CD-ROM features convenient customizing tools, Internet Information Server, Wallet, ActiveX SDK, Java SDK and more.

Build a Microsoft Intranet

$49.99, 624 pages, illustrated, part #: 1-56604-498-7

Streamline your Intranet design using Microsoft's uniquely integrated tools. Plan, install, configure and manage your Intranet. And use other Microsoft products to author and browse web pages. Includes CD-ROM supporting and reference documents, pointers to Internet resources.

VENTANA

Exploring Moving Worlds

$24.99, 288 pages, illustrated, part #: 1-56604-467-7

Where will the Moving Worlds standard lead? This overview points the way, with specifications and software examples to help developers create live content, animation and full motion on the Web. Features detailed specifications and software examples.

Exploring ActiveX

$24.99, 320 pages, illustrated, part #: 1-56604-526-6

Web developers, take control! ActiveX is changing how you work, and this book tells you how to adapt. Thoroughly explains ActiveX controls, documents and scripting, with guidelines for effective use. Tips, tricks and shortcuts throughout help you make the most of this powerful new Microsoft technology.

VENTANA

TO ORDER ANY VENTANA TITLE, COMPLETE THIS ORDER FORM AND MAIL OR FAX IT TO US, WITH PAYMENT, FOR QUICK SHIPMENT.

TITLE	PART #	QTY	PRICE	TOTAL

SHIPPING

For orders shipping within the United States, please add $4.95 for the first book, $1.50 for each additional book.
For "two-day air," add $7.95 for the first book, $3.00 for each additional book.
Email: vorders@kdc.com for exact shipping charges.
Note: Please include your local sales tax.

SUBTOTAL = $ _____

SHIPPING = $ _____

TAX = $ _____

TOTAL = $ _____

Mail to: International Thomson Publishing • 7625 Empire Drive • Florence, KY 41042
☎ **US orders 800/332-7450 • fax 606/283-0718**
☎ **International orders 606/282-5786 • Canadian orders 800/268-2222**

Name _____

E-mail_____ Daytime phone _____

Company _____

Address (No PO Box) _____

City_____ State_____ Zip_____

Payment enclosed ____VISA ____MC ____ Acc't # _____ Exp. date_____

Signature _____ Exact name on card _____

Check your local bookstore or software retailer for these and other bestselling titles, or call toll free:

800/332-7450

8:00 am - 6:00 pm EST